AMERICAN
TRANSPORTATION

STATION ON THE MORRIS & ESSEX RAILROAD by Edward Lamson Henry, oil, 11 x 20 inches, courtesy of the Chase Manhattan Bank, New York, New York.

AMERICAN TRANSPORTATION

ITS HISTORY AND MUSEUMS

Allan E. Lee

Hildesigns Press

Pan American Airways Boeing Clipper taking off. Photo courtesy of the
Smithsonian Institution, Washington, D.C.

Published by Hildesigns Press, 2855 Ridge Road
Charlottesville, VA 22901, telephone (804) 296-0885

Book design by Hilde G. Lee, Hildesigns. Cover design by Bill Bricker, Grey Market, Ltd.

Library of Congress Cataloging in Publication Data
ISBN 0-943231-57-4

Printed in the United States of America

First Printing

Contents

Introduction

Transportation is one of man's oldest activities, predating agriculture and shelter building. The earliest caveman carried his food, as well as wood and stone for tools, on his back to the family hearth. The animal-drawn travois and sled were probably the earliest land vehicles and the tree trunk the first water conveyance. The Egyptians are reported to have developed the first sailing ship around 2500 B.C. and the first wheeled vehicle, the horse-drawn chariot, around 1500 B.C.

Transportation has provided the arteries for every economy since history began. Through them has flowed the lifeblood of mankind—goods, food, materials, and people. As hard as it is to imagine, without modern transportation the world would still consist of isolated self-sufficient villages. Fortunately, technology has provided the means to build and improve upon the world's transportation systems—starting with horse-powered farm wagons and improved roads, and continuing through development of canals, railroads, automobiles, and airplanes.

America's economy began to develop as the rate of advancement in transportation technology was accelerating in Europe. The second half of the 1700s saw the first demonstrations of the steam-powered road vehicle and the hot-air balloon in France, as well as the emergence of the canal as an important means of transport in Europe. The steam locomotive and the steamboat made their appearance in England soon after the turn of the century. America, with its abundance of natural waterways, soon developed a thriving maritime industry, both on its inland waterways and radiating from its coastal ports. Canal fever created a network of artificial waterways east of the Mississippi River, which was soon followed by a network of railroads. As soon as self-powered road vehicles were developed in the early 1900s, the nation's modern road system began to evolve. While the nineteenth century gave birth to the modern ocean-shipping and railroad industries, the twentieth century belongs to the automobile and the aircraft.

My own interest in transportation started while I was growing up in one of the great intermodal transportation centers in the country, the San Francisco Bay area. From our family home in the hills of Berkeley, I remember observing the coming and going of steamships through the Golden Gate, as well as river steamers and ferryboats on the bay. I watched with fascination steam trains arriving from and departing to the north, south, and east almost continually along the eastern shore of the bay via the Southern Pacific, Santa Fe, and Western Pacific railroads. After school several of us frequently rode our bicycles down to the mainlines to watch at close hand the massive steam engines pound by. I always looked forward to a visit to my uncle's home in the hills of San Bruno, overlooking the San Francisco airport, as I could watch the planes landing and taking off. An actual visit to the airport was a special treat.

After graduating from the University of California with a degree in engineering, I went east to Harvard to obtain a masters degree in transportation economics. During the next several years I worked as a signal engineer for a western railroad, as a transportation economist for the old California Railroad Commission, and for several years supervised bulk oil shipments from a large oil refinery. In later years I became a management consultant and assisted a number of airlines and other transportation companies throughout the world. Thus, transportation has been in my blood since childhood, and continues to remain a fascination for me. Writing this book and visiting the museums included in it has been a labor of love from the start.

The original idea for this book germinated from my wife's and my enjoyment in visiting museums that focus on American history. We started taking notes about what we learned at each museum and classified museums according to the subject matter of the exhibits. In talking to friends and acquaintances, we found a mutual interest in visiting museums, but also a frustration that there were no adequate descriptions of them according to subject matter. Except in specialized fields, practically all museum directories classify museums by location and only secondarily by subject. We decided, therefore, to take what is currently available a step further by providing a brief history of individual subjects concerning American history as an introduction to a description of the important museums that deal with each subject.

Our initial list of 50 historical topics proved too unwieldy for a single book so, in cooperation with our publisher, we divided the topics into a five-volume series. This volume on transportation is the first of the series. Upcoming volumes will be titled: *American Military; Agriculture and Industry; Home and the Arts;* and *Social and Religious History.*

By providing a historical summary of each mode of transportation, I hope to provide the reader with an understanding of the evolution of each and a context for the exhibits presented at the 202 important museums listed.

I believe that all of the leading museums in each mode are included, as well as most of the modest-sized ones. Specific exclusions include broadly-focused museums with modest transportation-related exhibits. There are, for example, a number of county and regional museums that have small, but very worthwhile, carriage and automobile collections that we reluctantly had to leave out due to lack of space.

Naval and military aviation museums were left out since they are not, strictly speaking, involved primarily in transportation in the normal sense of the word. Several military aircraft museums are included, however, that provide an in-depth accounting of the history of aviation technology. The next volume in this series, which deals with the history of the nation's military, will include all of the significant military aircraft and ship museums in the United States.

I hope that readers interested in transportation history, as well as inveterate museum-goers, will find this book informative and useful. For their convenience I have included a list of museums by state and city in the back of the book. They are cross-referenced to the section of the book in which they are described.

I wish to thank all of the staff members at the museums who provided information for this book. Almost universally, I found them responsive to the concept of the book and to my requests for information. Their helpful editorial comments and suggestions are much valued. I would like to give special thanks to my wife, Hilde, whose help went far beyond that of a supportive soul mate. She contributed to the research, drafted the chapters on Carriages and Trails and Roads, and most important, performed the creative design function of bringing the manuscript into book form. While it has become a cliché, it is nevertheless true, without her participation this book would never have been published.

Allan E. Lee

To the Reader:

■ For your convenience, this book includes open times and admission fees for the museums mentioned herein. The opening and fee schedules shown were effective at the time each museum was contacted.

■ Since museums change their open times and fees regularly and, on occasion, without notice, the information should be considered as general guidelines. If the information is critical to the reader's travel schedule or budget, he or she should telephone or write ahead to obtain current information.

■ The general rules of thumb for larger museums are that they are closed on Mondays, while small ones may open only on weekends. Outdoor museums and small, regional museums typically close in off-season months or operate on reduced schedules. National parks and monuments are typically open every day during summer months.

■ Museums are listed in this book in alphabetical order by state within each subject section on maritime, railroads, automobiles, aviation, and the taverns portion of trails and roads. Trails and roads museums are listed in that section by trail or road in the order discussed in the text and east-to-west or north-to-south for each trail or road. Historical canals are listed alphabetically by state, while modern canals are listed by major waterways in the order discussed in the text.

*IN THE OLD STAGECOACH DAYS by E. L. Henry, oil, 24 x 28 inches,
courtesy of the R. W. Norton Art Gallery, Shreveport, Louisiana.*

Trails and Roads

During the first 150 years of colonial settlement of the eastern shores of America, travel was difficult and dangerous. The landscape was heavily wooded. Westward migration was blocked by rugged mountains, and the potential for encountering hostile Indians was high. In the earliest stages of colonial settlement, travel was on foot along established Indian trails or new trails blazed through the woods. In frontier days trails were known as traces or tracks—routes through the woods or mountains, marked only by tree blazes or stone cairns.

Indian Trails

The Indians maintained a variety of trails for different purposes. The expression "on the warpath" was a literal one. Warpaths were located at higher elevations than other trails to provide observation points for watching enemy tribe movements. Portage paths in the lowlands were used by Indians to carry their canoes overland from one stream to another. The Indians also had hunting trails that ran from their villages to nearby hunting grounds.

The most extensive Indian trails were the intervillage routes used in peaceful times for tribal gatherings and trade. These Indian paths were laid out with an almost uncanny directness between the points they connected.

Four of the most important Indian trading trails were the Wilderness Trail from Tennessee through the Cumberland Gap into Kentucky; the Natchez Trace from the Natchez, Mississippi, region to central Tennessee; the Great Trail from the Ohio River in eastern Ohio to the region around what is now Toledo and Detroit; and the Great Trading and Warpath Trail, which ran southwest from the Shenandoah Valley in Virginia through Tennessee into Georgia and Alabama.

As the settlers moved westward, Indian trails were gradually widened and improved to accommodate military and civilian travel. In addition, private road-building ventures were created in the form of toll roads. This network of trails and roads became vital to the opening of the western frontier, but it developed slowly over the first century and a half of colonial settlement.

Following the Revolutionary War, the new nation's leaders became acutely aware of the isolation felt by the pioneering settlers west of the Alleghenies in Ohio, Indiana, Kentucky, and Illinois. The British were still in the area trying to stir up trouble, and federal leaders feared that unless travel and trade were improved, the new territories might become independent of the original 13 states. As President George Washington put it, "The western states hang upon a pivot. The touch of a feather will turn them any way." Washington urged construction of new and improved roads across the Alleghenies in order to protect the viability of the new nation.

Braddock's and Forbes' Roads

The first major roads to the West from the eastern seaboard were built for military purposes in the 1750s, during the French and Indian Wars. British General Edward Braddock built a road, appropriately remembered as Braddock's Road, from Cumberland, Maryland, over the Alleghenies to enable him to attack French-held Fort Duquesne in what is now Pittsburgh. Braddock actually widened a trail that had been blazed a few years earlier to connect the Potomac and Monongahela rivers.

Braddock sent a detachment of several hundred men ahead of the main body of soldiers to open a 12-foot-wide wagon and artillery road. These men felled trees, bridged creeks, and laid causeways across the swamps. The strain of hauling heavy artillery equipment over the rough roadway killed many horses and frequently forced the men to pull wagons and guns out of the mud.

Despite the difficulties, General Braddock arrived within a few miles of Fort Duquesne, where his entire force walked into a French-Indian ambush. Braddock was killed, and his remaining troops retreated hastily.

Army scouts on an old Indian trail in the mountains. Etching collection of the author.

Consequently, the road-building project was cancelled after reaching what is now called Braddock, Pennsylvania.

Several years later, in 1758, General John Forbes successfully ousted the French from Fort Duquesne. To undertake this campaign, Forbes built a road further north than General Braddock's. Still called Forbes' Road, it runs from Bedford, Pennsylvania, to Pittsburgh. The road was constructed over a wagon trail opened in 1754 by James Burd of Shippensburg, Pennsylvania. After the cessation of the French and Indian Wars, the Braddock's and Forbes' Roads were abandoned and deteriorated rapidly. Following the Revolutionary War, however, they were resurrected by early immigrants venturing west, as they were the only established roads to the Ohio River from the coastal cities between New York and Philadelphia. The routes Generals Braddock and Forbes took are followed today by Interstate 40 and Interstate 30, respectively.

Wilderness Trail

The Wilderness Trail stretched from Fort Chisholm in the Shenandoah Valley of Virginia, through the Cumberland Gap, and on to Harrodsburg, Kentucky. A popular route for settlers after the Revolution, the trail was instrumental in opening Kentucky to settlement. Between 1776 and 1796, more than 200,000 people traveled into Kentucky over the Wilderness Trail. It is closely associated with Daniel Boone, who helped clear what was originally called the Boone Trace from the Cumberland Gap to the Kentucky River, southwest of what is now Lexington, Kentucky.

A large part of this trail was composed of a succession of irregular woodland paths created by wandering herds of buffalo and roving Indian hunters or war parties. Almost two-thirds of the 300-mile trail had to be opened and marked in order to guide a seemingly endless train of pioneers.

After Kentucky became a state in 1792, the trail was widened to handle wagons. Sections of the road were leased by the state government to private contractors who kept the road in repair in return for authorization to erect gates or turnpikes where tolls were collected. Troops established blockhouses along the road to protect travelers from marauding Indians and outlaws.

Natchez Trace

The Natchez Trace between Natchez, Mississippi, and Nashville, Tennessee, developed in colonial times from an old Indian trail into a major road connecting the lower Mississippi River valley with a road through Tennessee that led to the colonies on the East Coast. It was used extensively by Andrew Jackson in the War of 1812 and later was used to move the eastern Indian tribes to the Indian Territory west of the Mississippi River.

Before steam-powered riverboats were introduced on the Mississippi River, Ohio valley traders and farmers built rafts to float wheat, flour, pork, hides, furs, and tobacco down the Ohio and Mississippi rivers to Natchez. After selling their cargo and their rafts for lumber, they

An 1823 painting of the first McAdam road. Laborers broke stone into four-ounce pieces to be laid on the road in the McAdam method. Courtesy of the Federal Highway Administration, Washington, D.C.

returned on foot or horseback to the Ohio River valley via the Natchez Trace. These traders were called "Kaintucks," regardless of where they originated. In 1806 one of the early Kaintucks to walk the trace back to Kentucky was Thomas Lincoln, father of Abraham Lincoln.

Great Trail

The Great Trail was originally an Indian path that led from the forks of the Ohio River at present day Pittsburgh to the region around Detroit. It followed the northern bank of the Ohio River and then turned northwest passing near what is today Toledo. White traders with packhorses used the Great Trail to transport goods to the Indians and bring back furs.

During the latter part of the eighteenth century, it was the most important trail north of the Ohio River. The Great Trail continued to be used into the nineteenth century until eventually it was supplanted by the Cumberland Road, the Erie Canal, and later the railroads.

Great Trading and Warpath Trail

The Great Trading and Warpath Trail, originally a series of animal trails, was used by the Indians primarily for warfare and for trading during peaceful intervals. The trail ran southwest from the Shenandoah Valley to the area inhabited by the Cherokee Indians in Tennessee, where it connected with the warpath of the Creek Indians in Georgia and Alabama. The Iroquois and Shawnee of the North used this trail in their raids against the Cherokee and the Creek of the South.

In the late 1700s these war and trading paths were adopted by white settlers and traders on their migrations to the Southwest. They eventually became the basis for wagon roads and mail routes.

Early Road Building

The first record of a formal road-building program in America was one ordered by a Massachusetts Bay Company court in 1639. It decreed that each town select two or three men to join with two or three men from an adjacent town and lay out the most convenient "highway . . . so as to provide ease and safety of the traveler." As the colonies grew, their governments began to authorize construction of additional roads and bridges. Unfortunately, due to inadequate funds, authorization did not always yield results. Consequently, the colonies lacked an effective system of intercity and intercolony roads until well into the 1700s. Until then, intercity travel was mostly by foot or horse, and there was little intercity trade.

As the 1700s progressed, passenger and mail services by stagecoach began to develop between populated centers, which put increasing public pressure on colonial governments for more and better roads. Stage lines interconnected Boston, New York, and Philadelphia by 1755. By 1803 stagecoach service had extended from the northern cities south to Georgia, and the following year, service was introduced from Philadelphia to Pittsburgh.

At the time of the Revolutionary War, an extensive system of dirt and corduroy roads—roads built from logs laid side by side—had been constructed in the populated northeastern part of the country. The opening of Kentucky and the Northwest Territory following the war stimulated the need for roads across the Appalachian Mountains to the west.

By 1800 westward migration had begun to accelerate, and state and territorial governments were unable to keep pace with the growing need for new and improved roads. The introduction of the Conestoga wagon added further pressure for road construction, as it enabled farmers and merchants to expand their markets and settlers to pack up and move west. As the fourth decade of the 1800s began, commerce had expanded to the point that the shortage of adequate roads had become acute.

Early Road-Building Techniques

In the 1820s freight haulers were conducting regular schedules between Baltimore and central Ohio. Freight was being delivered to Ohio within one month of its leaving Baltimore by heavy-duty wagons pulled by four-horse teams. In 1820, more than 3,000 wagons made the run westward.

As the loads carried by wagons and carriages increased, it became evident that merely smoothing and grading a dirt surface was insuffi-cient to maintain serviceable roads. A Scotchman named John Loudon McAdam developed a more durable road by laying ten inches of crushed rock in layers of decreasing size on the natural surface. Over time the iron wheels of the wagons travel-ing the road crushed the stones and made a smooth surface. McAdam's technique was used in 1792 by the newly formed Philadelphia and Lancaster Turnpike Company to build a 66-mile toll road between those two cities in Pennsyl-vania. This macadamized road proved very popular and durable in all kinds of weather.

Macadamized roads became the standard for construction of major roads until the intro-duction of the automobile brought about the use of brick and later asphalt (crushed rock bound with heavy oil, a mixture that continued to be called macadam) in the early 1900s.

Planked Roads

Seizing on the need for roads, private investors started building toll roads. Desiring the quickest and least-expensive method of road construction, they adopted a technique used in Canada, although originally developed in Russia, of building planked roads. The planked road consisted of eight-foot planks, usually three inches thick, laid across the roadway on heavy log stringers.

The first such road was built in New York State between Syracuse and Oneida Lake in 1837. In 1848 a plank road was constructed in New York City and proved very profitable for its investors. Soon privately funded planked toll roads became fashionable, as investors found that they returned dividends almost immediately. Planked roads could be constructed at a cost of about $1,500 per mile, compared to a stone surfaced road which cost about $10,000 per mile. During the next ten years, 10,000 miles of planked toll roads were built throughout the East and Midwest.

Unfortunately, investors preferred quick dividends to long-term payouts, and without adequate maintenance, planked roads deterio-rated rapidly. After a few years many of these

Plank roads were popular for about ten years. Shown above are the offsets in the planking to allow wagons to climb back "on deck" after turning off to pass another team. Etching collection of the author.

roads disappeared into the mire or floated away during the wet seasons. Others simply rotted away. By 1865 there were few planked toll roads left in the country.

During the first half of the 1800s, most private investment funds for transportation went into canal construction. By the time the pace of canal construction slowed in 1850, investment in railroads had become popular, which further delayed the development of the nation's road system. In the main, rural roads continued to be blankets of dust in the dry months and seas of mud in the wet season.

In the 1860s and 1870s, most road improvements were limited to the larger cities. Cobblestone-paved streets had begun to appear in Boston and Philadelphia as early as the late 1700s, as a means of reducing dust and mud. They were used extensively in major cities until well into the 1900s. Cities tried various types of paving, including brick; granite blocks; packed gravel; packed sand and clay; creosoted wooden blocks; and in later years, macadam and concrete surfaces.

The introduction of the pedaled bicycle in America in 1866 put considerable pressure on politicians to provide funds for adequate paved roads in the cities. The bicycle appeared at about the time the northern and midwestern regions of America were shifting from a rural society to an urban one. Thus, it gave the urban worker the mobility needed to live in more pleasant surroundings removed from his place of work.

Improvements to rural roads continued to proceed at a slow pace until the early 1900s, when the introduction of the automobile accelerated the pace rapidly. In the 1880s brick-paved rural roads had begun to appear in Ohio and Indiana. Tar and gravel roads started becoming popular around 1906, and concrete roads first appeared in 1909. At that time there were approximately two million miles of roads in the United States, but only 150,000 miles had gravel or paved surfaces.

The federal government finally renewed its support of national road building when it passed the Federal Highway Act in 1916. Between then and 1925, the nation built 50,000 miles of federally financed paved interstate roads.

Zane's Trace

One of the first federally funded roads was Zane's Trace. In 1796 Congress authorized the president to contract with Ebenezer Zane to build a trace from the Ohio River, across from

Wheeling, Virginia (now West Virginia), to Limestone (now Maysville), Kentucky. The trace traveled west from Wheeling to what is now Zanesville, Ohio, then headed southwest through Lancaster and Chillicothe, finally terminating at the Ohio River across from Maysville, Kentucky. As a reward for locating and building the trace, Congress gave Zane three land warrants, totaling 1,920 acres along the Ohio River.

The main objective of federal financing of the Zane Trace was to enable mail to be carried west when the Ohio River was frozen in the winter. It quickly became the most traveled trail in Ohio. The path from Wheeling to Zanesville later became part of the National Road.

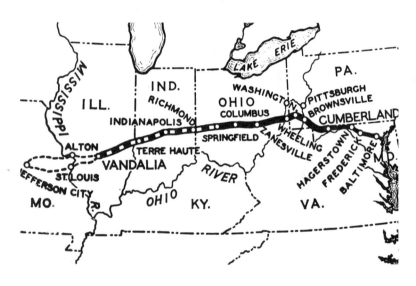

The National Road, 1840. Collection of the author.

National Road

Probably no road built in this country captured the imagination and pride of its users, nor met the needs of the times, as did the National Road. Its importance in its time rivaled that of the Erie Canal and the transcontinental railroad in theirs. Also, probably no other federally sponsored project raised as much political controversy or took as long to become a reality. Issues were fought in Congress over its starting point, route, method of construction, and its financing.

The constitutionality of funding the road with federal dollars became a major controversy between President James Madison and Congress. Congressional supporters of the road included Senators Henry Clay of Kentucky and John C. Calhoun of South Carolina.

Pressure to establish a road from the eastern seaboard across the Alleghenies to the upper section of the Ohio River started soon after the close of the War for Independence. Settlers in western Pennsylvania and the Ohio River valley were demanding access to eastern markets. War veterans who had been given land warrants in the newly created Northwest Territory as reward for their service in the Revolutionary War became increasingly vocal about having the government build roads to the lands west of the Ohio River. Virginia and Maryland politicians and businessmen wanted better access to the region in order to head off competition from their counterparts in Pennsylvania and New York.

Even though he died before construction was authorized, President George Washington was one of the leading proponents of the road and participated in its early planning. He had traveled the future course of the road in his own efforts to drive the French from the Pittsburgh area in 1753 and again in 1754. Washington had a personal interest in making the area more accessible, since after the War of Independence he had been granted 20,000 acres in what is now West Virginia by a grateful federal government.

Washington's efforts to put down the Whiskey Rebellion by farmers in the Ohio valley in 1791 further convinced him of the military value of the National Road. The lack of an adequate road across the Alleghenies was, in large

A six-horse conestoga wagon heading west passes a stagecoach arriving from the Ohio River valley on the National Road, 1840. Painting courtesy of the Federal Highway Administration, Washington, D.C.

part, the reason for the Whiskey Rebellion. Due to the high cost of transporting grain from the Ohio River valley to eastern markets by pack animal over existing trails, farmers found it more expedient to convert the corn to whiskey. Instead of loading each pack animal with about four bushels of grain valued at $70, the farmer chose to make moonshine and transport the equivalent of 24 bushels on each animal, valued at more than ten-fold that of the raw grain. Secretary of the Treasury Alexander Hamilton's whiskey tax took the profit out of this practice, and the farmers in the Ohio River valley rebelled.

The beginnings of the National Road started in 1802 with Congressional authorization for the Cumberland Road from Cumberland, Maryland, to Wheeling, West Virginia. Before construction actually began in 1806, Congress created the concept of a national road and extended the scope of the Cumberland Road to reach from the Atlantic Ocean to the Mississippi River at St. Louis, Missouri.

The National Road Law prescribed the method of construction. It specified that no slope on the road could be steeper than five degrees, a 66-foot-wide right-of-way was to be cleared of trees, and a 20-foot-wide center strip was to be "covered with stone, earth, or gravel and sand, or a combination of some or all of them." The roadbed developed by John McAdam had not yet been tested.

Construction of the National Road finally started in 1811 at Cumberland, the head of navigation on the Potomac River. It reached the Ohio River at Wheeling in 1818, and immediately became the most popular route across the Alleghenies. It was not until 1825, however, that Congress authorized extension of the road to Zanesville, Ohio. Following the previously built Zane's Trace, the National Road reached Zanesville in 1830, and Columbus, Ohio, by 1833. The first section of the National Road, from Cumberland to Wheeling, is still frequently referred to as the Cumberland Road.

Conveyances on the National Road ranged from stagecoaches to Conestoga wagons, and later even to bicycles. Western farmers drove herds of cattle, hogs, sheep, and often turkeys to eastern markets over the road. The U.S. Post Office operated a pony express over a segment of the road in Ohio for several years. Taverns sprang up along the road at an average of one per mile. They were all too eager to "water the horses" so that they could "brandy the gentlemen."

Although the intended terminus of the road had been St. Louis, political stalemates eventually caused termination in Vandelia, Illinois. The last federal funds were appropriated in 1838, and the road finally reached Vandelia in 1839, twenty-eight years after construction had started. In the 1830s road repair had become a major government expenditure, which caused Congress to again raise the issue of the constitutionality of federally financed roads. As a result the federal government started a program of turning the road over to the individual states through which it ran; they had already been doing much of the final construction and all of the maintenance.

By 1850 the railroads had reached the Mississippi River, and there was little support for extending the National Road with federal funds. In fact the federal government withdrew support of all road construction and maintenance, except for purely military roads, until the passage of the Federal Highway Act in 1916.

Road Development in the West

While road development east of the Mississippi progressed at a slow pace during the 1800s, development west of the Mississippi remained almost nonexistent. Until late in the 1800s, few population centers existed west of the Mississippi River, except on the West Coast. Distances between centers were many times greater than in the East, making overland transport extremely costly and mostly limited to mining equipment and supplies. The westward migration of settlers brought about some improvements to western wagon trails, but the principal federal investment in the West was in the construction of U.S. Army forts along the wagon trails to protect immigrants and settlers

from Indian raids. Because of the distances involved and the sparseness of the population, federal support of the western transportation system in the late 1800s focused on creating transcontinental railroads.

Except for mining towns, to which new trails and roads had to be built by the mining companies, settlements tended to develop at the uppermost points of navigation on rivers, as well as at the foot of rapids, falls, or other obstacles where portages were necessary. Settlements on the Missouri and Mississippi rivers became the starting points for famous trails, such as the Santa Fe and Oregon trails.

Old Spanish Trail

The Old Spanish Trail predated westward migration. Developed by the Spanish during the 1770s, it snaked west from Santa Fe, New Mexico, to connect with the Spanish missions in Southern California. Two Franciscan monks first traveled and marked most of the trail. Father Garcés traveled the western section in 1775-76, and Father Escalante the eastern portion in 1776.

To avoid difficult mountain terrain, including the Grand Canyon, the trail followed a

Mule train crossing the Sierras, photogravure from a painting by Frederic Remington. Collection of the author.

circuitous route into central Utah and then southwest through what is now Las Vegas, Nevada, to the Los Angeles basin (roughly paralleling Interstate 70 and Interstate 15). In the early 1800s the trail was traveled by white traders who went to California to obtain mules and other draft animals (sometimes illegally) for the Santa Fe Trail trade. By the 1850s the Old Spanish Trail had become an important route for immigrants into Southern California.

Santa Fe Trail

The Santa Fe Trail was originally an old Indian trail that ran from the lower Missouri River at its junction with the Kansas River at what is now Kansas City, Missouri, to Santa Fe and Taos, New Mexico. As developed by white traders, the Santa Fe Trail initially started near St. Louis. When riverboats navigated further up the Missouri, the transfer point also moved upstream until it finally reached Kansas City. At the transfer point supplies and trading goods were loaded from riverboats onto wagons for the 800- to 900-mile journey. The trail wound west and southwest from the Missouri River through Kansas and southwestern Colorado.

Trade opportunities in Santa Fe were first publicized by Lieutenant Zebulon Pike, who had been captured by the Spanish in 1807, when he wandered into the area while looking for a navigable route to the West Coast via the Arkansas River. The Spanish did not permit American traders into Santa Fe even though this trade route was shorter and more efficient than the old method used by the Spanish of hauling goods by packtrain from supply points in central Mexico.

Because of Spanish resistance to American traders, the Santa Fe Trail did not become an important trade route until after Mexico took over the territory in 1821, following its independence from Spain. The official trail route was established by William Becknell of Arrow Rock, Missouri, who was one of the first traders to reach Santa Fe in late 1821. Wagon trains continued to transport goods to Santa Fe over the trail, bringing back silver from New Mexico mines, until 1880.

Initially, early traders transported their goods by packhorse. Becknell, on his second journey, experimented with carrying part of his merchandise in wagons. The experiment proved successful, and after that wagons were generally employed. Merchants traveled in caravans, and the wagons moved in parallel columns so that they could be quickly formed into a circle to repel Indian attack. Any livestock was placed inside the wagon circle for protection.

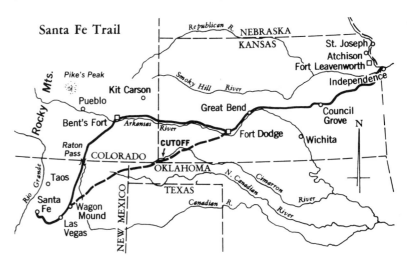

The Santa Fe Trail is the oldest road west of the Missouri River. Map courtesy of the author.

At the time there were no stage stations on the entire 860-mile route and no inhabitants other than Indians. At noon the wagon train stopped for a meal of cold food. The mules were given grain and allowed to graze for an hour or two. Before dark each evening, camp was made in some spot where there was water, grass for the mules, and the least danger of Indian attacks. Depending on the size of the wagon train, the

The Oregon stagecoach continued to operate after the advent of railroads. Etching collection of the author.

vehicles were pulled into a circle or triangle for fortification. A fire was built, beans boiled, salt pork fried, and corn bread baked in the fat. Two-man relays stood guard through the night while others rolled in blankets slept on the ground with their feet toward the fire.

The Santa Fe Trail was often dangerous and always difficult. Indians raided the wagon trains periodically during most of the life of the trail. Wagons passed through long stretches of desert where no water was available. Feed was scarce; only the first trains that left the Missouri River in the early spring found sufficient grazing for the animals along the trail. Sudden storms would frequently turn sections of the trail into a quagmire. The story is told about a traveler on the trail who happened on a wagon sunk to its axles in mud. The traveler commented that it looked like the drover was in a bad fix. The drover replied, "Oh no, I am all right, but there are two wagons below mine, and those fellows down there are having a hell of a time."

Oregon Trail

The most heavily traveled of the overland immigrant routes to the West Coast was the Oregon Trail. The trek westward over the Oregon Trail, which took eight months, is considered to be the largest and longest human migration by land in the history of mankind.

The eastern half of the trail was created by fur traders seeking pelts in the Rocky Mountains in the 1700s. It was first publicized by Meriwether Lewis and William Clark, who explored the region in the early 1800s.

While there were several alternate starting points, the trail basically originated in Independence, Missouri, and ended in Portland, Oregon, at the confluence of the Willamette and Columbia rivers, a total distance of 2,100 miles. Generally, it followed the Platte and North Platte rivers through Nebraska and into Wyoming, then headed west through South Pass, the crossing point of the Continental Divide. The trail then headed southwest to Fort Bridger, where it turned northwest to join the Snake River in Idaho and finally met the Columbia River in eastern Oregon. Travel down the Columbia was frequently undertaken by raft.

Many of the immigrant wagon trains began in St. Joseph, Missouri, or Council Bluffs, Iowa, both towns along the Missouri River. The immigrants and their prairie schooners gathered at these locations during the late winter and early spring. When the spring grass was high enough on the Plains so that livestock could graze en route, the wagon trains departed. There were no roads so the immigrants followed the ruts of previous wagon trains. As the ruts became too deep, new ones were started. Ruts created by thousands of wagon wheels in the mid-1800s can still be found, spread across several miles of open plains.

The immigrant flow started around 1842, just as the fur trade was declining. In 1843 a thousand immigrants reportedly passed by Fort Laramie, Wyoming, on their way to California and the Northwest; by 1851 the number had increased to a staggering 55,000. Between 1840 and 1860, more than 300,000 settlers traveled through South Pass.

Fort Laramie in southeastern Wyoming and Fort Bridger in southwestern Wyoming played important roles on the Oregon Trail. Both forts started out as private enterprises. Fort Laramie, originally a fur-trading post built in 1834, became part of Jacob Astor's American Fur Trading Company soon thereafter. By 1840 it was an important resupply post for wagon trains on the Oregon Trail. Fort Laramie was 667 miles west of Independence, Missouri, which placed it roughly a third of the way along the total distance of the trail.

Jim Bridger, who had been involved in fur trading at Fort Laramie, built Fort Bridger in 1843 as a resupply station for wagon trains. He built his station 450 miles west of Fort Laramie at the point where the Oregon Trail headed northwest and the Mormon Trail to the Salt Lake and California branched to the southwest. The Mormons took over Fort Bridger in 1853, but it was captured by the U.S. Army in 1857 as part of the Utah (Mormon) War.

Life on the Trail

On the trail, men's and women's work was divided. The men tended the stock and the wagons, selected the route and the campgrounds, and were responsible for the safety of the wagon train. The women cooked, washed, and took care of the children—all familiar household tasks, but quite different and more complicated on the journey westward. They had to learn to cook over an open fire, frequently made with buffalo chips, which they had to gather. Their meals were limited to the provisions aboard the wagon; the wild plants, fruits, and berries picked along the way; and the wild game shot by their husbands. Clothing was washed whenever there was a stream near their campground.

Wagon train stopping at a lone frontier cabin on the trail. Etching collection of the author.

The difficult and dangerous journey tested human endurance. Many times along the way, precious possessions had to be discarded. Worn-out draft animals, as well as the family cow being driven to a new home, died along the way. The trail was littered with carcasses of dead cattle, horses, and mules, and shallow graves of the immigrants who succumbed along the way.

During the California Gold Rush in 1849, the California Trail left the Oregon Trail at Soda Springs, Idaho (approximately 150 miles northwest of Fort Bridger), and headed southwest, entering California over Donner Pass. The pony express in 1860 also used the Oregon Trail. Its route from Independence, Missouri, to Sacramento, California, essentially followed the

Oregon Trail to Fort Bridger, then the Mormon Trail to Salt Lake, and finally the California Trail through Fort Churchill, Nevada, and over Carson Pass into California.

Bozeman Trail

In 1862 gold was discovered in Montana near Virginia City, attracting prospectors and miners, who traveled the Oregon Trail into Idaho and then headed north to Montana. John Bozeman found a more direct route to the gold fields from the Oregon Trail west of Fort Laramie at Fort Fetterman. Unfortunately, the Bozeman Trail ran through the heart of Sioux country, which set off the Red Cloud War.

The Army built several forts along the trail to protect travelers and wagon trains, the most important of which were Fort Phil Kearny and Fort Reno, both in Wyoming, and Fort C. F. Smith in Montana. The Bozeman Trail proved too costly to maintain, however, with constant forays by bands of Indians led by Chiefs Red Cloud, White Cloud, and Crazy Horse. The Army finally withdrew from the forts and closed the trail in 1865. The Sioux celebrated the victory by burning down the forts as the soldiers rode away. Following the suppression of the Sioux in 1877, however, the Bozeman Trail became an important route for cattle drives from Texas into Wyoming and Montana.

Stagecoach Travel in the West

Stagecoaches in the West usually traveled at a gallop whenever possible. During the heyday of the western stagecoaches around 1870, it was feasible for a passenger, if he or she could stand the rigorous and extremely tiring ride, to travel from St. Louis to San Francisco in 23 days. The travel day usually started at 3 a.m.

Traveling at a gallop by stagecoach on a rough road. Etching collection of the author.

and continued until dark with only 20- to 40-minute stops for breakfast and lunch. Horses were changed every 10 to 15 miles and drivers every 30 to 45 miles. While these stops typically lasted for only a few minutes, passengers were urged to get out and exercise. Sleeping accommodations at night were found at primitive stations, above saloons in frontier towns, or frequently in the stagecoach itself.

After several days on the road, passengers were urged to stop at major stations where food and bedding were available. Cases on record describe some passengers going insane because they tried to accomplish the trip without stopping. In addition to the constant swaying and jolting, the passengers endured sleeplessness, intense heat and dust, torrential rains, collapsed bridges, and occasional Indian raids.

In the summer the stagecoach was constantly surrounded by clouds of dust. In crossing the prairies the heat inside a stagecoach often rose to above 110 degrees Fahrenheit. After even an hour's ride on a dry, hot day, passengers looked like soft-coal miners coming off a shift. They were covered from head to toe with grime, their faces streaked with rivulets of mud from trickling sweat or tears from dust-inflamed eyes.

In the winter snow seeped in around the curtains and covered the floor, the seats, and the passengers. Night temperatures often dropped below zero. When the passengers had to sleep in the stagecoach, they covered themselves with buffalo robes and huddled close together to conserve as much body heat as possible. At the relay stops the passengers crawled out half frozen to stamp their feet and revive their circulation.

Spring was even worse, because the thaw turned the black soil of the Plains into a morass of deep, sticky mud. It was all six horses could do to drag an empty Concord coach through the worst stretches. Passengers usually had to get out and slosh through the mire for often a mile or more until solid ground was reached.

To break the monotony of the journey, the passengers sang hymns, recounted their own experiences, or bored fellow travelers with tales of their misfortunes. Passengers were expected to participate in seeing that the stagecoach kept on schedule. When rounding curves at a gallop, they had to respond quickly when the driver yelled, "Gentlemen lean left" or "Gentlemen lean right," to avoid causing the stagecoach to tip over. (Presumably lady passengers followed suit.) Male passengers handled the belaying rope to ease the coach down a steep decline or gathered poles to lever the coach out of the mud. The "gentlemen" passengers were also instructed to keep their firearms handy to ward off marauding Indians or bandits. All-in-all it was an exciting and sometimes tragic experience to travel by stagecoach in the West during the mid-1800s.

Accommodations for Travelers

In the early days of the colonies, it was the practice to accommodate a traveler who came into the community in a private home. Most people at that time traveled on foot or by horse-back. Women traveled infrequently and were most often accompanied by a male member of the family.

As travel in the North increased, the inconvenience and additional expense of providing lodging and food for strangers eventually justified the need for public accommodations. In the South, however, where plantation homes were far apart, strangers were welcomed, because they often brought news of the outside world. The same was true on the frontier.

Travelers venturing west of the Mississippi River in the mid-1800s were not so fortunate, since settlements and settlers were few and far between. Accommodations ranged from rooms above saloons, to bunks in the relay stations, a bed of hay in a barn, in the coach, or simply the bare ground.

Eastern Taverns

East of the Appalachian Mountains taverns played a vital role in providing lodging for the weary traveler until well into the 1800s. By definition a tavern was a house that offered drink, food, and usually overnight accommodations to the public. Since the majority of the early settlers hailed from rural areas of England, they had brought the traditions of English

Unknown artist's rendition of Mount Washington Tavern, Farmington, Pennsylvania, courtesy of National Park Service, Fort Necessity National Historic Site, Farmington, Pennsylvania.

taverns with them, and the tavern also became the center of community life. Taverns were well-established throughout the New England and Middle Atlantic colonies by 1720.

Most of the tavern laws passed in the colonies were intended to curb drinking by limiting the time one spent in a tavern. In Massachusetts tavern laws forbade travelers from enjoying more than one gill (four ounces) of liquor while staying at a tavern. Maryland laws, on the other hand, encouraged tavern keeping for the entertainment of "all persons as well as strangers."

The location of the tavern was an important consideration in granting tavern licenses. Some colonies decreed that ferry operators establish and run taverns at their terminals for the convenience of their customers. Most colonies required that tavern locations be convenient for both local inhabitants and travelers. Stagecoach lines expanded throughout the Northeast and beyond the Allegheny Mountains. Called "accommodations," these coaches operated on regular schedules, stopped frequently, and allowed for overnight stops. Tavern keepers were frequently part owners of stagecoach lines, and each stage stopped at its own set of taverns. Thus, there were competing taverns scattered along the major roads of the eastern United States until the mid- to late-1800s. By then the railroads had captured the bulk of the nation's passenger transportation.

The best sites for taverns were in the main part of town near places of public business, on major roads, or at crossroads. In rural areas they were located eight to ten miles apart. The quality of taverns in the South was poor outside of Charleston and Savannah. Travelers in the South relied on the hospitality of rural homeowners until the late 1800s.

Travel in colonial America was hazardous and tiring. Bad weather and road conditions frequently delayed the traveler. As a result a person did not have to travel a great distance to need the services of a tavern. A trip ten miles outside of Boston, for example, required an overnight stay. The only landmarks along the roads, other than natural ones, were taverns, and travelers measured their journeys in the time it took to travel from one tavern to another. Travelers relied on word-of-mouth recommendations for overnight lodgings, since road maps and travel information were nonexistent.

A few of the colonies attempted to set standards for tavern fare and lodgings. Maryland required that a tavern keeper maintain a set number of beds for guests. The prices charged for food and lodging in a licensed tavern were regulated by law. Before the Revolutionary War travelers were customarily charged between 75 cents and one dollar for a night's lodging, three meals, and beer. Following the war, tavern keepers began charging separately for meals, with dinner costing 75 cents and breakfast 50 cents.

The quality and extent of sleeping accommodations varied widely. In the seventeenth and into the eighteenth century, it was common practice to place beds in every room of the house and in the public rooms of the tavern. Outside the urban areas taverns were usually residences that had been turned into inns, and travelers shared the rooms with the tavern keeper's family.

Even after the establishment of separate bedrooms, usually one for men and one for ladies, guests commonly shared a bed, sometimes as many as six persons sleeping crosswise. If there were insufficient beds, straw pallets would be placed on the floor to accommodate the latecomers. Most taverns were equipped with six to eight beds. The Raleigh Tavern in Williamsburg, Virginia, was an exception, listing 38 beds in its inventory. Although women travelers usually slept in separate beds or even separate rooms, they were occasionally forced to share sleeping accommodations with the men.

By the late 1700s an emphasis was placed on improving lodging conditions and privacy. However, it was not until the latter part of the nineteenth century that some of today's standards of privacy and cleanliness were widely adopted.

An 1860s photograph of Rock Creek Station. This "road ranch" catered to stagecoaches, freight lines, and immigrant traffic on the Oregon Trail. Photo courtesy of Rock Creek Station Historical Park, Fairbury, Nebraska.

Stagecoach Stops in the West

Accommodations for stagecoach travelers west of the Mississippi were far below those in the East. Oftentimes the stagecoach driver merely stopped along the road for the night. Passengers slept in the coach or, if the weather was warm, slept on the ground. Frequently the stagecoach line would provide passengers with pneumatic pillows that they could inflate for a more comfortable night's sleep on the coach.

If the stagecoach also traveled at night, passengers usually had no sleep for the first night or two as they sat bolt upright bumping along over the prairie. However, if the passenger desired he could lay over at a relay station or ranch house. In pleasant weather passengers would sleep on top of the coach. To keep from being jolted off by its motion, they tied themselves on with a rope or strap.

On most western roads two types of relay stations existed: smaller "swing" stations, and larger "home" stations. The "swing" stations had no passenger facilities and only provided for a change of horses or mules for the stagecoach. The "home" station provided new drivers and sometimes facilities for passengers.

In the early 1860s the Leavenworth & Pike's Peak Express Company established the first series of relay stations with the traveler's comfort in mind. Twenty-five of the larger stations were maintained as "home" stations which provided excellent meals and lodging for the passengers.

By the mid-1860s a number of ranches were established along the stagecoach routes adjoining the stage stations. Although the ranchers raised some livestock, they primarily provided food and lodging for stagecoach travelers. Several of the ranch houses also had a section termed the "pilgrim quarters." Here the travelers could sleep on the floor and do their own cooking in an open fireplace.

Prices for meals at "home" stations and ranch houses varied from $0.60 to $1.50. The food was generally bad, primarily consisting of beans, bacon, hominy, sorghum, and an abundance of buffalo and antelope steaks. Dried apple pies were the norm for dessert. One traveler expressed his feelings about these pies in this manner:

> I loathe! abhor! detest! despise!
> Abominate dried apple pies . . .
> The farmer takes his gnarliest fruit,
> Tis wormy, bitter, and hard, to boot;
>
> He leaves the hulls to make us cough,
> And don't take half the peelings off . . .
>
> Tread on my corns, or tell me lies,
> But don't pass me dried apple pies.

Trail, Road, and Accommodation Museums

Trail and Road Museums (museums listed east to west by individual trail or road)

Braddock's and Forbes' Roads

❖ *FORT NECESSITY NATIONAL BATTLEFIELD, U.S. Route 40, Farmington, Pennsylvania 15437. Tel: 412-329-5512. Open daily 10:30-5, except Christmas. Admission $1, family discount.*

Located 11 miles east of Uniontown, Pennsylvania, on U. S. Route 40, Fort Necessity was established as a national historic site in 1931. It is operated by the National Park Service and contains two entities: the reconstructed Fort Necessity stockade and the adjacent Mount Washington Tavern. General Edward Braddock is buried nearby, having died in an ambush near Fort Duquesne. Today's Interstate 40 generally follows the original Braddock's Road on which Fort Necessity was constructed.

Fort Necessity was built by George Washington in 1754. In July of that year, Washington and his Virginia and South Carolina militiamen were quickly overwhelmed by French and Indians from Fort Duquesne in a battle and were forced to return to Virginia.

In addition to the reconstructed stockade the battlefield site also consists of troop entrenchments and earthworks. A visitor center exhibits the conditions and events at the time of the battle, along with a brief slide show.

❖ *FORT LIGONIER, U.S. Route 30, Ligonier, Pennsylvania, 15658. Tel: 412-238-9701. Open daily 10-5, April through October. Admission $4, senior and youth discounts.*

General John Forbes built a fort at Ligonier in 1758 as a defense of his road. The fort, which has been reconstructed and is open to the public, contains interpretive exhibits of the original fort. Two of the rooms are furnished with period artifacts.

❖ *FORT PITT MUSEUM AND BLOCKHOUSE, Point State Park, Pittsburgh, Pennsylvania 15222. Tel: 412-281-9284. Open Tuesday through Saturday 10-4:30, Sunday noon-4:30, closed on certain holidays. Admission $3, senior and youth discounts.*

Fort Pitt was located at the junction of the Allegheny, Ohio, and Monongahela rivers in what is now downtown Pittsburgh. Its strategic location allowed defenders to control river traffic down the Ohio River. It also became an important terminus of overland roads from the East. The British built Fort Pitt in 1758, after they had captured the French-held Fort Duquesne near the same location. After the British abandoned the fort in 1772, the Colonists continued to

defend it against the Indians, who were attacking the increasing number of settlers.

Fort Pitt Museum was opened by the Commonwealth of Pennsylvania in 1964 within Point State Park and is housed in a reproduction of a portion of the original fort. The museum, which uses dioramas to describe the early frontier in the region and the various conflicts between the British and French, also contains artifacts from the period.

Wilderness Trail

❖ *CUMBERLAND GAP NATIONAL HISTORIC PARK, U.S. Route 25E, Middlesboro, Kentucky. Tel: 606-248-2817. Open daily 8-5. Admission free.*

The Cumberland Gap National Historic Park, which encompasses more than 21,000 acres, was established in 1959 and is operated by the National Park Service. The park's visitor center is located on U. S. Route 25E/State Route 58, southeast of Middlesboro on the Kentucky side of the gap. It contains interesting exhibits regarding the history of the gap and the Wilderness Trail, highlighting the importance of the Cumberland Gap in opening the Old Northwest Territory.

Daniel Boone Homestead. Photo courtesy of the Pennsylvania Historical and Museum Commission, Birdsboro, Pennsylvania.

❖ *DANIEL BOONE HOMESTEAD, Daniel Boone Road, Birdsboro, Pennsylvania 19508. Tel: 215-582-4900. Open Tuesday through Saturday 9-5, Sunday noon-5, closed major holidays except Memorial Day, July 4, and Labor Day. Admission $3, senior, youth, and group discounts.*

The Daniel Boone Homestead preserves the family home where the American pioneer was born in 1734. The home, which is nine miles east of Reading, Pennsylvania, just north of U.S. Route 422, was established as a state historic site in 1937. The homestead consists of the foundation of the original log cabin built in 1730 by Squire and Sarah Boone, Daniel's English Quaker parents. The house has been restored and is furnished with antiques.

Also included on the property are a restored barn, sawmill, blacksmith shop, Germanic log cabin, bake house, and smoke house. The visitor center provides exhibits on the life of Daniel Boone and the Boone family.

In 1767 Boone led a group of settlers through the Cumberland Gap into Kentucky. In 1775, while employed by the Transylvania Land Company, he blazed a trail and guided another group of settlers into Kentucky. Boone helped found a settlement, which later was named Boonesboro. Around 1800 Boone lost his property through faulty registration and joined his son in Defiance, Missouri, where he lived for the rest of his life. He died in Defiance in 1820 at the age of 86. His home in Defiance is also preserved and open to the public.

Natchez Trace

❖ *NATCHEZ TRACE PARKWAY, Tupelo Visitor Center, Tupelo, Mississippi 38801. Tel: 601-842-1572. Open daily 8-5. Admission free.*

❖ *NATCHEZ TRACE PARKWAY, Natchez Visitor Center, Mount Locust, Mississippi 39120. Tel: 601-445-4211. Open daily 8:30-5, February through November. Admission free.*

The National Park Service is developing the Natchez Trace into a parkway to commemorate the importance of the Natchez Trace in the development of the country. There are two visitor centers: one near Tupelo, Mississippi, and the other near Natchez). They, and various historical markers along the 400 miles of completed parkway, present the story of the trace.

The Tupelo Visitor Center, located at milestone 266, was founded in 1938 and features exhibits on the history of the trace, including a 12-minute slide show.

The Mount Locust Visitor Center, located at milestone 15.5, is in the only inn remaining from the original trace. This center provides exhibits on the trace as well as the modern parkway, and Park Service rangers give regular talks on the history of the trace.

National Road

❖ *NATIONAL ROAD-ZANE GREY MUSEUM, east on U.S. Route 40, Zanesville, Ohio 43702. Tel: 614-872-3143. Open Wednesday through Saturday 9:30-5, Sunday noon-5, March, April, October, and November; Monday through Saturday 9:30-5, Sunday noon-5, May through September. Admission $3, senior and children discounts.*

The National Road-Zane Grey Museum is located east of Zanesville, Ohio, on the old National Road. The museum, operated by the Ohio Historical Society, provides various exhibits on the history of Zane's Trace and the National Road. A 136-foot diorama portrays the development of the National Road from the time the first trees were felled to the arrival of the automobile. Other exhibits illustrate how vehicle technology prompted road-surface improvements from gravel to concrete. A Conestoga wagon, a stagecoach, early bicycles, and early automobiles are also on display.

The museum displays life-size reconstructions of typical scenes along the National Road during the nineteenth century. Featured are a blacksmith shop, a wheelwright, and various tavern scenes. A wing of the museum displays memorabilia relating to the western writer, Zane Grey, who was born in Zanesville.

Santa Fe Trail

❖ *ARROW ROCK STATE HISTORIC SITE, State Route 41, Arrow Rock, Missouri 65320. Tel: 816-837-3330. Open Monday through Saturday 10-4, Sunday noon-5; closed major holidays. Admission free.*

Originally named New Philadelphia in 1829, the town of Arrow Rock is located midway between St. Louis and Kansas City on the Missouri River. A trading center for area farmers, the town was one of the early starting points of the Santa Fe Trail. However, as the riverboats loaded with supplies and settlers destined for the Santa Fe Trail found ways to navigate further upstream to Independence and beyond, Arrow Rock lost its significance and became another sleepy river town.

Arrow Rock State Historic Site, established by the State of Missouri in 1923, commemorates the historical importance of this river port. A number of the original buildings have been restored to the town's period of glory, including the courthouse and jail, the town general store, Arrow Rock Tavern, and several historic homes.

The tavern dates back to 1834. It was built by Joseph Huston, a Virginian, who saw the need for a tavern to house weary travelers passing through town. The taproom of the tavern contains a museum exhibiting artifacts associated with the heritage of the town. The tavern's restaurant specializes in traditional country-style dishes.

Arrow Rock was home to the famous pioneer genre artist, George Caleb Bingham. The brick house Bingham occupied from 1837 to 1845 has been restored and is furnished with items appropriate to the period.

❖   *FORT LARNED NATIONAL HISTORIC SITE, west on State Route 156, Larned, Kansas 67550. Tel: 316-285-6911. Open year-round 8:30-5, extended in summer months until 6. Admission $1 for adults, under 16 and over 62 free.*

Fort Larned National Historic Site, six miles west of Larned, was established by the National Park Service in 1966. It is judged to be the best-preserved fort of those built during the Plains Indian wars in the 1860s and 1870s.

Fort Larned, Kansas, was built in 1859 to protect wagon trains on the Santa Fe Trail and was active until 1878. Situated almost midway between Independence, Missouri, and Santa Fe, the fort provided vital protection to travelers on the trail and attempted to keep the peace between Indians and settlers in the region. The U.S. Indian Bureau maintained an agency here during the 1860s.

The restored buildings at the Fort Larned National Historic Site include two barracks, a blacksmith's shop, a baker's shop, a carpenter and wheelwright's shop, a schoolhouse, an officers' quarters, and a quartermaster's warehouse. The blockhouse has been reconstructed to resemble its original appearance. One of the barracks serves as the visitor center, which contains military artifacts and historical exhibits. A section of the Santa Fe Trail containing ruts created by the thousands of wagons that traversed the trail can be seen near the fort.

❖   *SANTA FE TRAIL CENTER MUSEUM, west on State Route 156, Larned, Kansas 67550. Tel: 316-285-2054. Open daily 9-5, except major holidays and Mondays, Labor Day through Memorial Day. Admission $3, children discounts.*

The Santa Fe Trail Museum, located two miles west of Larned, was opened in 1974 by the Fort Larned Historical Society. On display are a number of local artifacts from the active days of the Santa Fe Trail. Exhibits include replicas of an Indian hunting lodge, a dugout, and a settler's sod house. The museum also maintains a library of publications relating to the Santa Fe Trail and the local region.

❖   *BENT'S OLD FORT NATIONAL HISTORIC SITE, east on State Route 194, La Junta, Colorado 81050. Tel: 719-384-2596. Open Memorial Day to Labor Day 8-6, rest of the year 8-4:30. Admission $1, seniors and children free.*

Bent's Old Fort on the Arkansas River in southeastern Colorado was once the frontier hub from which American trade and influence extended south into Mexico, west into the Great Basin, and north to southern Wyoming. The fort, built in 1833 by Charles and William Bent and Ceran St. Vrain, became an important fur-trading post along the trail. For more than 17 years, the Bents and St. Vrain successfully maintained a trading operation that brought manufactured goods from the East into the Mexican territory and, in reverse, brought

Mexican and Navajo goods to the fort for shipment on to Missouri. In addition, Indian tribes of the area traded their furs for goods, and mountain men bartered beaver pelts and other furs for equipment and supplies. Kit Carson was employed by the fort as a hunter and scout for more than ten years.

Bent's Old Fort, a two-story adobe complex, has been reconstructed to its appearance in 1845-46. The rooms are furnished with antiques and reproductions of the period. Included in the complex are a kitchen, dining room, trade and council room, living quarters, military quarters, and warehouses. Bent's Old Fort is operated by the National Park Service.

❖ *PIONEER MUSEUM, 300 East Main Street, Trinidad, Colorado 81082. Tel: 719-846-7217. Open Monday through Saturday 10-4, Sunday 1-4, Memorial Day to Labor Day; by appointment, rest of year. Admission $1, children and senior discounts.*

The Pioneer Museum in Trinidad is part of a complex operated by the state of Colorado in cooperation with the Colorado Historical Society. Trinidad was a major supply depot on the western half of the Santa Fe Trail. It is located at the foot of Fisher's Peak, a famous landmark on the trail.

The museum complex includes the museum plus the Baca House, a two-story adobe structure built in the mid-1860s and purchased in 1870 by Felipe Baca, a prosperous sheep rancher and politician.

A one-story adobe building houses the museum, which provides exhibits dealing with the Santa Fe Trail such as wagons and tools used on the trail. It also features exhibits on local ranching history. The Baca House contains exhibits on regional history, particularly the local Hispanic culture, and includes an interpretative program on the history of the Santa Fe Trail from 1821 to 1880.

❖ *FORT UNION NATIONAL MONUMENT, north on U.S. Route 25, Watrous, New Mexico 87753. Tel: 505-425-8025. Open 8-6 Memorial Day to Labor Day; daily 8-5, rest of year. Admission $1, under 16 and over 62 free.*

Fort Union National Monument was established in 1956 and is administered by the National Park Service. It is located where the western ends of the Mountain and Cimarron Cutoff branches of the Santa Fe Trail merge. The Cimarron Cutoff shortened the distance considerably by avoiding crossing over Raton Pass. However, it presented problems to wagon masters due to the route's shortage of water and food for the animals.

Fort Union, the largest Army installation on the southwestern frontier, was established in 1851 as a supply depot for nearly 50 other southwestern forts. It served as as a guard station on the Santa Fe Trail until the railroad reached the region in 1891. The only Civil War battle fought in the Southwest took place 60 miles from Fort Union when Confederate troops tried to intercept freight bound for the fort.

The sprawling installation, which took six years to complete, was the most extensive in the Southwest Territory. It included not only a military post, but a separate quartermaster's depot with warehouses, corrals, shops, offices, and quarters. The supply function overshadowed that of the military, although throughout the 1860s and 1870s troops from Fort Union continued to participate in operations against hostile Indians. By 1891 the fort had outlived its usefulness and was abandoned.

The visitor center and museum at this national monument contain exhibits describing the activities of the infantry, cavalry, and artillery units stationed here, including their weapons and

Interior of Mechanics Corral, Fort Union Depot, New Mexico. Photograph courtesy of Fort Union National Monument, Watrous, New Mexico.

other artifacts. Part of the exhibit describes the role of the fort in the development of the Santa Fe Trail. A self-guided tour can be taken around the ruins of the original buildings. The stone foundations of the buildings are still visible, as are some of the adobe walls.

❖ *PALACE OF GOVERNORS, on the Plaza, Santa Fe, New Mexico 87501. Tel: 505-827-6483. Open daily 10-5. Admission $3.50, senior discount, under 16 free.*

Built by the Spanish on the central plaza in 1609, the Spanish-style Palace of Governors successively became the seat of government under Spanish, Indian, Mexican, and United States territorial rule until 1909. At that time the State of New Mexico converted it into a museum, which it now operates with the assistance of a local historical society.

The Palace of Governors contains displays of life in the region under its various rulers. An extensive collection of artifacts from the various periods includes firearms, pottery, silver, furniture, and religious art. Also on display are trail markers and stagecoaches that traveled the Santa Fe Trail around 1880. The palace library houses a large collection of publications and photographs dealing with the history of the region, including the Santa Fe Trail.

Oregon Trail

❖ *ROCK CREEK STATION STATE HISTORIC PARK, southeast on State Route 8, Fairbury, Nebraska 68352. Tel: 402-729-5777. Visitor Center is open daily 9-5 Memorial Day to Labor Day; weekends 9-5, rest of year. The grounds of the park are open year-round. Admission $2 per car.*

This historic park, located approximately seven miles east of Fairbury, was founded by the state of Nebraska in 1980. Rock Creek Station was originally an important stopping place and resupply point on the Oregon Trail. Its fame in western lore was established when James "Wild Bill" Hickok killed the owner of the station, David McCanles, and two of his hired hands on July 12, 1861, for reasons that apparently remain obscure to this day. At the time of the brawl,

Hickok was an employee of a stagecoach company and had been sent to Rock Creek as assistant stock tender and stable hand.

Nebraska is in the process of restoring several of the important ranch buildings. The east ranch house and the west ranch house have been restored according to 1861 photographs. Also restored are the bunkhouse, pony express barn, sleeping quarters, and blacksmith shop where demonstrations are held. Undergoing restoration is the toll bridge cabin where tolls were collected. The visitor center offers historical and interpretive displays of the function of the ranch station. There are displays of wagons and livestock.

❖ *FORT KEARNY STATE HISTORICAL PARK, south on State Route 44, Kearney, Nebraska 68847. Tel: 308-234-9513. Open daily 9-5, Memorial Day through Labor Day. Admission $2 for park permit.*

Fort Kearny is in south-central Nebraska on the Platte River near Kearney. The fort was established by the Army in 1848 to provide protection to wagon trains heading west on the Oregon Trail and continued in this role until 1871. The state of Nebraska established this historical park at the site of the original fort in 1929.

During its 23 years of operation Fort Kearny served as headquarters for military and civil governments and was an important stagecoach stop, a home station for the pony express, and a supply base for the Army's numerous Indian campaigns. The California Gold Rush of 1849 increased travel on the Santa Fe Trail, although the years immediately following the Civil War saw the fort's peak activity. However, as the scene of Indian wars shifted further west, Fort Kearny became less essential to the military. The last function of the fort was to protect the crews constructing the Union Pacific Railroad.

Several of the fort's buildings, including the carpenter's shop and the powder magazine, have been restored. In addition there are replicas of the stockade and a sod blacksmith shop. A visitor center provides a history of the fort and includes a collection of artifacts, as well as a slide presentation of activities at the original fort and its relation to the Oregon Trail. Visitors can take a self-guided tour of the ruins of the original fort, which covers 40 acres.

❖ *FORT LARAMIE NATIONAL HISTORIC SITE, south on State Route 160, Fort Laramie, Wyoming 82212. Tel: 307-837-2221. Open 8-4:30 in the winter and 8-7 in the summer. Admission $1, seniors and children free.*

Fort Laramie is located at the confluence of the Laramie and North Platte rivers on the Oregon Trail. It was named a National Historic Site in 1938 and is operated by the National Park Service.

The fort was originally established as a fur-trading post in 1834 and operated as part of John Jacob Astor's American Fur Company until the Army acquired it in 1849. The army maintained troops at Fort Laramie to keep the peace along the Oregon Trail until 1890 when this function was no longer needed. The fort served as a pony express stop for the Cheyenne to Deadwood Express.

Although no remnants of the original fur-trading post remain, partial ruins and 13 historic structures pertaining to the military fort have been reconstructed. Eleven of the buildings are furnished according to period styles.

Jim Bridger's original trading post on the Oregon Trail. Photo courtesy of the Wyoming State Museum, Cheyenne, Wyoming.

❖ *FORT BRIDGER STATE MUSEUM, Fort Bridger, Wyoming 82933. Tel: 307-782-3842. Open 9-4:30 April 15 to Labor Day, with extended hours in June, July, and August. Open 9-4:30 on weekends rest of year. Admission $1 for adults.*

Fort Bridger, in southwestern Wyoming, was founded as a trading post in 1842 by Jim Bridger and Louis Vasquez. The trading post became an important outfitting point for the immigrants and Mormons traveling on the Oregon Trail. Many immigrants camped near the trading post for a while and obtained fresh oxen and mules for the rest of their journey.

Mormons, who were fleeing persecution in the East, built Fort Supply 12 miles south of Fort Bridger. They purchased the Bridger trading post in 1855 from Vasquez and used both posts as supply points. After two years, friction developed between the Mormons and the U.S. government. The Mormons burned both

installations and retreated to Salt Lake City, Utah. By 1859 the Army had taken over the Bridger trading post as a fort and expanded the facility to 29 buildings.

Although some of the fort's original buildings are in ruins, many have been reconstructed or restored. Jim Bridger's trading post has been excavated and reconstructed. A guardhouse, milk house, and laundry have been restored. The first schoolhouse in Wyoming still stands on the post. The officer's quarters are furnished with typical frontier furniture, and the pony express relay station and Overland Stage barns remain complete with wagons, buggies, and harnesses.

❖ *EMIGRANT TRAIL MUSEUM, DONNER MEMORIAL STATE PARK, 12593 Donner Pass Road, Truckee, California 96162. Tel: 916-587-3841. Open daily 10-12 and 1-4, closed major holidays. Admission $2, student discounts.*

The Donner Party is commemorated by the Donner Memorial State Park and its Emigrant Trail Museum near Donner Lake at the foot of Donner Pass near Truckee, California. The museum, which was completed in 1962, includes exhibits on the overland immigration of the 1840s, the Donner tragedy, construction of the transcontinental railroad, and the natural history of the Truckee Basin. A slide show depicting the history of the Donner Party is shown every hour on the hour.

The Donner Party was formed by two Illinois brothers, both prosperous farmers, named George and Jacob Donner. In April 1846, the Donners, their families, and their friends, the James Reed family, packed their possessions into six wagons and joined the stream of people bound for California. In late October the Donner Party, which by then had expanded to 20 wagons and 89 people, reached Truckee Meadows, near present-day Reno, Nevada. Fearful of the difficult mountain crossing up ahead, the group decided to rest for a week to gather strength. The delay proved to be fatal. Winter came early to the Sierra Nevada that year. The Donner Party became snowbound.

Efforts to rescue the Donner Party were hampered by bad weather, and rescue operations were not completed until April—five months after the Donner Party had been stranded. Only 47 of the original 89 had survived and most of those had done so by subsisting on the dead bodies of their companions.

About 100 yards south of the museum is the Murphy cabin site. Sixteen members of the Murphy, Foster, and Eddy families spent the winter in this dirt-floored cabin, which was approximately 25 feet long, and 18 feet wide.

Bozeman Trail

❖ *FORT PHIL KEARNY STATE HISTORIC SITE, U.S. Route 90 at exit 44, Story, Wyoming 82842. Tel: 307-684-7629. Open Wednesday through Sunday noon-4 and by appointment. Admission free.*

Fort Phil Kearny, located in Northern Wyoming, took the heaviest blows from the Indians in defense of the Bozeman Trail. It is commemorated by the Fort Phil Kearny State Historic Site in Story, Wyoming. A visitor center at the site of the fort houses displays and photographs pertaining to the operation of the fort.

❖ *FORT FETTERMAN STATE HISTORIC SITE, north on State Route 93, Douglas, Wyoming 82366. Tel: 307-358-2864. Open daily 9-5. Admission free.*

Fort Fetterman served as the starting point of the Bozeman Trail, and is commemorated as a State Historic Site. The fort was named after Captain William Fetterman, who died in what is called the Fetterman Massacre while defending a wood-gathering party sent out from Fort Phil Kearny.

Two original buildings remain from the fort; one of which houses the museum containing artifacts from the fort. Detailed markers identify the foundations of the buildings in the fort and serve as narrative for a self-guided tour.

Tavern and Inn Museums (listed alphabetically by state and city)

❖ *KEELER TAVERN PRESERVATION SOCIETY, 132 Main Street, Ridgefield, Connecticut 06877. Tel: 203-438-5485. Open Wednesday, Saturday, and Sunday 1-4; other times by appointment. Admission $3, student and senior discounts.*

Keeler Tavern was built as a home in the late 1720s by Benjamin Hoyt. Timothy Keeler purchased the house in 1769 and three years later turned it into a tavern and stagecoach stop. Keeler Tavern remained in continuous operation by the Keeler family as an inn for 135 years. The establishment developed a reputation for exceptional hospitality and was a regular stop on the coach route between New York and Boston.

During the Revolutionary War Keeler Tavern became a rallying place for supporters of the colonial cause. On April 27, 1777, British troops fired on the tavern because patriots were reported to be making musket balls in the basement. A small cannonball fired that day is still imbedded in a corner post of the house.

In 1966 a group of Ridgefield citizens purchased the property and formed the Keeler Tavern Preservation Society. All of the rooms are

Keeler Tavern Museum. The stone platform near the gate was used to make entering and exiting a stagecoach more convienent. Photo courtesy of the Keeler Tavern Museum, Ridgefield, Connecticut.

now furnished according to the period, many with original furnishings from the Keeler family. A collection of cooking utensils and household items provides a picture of domestic life in eighteenth century New England.

❖ *HUDDLESTON FARMHOUSE INN MUSEUM, U.S. Route 40W, Cambridge City, Indiana 47327. Tel: 317-478-3172. Open Tuesday through Saturday 10-4 and Sunday 1-4, May through August; Tuesday through Saturday 10-4, rest of year. Admission is by donation, $2 suggested.*

The Huddleston Farmhouse Inn Museum is located on the old National Road. John Huddleston, his wife Susannah, and their children—eventually numbering 11, established a thriving 78-acre farm west of Cambridge City in 1838. Weary travelers seeking shelter, food, wagon repairs, and rest for their horses found respite at the Huddleston farm.

Although the Huddleston house sheltered weary travelers, it was not exactly comfortable. Families brought food to prepare in the public kitchens on the farmhouse's lower level or paid to eat at the Huddlestons' table.

Huddleston also sold food for the travelers' animals. In inclement weather travelers slept in the barn, on the house's porch, or in the basement. During pleasant weather they usually slept in their own wagons parked in the barnyard.

In the 1960s through a generous gift of pharmaceutical philanthropist Eli Lilly, the Historical Landmarks Foundation was established to purchase the farm and restore the buildings. The furnishings are replicas of ones used in the mid-1800s, during the peak days of the National Road.

❖ *MOUNT WASHINGTON TAVERN, U.S. Route 40, Fort Necessity National Battlefield, Farmington, Pennsylvania 15437. Tel: 412-329-5512. Open daily 10:30-5, mid-spring to late fall, extended hours June through August; Saturday and Sunday 10:30-5, rest of year. Admission $1, family discount.*

In the 1820s Judge Nathaniel Ewing of Uniontown, Pennsylvania, built a stagecoach inn at Mount Washington, Pennsylvania. The inn was located a few feet back from the National Road in a two-acre apple orchard. The large brick-and-stone structure contained 11 rooms in two stories with an attic and a basement.

Mount Washington became a famous tavern on the National Road almost from the time it opened. It was one of the stops on the Good Intent Stage Line, one of the dozen or so stage lines that operated on the National Road. Mount Washington Tavern kept nine pairs of horses waiting in its stables at all times as relays for incoming coaches. It is surmised that the tavern also served other stage lines as records show that one morning 72 stage passengers were served breakfast.

The tavern is open to the public, and the parlor, ordinary room, kitchen, and bedrooms have been refurnished with period furnishings to show the type of accommodations available to stagecoach passengers at the time. An exhibit about the National Road is on display in the dining room of the tavern. The site is administered by the National Park Service.

❖ *THE COMPASS INN MUSEUM, Town Center, Laughintown, Pennsylvania 15658. Tel: 412-238-4983. Open Tuesday through Sunday 11-4, May 1 through late October. Admission $3, student discount.*

Located on the original General Forbes' Road, the Compass Inn and Tavern was built in 1799, when Forbes' Road had become the Philadelphia and Pittsburgh Turnpike. The inn is located near Ligonier, Pennsylvania, about 30 miles east of Pittsburgh, and was a stopping place for stagecoaches and drovers.

The inn has been restored by a local historical group and furnished with period artifacts. The barn adjacent to the inn contains an antique Conestoga wagon and a stagecoach used on the original turnpike. The blacksmith's shop and cooks' house contain implements used at the time.

❖ *PACKWOOD HOUSE MUSEUM, 10 Market Street, Lewisburg, Pennsylvania 17837. Tel: 717-524-0323. Open Tuesday to Friday 10-5, Saturday 1-5, Sunday 2-5, closed major holidays. Admission $4, senior and student discounts.*

The building known as the Packwood House was built as a log structure at the close of the eighteenth century. In the early 1800s it evolved into a massive three-story brick building that served as an inn for land, river, and canal travelers in the Susquehanna Valley. The inn remained in operation until 1886.

The Packwood House Museum was founded in 1972. Today 27 of the rooms are on exhibit and contain American and central-Pennsylvania artifacts.

Parlor in the 1850 Wade House, a stagecoach inn. Photo courtesy of The State Historical Society of Wisconsin, Madison, Wisconsin.

❖ *HISTORIC MICHIE TAVERN, State Route 53, Monticello Mountain, Charlottesville, Virginia 22902. Tel: 804-977-1234. Open daily 9-5, except major holidays. Admission $5.50, senior and school-age discounts.*

Michie Tavern was originally located on the William Michie family farm on Bucks Mountain in Albemarle County, Virginia. At the time the Buck Mountain Road was a stagecoach route from the Virginia coast to the new frontier in the Shenandoah Valley and the Allegheny Mountains. The family cabin became a convenient stopping place to spend the night before crossing the Blue Ridge Mountains. Often William Michie gave up his own bed to strangers.

As visitors became more frequent, Michie decided to build a proper tavern that could offer respectable accommodations and food. The tavern became so popular that Michie built a "hyphen" or connecting corridor between the tavern and his own cabin, thus adding two more sleeping rooms. William Michie died in 1811 and left the tavern to his son, William Jr., who operated the tavern until 1850.

In 1927 a local businesswoman, Mrs. Mark Henderson, purchased the tavern from the subsequent owners to house her vast collection of antiques. As the building was in disrepair and situated in a remote location, Mrs. Henderson

Historic Michie Tavern. Photo courtesty of Historic Michie Tavern, Charlottesville, Virginia.

moved the tavern to a more accessible site at the foot of Carter Mountain, one-half mile from Monticello, the home of Thomas Jefferson.

Today, the restored tavern serves as a museum. Visitors proceed through the building and listen to audio descriptions of each room. The gentlemens' and ladies' parlors, as well as the keeping room, bedroom, and ballroom are furnished with period antiques. The detached kitchen and other outbuildings are also open for viewing. The tavern building also contains a popular luncheon restaurant.

❖ *OLD WADE HOUSE AND WISCONSIN CARRIAGE MUSEUM, W7747 Plank Road, Greenbush, Wisconsin 53026. Tel: 414-526-3271. Open daily 9-5, May through October. Admission $4, senior and school-age discounts.*

Built in 1850 to serve the traffic on the busy Sheboygan and Fond du Lac Plank Road, the Wade House Stagecoach Inn was constructed by Sylanus and Betsey Wade. They furnished the inn with the latest styles of the time and provided accommodations and food for travelers in the area.

Since 1953, when the restored buildings were donated to the people of Wisconsin by the Kohler Foundation, the Wade House, along with

its adjacent carriage museum, has been operated by the State Historical Society of Wisconsin. Visitors to the Wade House can view the accommodations that awaited stagecoach travelers of more than a century ago. Depending upon the season, visitors can also see demonstrations of fireplace cooking and baking, food preservation, and candle making. (See the chapter on horse-drawn carriages for a description of the Wisconsin Carriage Museum.)

FAIRMAN ROGERS' FOUR IN HAND by Thomas Eakins, oil, 24 x 36 inches, courtesy of the Philadelphia Museum of Art, Philadelphia, Pennsylvania, given by Mr. William Alexander Dick.

Wagons and Carriages

Until the American Revolution the American colonies constituted a thin ribbon of settlements along the Atlantic Coast. In the more than 150 years between the settlement of Jamestown and the American Revolution, the frontier had only been pushed 200 miles inland from the Atlantic Ocean. The colonists traveled primarily on horseback or by boat on coastal waters and rivers. Stagecoach service, however, interconnected Boston, New York, and Philadelphia by the mid-1700s.

In the South the population was mainly agricultural with many settlers owning large plantations. There was little need for public transportation. Goods such as tobacco and cotton were carried by wagons to one of the innumerable rivers and rafted downstream to the seaport. Following the Revolutionary War, commerce developed between northern and southern states, and by 1800 stagecoach service had been initiated between Savannah, Georgia, and Philadelphia.

The earliest vehicles used in America were simply-made carts or wagons constructed by carpenters and farmers for farm work. They were used only incidentally to transport families from home to church, and to visit neighbors. When needed to transport passengers, the wagon was fitted with portable seats. Fancy carriages, imported from England, began to appear on the streets of Boston as early as 1700. Public coaches appeared in the 1720s.

In 1775 Daniel Boone blazed the Wilderness Trail from Virginia across the Allegheny Mountains to present-day Kentucky. As the number of immigrants moving west accelerated following the Revolutionary War, the Wilderness Trail and other similar trails leading west across the Alleghenies were upgraded to wagon roads. The opening of the old Northwest Territory in the 1790s and the Louisiana Purchase of 1803 spurred the movement westward and led to the creation of the National Road from Philadelphia to Ohio in the 1820s.

Conestoga Wagon

Conestoga wagons have been called "Empire Builders," because they were instrumental in helping to develop the lands west of the Allegheny Mountains. They were originally created in the mid-1700s by Pennsylvania German wagonmakers in the Conestoga valley to transport farm goods to market. Following the Revolutionary War, settlers adopted them to move their families westward into the new lands of Ohio and Indiana. Commercial freight forwarders used hundreds of Conestoga wagons to ship goods and produce on the Philadelphia and Lancaster Turnpike and the Cumberland Road during the late 1700s and early 1800s. The heyday of the Conestogas was over by the mid-1850s as canals and railroads expanded.

The Conestoga also found its way into North and South Carolina. Settlers traveled down what was called The Great Philadelphia Wagon Road, which started west of Philadelphia and continued south along the route now followed by U.S. Route 29 through Virginia and North Carolina into South Carolina. German and Scotch-Irish immigrants who settled in the back country of the Carolinas disembarked primarily in Baltimore and Philadelphia and were the major users of this overland route. As soon as the farming economy of the Carolinas began to develop, these immigrants started producing Conestoga wagons for local use.

The design of the Conestoga wagon is strictly American, with its ship-like appearance and hoop-shaped canvas cover. The ship-like appearance was no coincidence since the wagon was designed to be floated across rivers too deep to forge. They were ruggedly built to withstand the arduous journeys across the eastern mountains. Their low centers and high ends were designed to keep the contents from falling out on steep roads. Because of the heavy loads the Conestoga wagon was capable of carrying, its

Conestoga wagon passing a local inn, circa 1820. Sketch courtesy of the Smithsonian Institution, Washington, D.C.

wheels were up to six inches wide. Their width kept the wagon from sinking into the dirt roadways of the period.

The largest Conestoga wagon ever made stood 10 feet tall and was 20 feet long. It weighed 3,000 pounds and could carry three to four tons. To pull such heavy loads required a team of six horses or oxen. The driver typically rode one of the lead horses or walked beside the team.

Historians claim that the Conestoga wagon is the reason people drive on the right-hand side of the road in North America. Because of its design, the wagon had a tendency to pull to the right, and drivers found it easier to keep the wagon on the right side of the road.

Prairie Schooner

The Conestoga wagon of Pennsylvania was the forerunner of the covered wagons used by the pioneer settlers traveling west across the plains and mountains toward the Pacific Coast. The western version, called a prairie schooner, derived its name from the impression it gave of a ship sailing across the vast expanse of the level prairie. The prairie schooner was first developed in 1821 for use on the Santa Fe Trail. Most were built in St. Louis, Missouri, and were originally called Murphy wagons after a builder of wagons in that city. A large number of them were

manufactured by the Studebaker Brothers Manufacturing Company in South Bend, Indiana. The company also built the wagons used by the Borax Company to haul borax out of Death Valley, California, behind the famous 20-mule teams. Other prairie schooners were produced in Chicago; Indianapolis, Indiana; and Kenosha, Wisconsin.

The prairie schooner was pulled by four to six oxen or mules. The larger freight wagons used anywhere from six to twelve oxen depending on the weight of the load. Several extra oxen were driven along as reserves. Horses were seldom used as they were high-strung and did not have the stamina of oxen or mules. Additionally, horses were much in demand by the Indians and therefore attracted raiding parties.

Canvas sheets were placed over the bows and down the sides of the wagon bed to prevent rain from blowing into the cracks. Some of the trading wagons going west had a double canvas top, with wool blankets between the top canvases. The blankets not only kept the top dry, but enabled the trader to smuggle blankets past customs officers in New Mexico. Some of the wagons sported names, such as Constitution, President, The Republic, and Old Kentuck, on the white cover.

Necessities carried by most wagons for the long journey across the plains included an extra wagon tongue, one or two extra yokes, and

Wagon train of prairie schooners going west. Photo courtesy of the Smithsonian Institution, Washington, D.C.

one to two axles. The wagon's water keg was a necessity and was filled at every watering place. A chip-sack hung on a hook on the side of the wagon. It was filled with buffalo chips during the day to be ready for the evening campfire. A tar bucket also hung on the wagon and was used regularly to grease the axles.

Stagecoaches

Stagecoach service in America started to develop around 1750. The English allegedly invented the name "stagecoach" to describe a mode of overland travel where passengers transferred from coach-to-coach as they proceeded on their journeys in stages.

Stagecoach travel expanded after the Revolutionary War as new roads and territories were opened. The establishment of overland mail routes and the westward expansion spawned by the California Gold Rush of 1849 increased the use of stagecoaches. Their use peaked around 1870 as railroads expanded coast to coast.

The earliest public stagecoaches for long-distance travel were box-like, open wagons with bench seats. Permanent roofs and side curtains were added to protect the passengers from bad weather. During the first quarter of the nineteenth century, an increasing number of American stagecoaches were constructed with enclosed bodies and sturdier suspension systems.

The most popular stagecoach in the West was the Concord, so named because it originated with Abbot-Downing Company of Concord, New Hampshire. The Concord is the stagecoach frequently seen in movie and television Westerns. It has an egg-shaped body, and is pulled by a team of six horses. The driver sits on top holding six reigns in one hand, a whip in the other, and his foot on the brake. While the Concord was designed to accommodate 11 passengers, nine inside and one on either side of the driver, it frequently carried 15 or more clinging to the top and sides. The record number of passengers on a regular run is reported to have been 35. Seat belts and grab hooks were standard equipment on most Concord stagecoaches.

Abbot-Downing built its first Concord in 1827 and the stagecoach remained popular into the 1900s. Unlike other carriage builders, the Abbott-Downing Company continued to construct its vehicles almost entirely by hand. Instead of iron or steel springs, the company used

Stagecoaches used in America in the late eighteenth and early nineteenth centuries. 1. Stagecoach used in New England, 1795. 2. Stagecoach used in the Midwest, 1820. Photos courtesy of the Smithsonian Institution, Washington, D.C.

heavy leather eight-ply throughbraces on which the body was cradled. This sturdy suspension system was well-suited to the rugged terrain, but traveling by Concord was still a rough ride with the horses at a gallop on mountain roads full of potholes and jutting rocks. Because of its excellent design and careful construction, the Concord was in demand throughout the world and was exported to South Africa, Australia, South America, and even to England.

Freight Wagons

As the nation's commerce and industry became more complex during the 1800s, so did the design of wagons used to transport a wide variety of merchandise. Unbelievably large loads of freight were moved by horse and wagon in the nineteenth century. For example, a team of six horses and a wagon could transport a 20-ton marble slab from the quarry to a building site dozens of miles away. As mining developed in the West, freighters moved massive mining equipment up rugged mountain trails. Logging, a major industry around the Great Lakes and in the Pacific Northwest, required specialized flat-bed wagons or sleighs to haul lumber to nearby rivers for further transport.

In the major cities specialized wagons were used to deliver every conceivable commodity, including coal, ice, pickle and beer barrels, meat, groceries, bakery goods, milk, mail, department store packages, farm produce, and even laundered sheets and towels. Most of these merchandise wagons were relatively lightweight four-wheelers, although they varied in length, depending on their purpose. Two-wheel wagons were used for carrying small loads and had the advantage of being able to navigate in heavy urban traffic. Flatbed wagons, the forerunners of the stake truck, transported heavy and bulky merchandise. They were usually pulled by teams of four to six horses. More refined items were carried in smaller enclosed wagons fitted with shelves or bins, depending on the merchandise, and pulled by one or two horses.

Businesses quickly became aware of the advertising potential of the exterior panels of their wagons. They specified fancy and colorful lettering, trademarks, slogans, and scenes of product-related subjects on the sides of their wagons. Lunch wagons were pulled to a factory site where quick meals were provided for the workers. Two of the most popular fast-snack vehicles were the popcorn wagon and the ice-cream wagon. Both of these wagons were usually stationed in city parks, where they were patronized by strollers and people in passing carriages.

Some trade vehicles were even shaped to resemble the product of a specific company. The H.J. Heinz Company, for instance, had a specialized rig shaped like a huge pickle bottle. A novel two-wheeler in the shape of a top hat was used to deliver top hats. The body of a jeweler's cart was shaped like a small, round alarm clock and was constructed from bent wheel rims with a clock face painted on the side.

Other businesses went even further and developed show wagons with exceptional teams of horses. Armour and Company, for example, maintained a beautiful team of six dapple-gray Percherons, which were featured attractions at fairs and circuses in the early 1900s. The Anheuser-Busch Brewery continues to show its team of eight Clydesdales, a practice that started in the late 1800s. A furniture company in Stockton, California, maintained a team of eight strawberry-roan Belgians, which they showed throughout the West for a number of years. All of these equestrian splendors were designed to promote their sponsors by capitalizing on the American public's love of fine horses, a love that was transferred to the automobile in the 1920s.

Connecticut Pie Company's wagons ready for their morning deliveries. Photo courtesy of the Smithsonian Institution, Washington, D.C.

Rural Free Delivery Mail Service

Long-distance mail was being carried on stage lines or by riders fairly early in the 1800s. However, regular local delivery of mail to rural recipients did not begin until 1896. Before then, farmers and other country dwellers were forced to travel to an urban center, usually a one- or two-day trip, to pick up their mail. The U.S. Post Office initiated Rural Free Delivery (RFD) service in West Virginia and near China Grove, North Carolina, in 1896. The Post Office gradually extended service to other parts of the country over the next decade.

RFD service was offered year-round, and sleighs were used to transport mail during the winter months in the northern states. In the beginning of the service, mail carriers were required to furnish their own vehicles and animals, but the Post Office provided specially designed RFD buggies by the early 1900s.

The RFD buggy was unique and easily recognized as it slowly wended its way along country roads. An enclosed, lightweight surrey with a wooden frame, metal siding, and canvas top, it was typically painted white on the sides and black on the front and back. Others had a blue lower body, white upper, and red rear. The carrier sat on a straw-cushioned seat and drove while holding the reigns, which came through a notch in the front window. The interior of the wagon had a desk with a drawer and a number of pigeonholes above for mail. A rear luggage rack was often added for parcel delivery. In northern states during winter months, carriers frequently added small wood stoves for warmth.

RFD mail carriers at the turn of the century had a difficult and sometimes dangerous task. Roads were undeveloped and full of ruts.

Rain and snow could make them all but impassable. These conditions were also stressful to horses, so most mail carriers kept several horses that were rotated on alternate days. Routes were typically 30 to 50 miles in length, and carriers labored long hours, frequently from dawn to long after sunset.

Horse-drawn buggies continued to be used until the 1920s, when the Post Office finally replaced them with motor vehicles.

Private Carriages

Although most early transportation in the American colonies was by horse or utilitarian farm wagons, the wealthy men of the colonies, such as governors, successful merchants, and plantation owners, imported carriages from Europe for their personal transportation. In the latter part of the seventeenth and in the early eighteenth century, several types of small, open carriages began to be manufactured in America.

The manufacture in America of private carriages on a par with imported European-made ones began during the mid-eighteenth century in Boston, New York, and Philadelphia. The undertaking required the labor of numerous craftsmen—woodworkers, blacksmiths, wheelwrights, upholsterers, and painters. It also involved a considerable investment in materials. The first carriage makers were European immigrants who had learned their trade in Europe and produced vehicles based on European designs. The American Revolution curtailed the production of luxury items, but after the war domestic carriage-making was encouraged by protective legislation.

Carriages remained very expensive during the 1800s. Only the affluent owned their own carriages and maintained their own stables. The average family continued to travel on foot, by horseback, or by stagecoaches that were available in the more settled areas of the East Coast.

Unlike the commercial wagon, which was designed solely for utilitarian purposes, private carriages became statements of their owners' social and financial status. Consequently, they were constructed in a wide variety of sizes, shapes, and degrees of ornateness. They varied in size from the self-driven, two-wheel buggy to the ornate Grand Victoria, which was equipped with several uniformed attendants. In general, private carriages were owned primarily by wealthy merchants, bankers, lawyers, and doctors, all of whom lived principally in urban areas. Salesmen (then called drummers) and occasional users of private vehicles typically rented an appropriate carriage from a local livery stable.

One of the first carriage styles developed in America was the pleasure wagon, produced in New England at the beginning of the nineteenth century. It combined the functions of a work vehicle with that of a passenger vehicle because it had removable seats. The body of the wagon was boat-shaped to prevent the cargo from slipping out. Depending on the size of the body, one or two seats, each accommodating two passengers, could be installed quickly. The smaller pleasure wagons were often equipped with a collapsible hood, called a "half," which could be raised in inclement weather.

During the second half of the nineteenth century with standardization of production, interchangeabililty of parts, and reduced production costs, horse-drawn carriages became affordable to the upper middle class. Carriages were produced in large factories and shipped to sales rooms, called repositories, in major American cities. Some dealers also offered used vehicles for sale, much like today's automobile dealers.

By the beginning of the twentieth century, mass production had lowered the price of horse-drawn vehicles so substantially that they were advertised in mail-order catalogs for $20 each. By comparison, beef steak cost 13 cents a pound at the time. Thus a modest carriage or wagon cost the same as a calf. In 1900 more than 900,000 horse-drawn vehicles were manufactured in the United States.

The design of the early hooded buggies was derived from the one-bench pleasure vehicle. By the late nineteenth century, the buggy, a light,

Sunday afternoon carriage excursions in the park, circa 1875. Photogravure from a painting by Victor Perad. Collection of the author.

four-wheeled carriage accommodating one or two passengers, had become the most popular vehicle in America. Many of the buggies at the time had either a collapsible hood or a roof that could be removed in fair weather. Some buggies, such as the doctor's buggy, were constructed so that the doctor could be completely enclosed during inclement weather.

Although the buggy was the most popular American carriage, there were other carriages on the streets and roads of late nineteenth- and early twentieth-century America. Two popular four-wheel carriages were the runabout and the rockaway. The open carriage runabout could seat two and had a space under the seat and in the back for packages and parcels. The rockaway, developed by a carriage maker in Jamaica, New York, in the 1830s, was named in honor of the town of Rockaway on Long Island. Later models of this enclosed carriage provided a front seat for the driver.

Among the popular two-wheel carriages was the cabriolet, which was drawn by a single horse, had a fold-back hood, and seated two people. The term "cabriolet" was derived from the Latin word for goat and was first used in seventeenth-century Italy to describe two-wheeled vehicles pulled by a goat. By the nineteenth century it had become the name for a very chic gentleman's carriage.

One of the most significant developments in carriage design was the phaeton. The term "phaeton" was first used in 1742 and was applied to vehicles with precariously high suspension systems, open bodies, and forward-facing seats. The term probably was derived from the mythological Greek figure Phaeton, the son of the sun-god Helios, whose reckless driving of his father's chariot nearly set the world on fire.

By the mid-nineteenth century phaetons were considerably lower in design, and the term was applied to more than a dozen different styles of carriages, including the mail phaeton, with a square body and folding top over the driver's seat; the spider phaeton, a pleasure vehicle used for competitive driving; and a basket phaeton, which had a wicker body and a fringed parasol top.

As carriages were mass-produced and became more affordable for the American middle class, the wealthier populace turned to luxury vehicles, many of which were designed to be driven by coachmen. Although the exteriors of many of these private coaches were somber in appearance, the luxurious interiors were decorated in silk, velvet, satin, and soft leather. There were optional accessories, such as cigar boxes, folding vanities, and flower vases—all of which could be ordered from the manufacturer.

During the late 1800s and early 1900s, luxury coaches filled the carriage houses in the cities and fashionable summer resorts. The vehicles, the horses, and the coachmen became integral parts of the social scene. Published social guides listed the size of a family's horses, the style of its carriage, the type and fit of the harness, and the decorum of the coachman. The size, weight, and appearance of the coachman was dictated by fashion to conform to the appearance of the carriage.

City parks were developed during this time, partly to satisfy the public's demand for healthful recreation, but also to provide a place for high society to promenade their families, carriages, and horses. New York's Central Park, built between 1857 and 1876, was designed as much for carriage paths as for pedestrian walkways. The Sunday carriage promenade in the park by wealthy men to show off their carriages, teams of horses, and wives' finery was an accepted custom in the 1800s.

One of the most popular coachman-driven vehicles was the brougham. This box-like carriage seated two to four persons, with a front perch on the outside for the driver. A smaller version, seating only two, was known as a coupé, although in later years both types were referred to as broughams. A bell pull inside on a sidewall panel connected to a bell beneath the driver's seat

Rockaways, first produced about 1830 and of American design, were created to keep both passenger and driver under cover. The profile of this horse-drawn vehicle was eventually incorporated into early limousine auto bodies. Photo of an 1880 rockaway courtesy of the Owls Head Transportation Museum, Rockland, Maine.

and was used to signal the coachman. Some summer broughams could be converted to open vehicles by removing the upper panels and lowering the windows into the door panels.

Coaches varied in size, but typically seated four to six comfortably. Some coaches also had an exterior seat at the back for a footman. There was frequently a compartment for luggage under the driver's seat. The larger coaches were used for extensive trips, such as transporting the owners and their families to their summer residences.

Several open, coachman-driven carriages also existed. One of the most popular was a variation of the cabriolet with a fold-back top and a graceful low-slung body that extended into the driver's seat. These carriages became known as Victorias. They were preferred for park driving since the body of the carriage and the folding hood presented a good view of the passengers. For very formal occasions the Victoria was accompanied by a postilion (one who rides the leading left-hand horse in a team of four).

The landau, a low-slung, sporty vehicle, had two seats for four passengers. The coachman's perch was often above the heads of the passengers. The top of the carriage was made in two parts so that it could be folded back, half of it resting above the front seat and the other half above the back seat.

Another popular sporting coach was the drag, also called a "Tally-Ho" and a "four-in-hand," although this latter term was a general one used for any coach pulled by four horses. The drag served as a road coach, as well as a private coach for outings. It had four bench seats on top with an imperial in the center. The imperial was a box that could store equipment, food, and drink, and could be opened to make a table. The rear boot of the drag also opened into a serving table and provided additional space for food, drink, picnic utensils, and glassware. The drag was popular at spectator events such as horse races since the passengers could sit on top to watch the races over the heads of the crowd. On the way to such outings, the servants usually rode inside the coach.

In the smaller gentlemen's drags the passengers rode to the spectator events inside the carriage. Upon arriving at the event, the driver would pull out the ladder, which was stored underneath the carriage, and put it in place so that the passengers could climb to the top seats and watch the races. The tailgate section at the back of this type of carriage also had storage compartments for utensils and food.

Owning a carriage in the 1800s and early 1900s was not as simple as having a car today. In addition to a garage for the carriages, the owner needed a stable and feed for the horses and a tack room to store harnesses and other equipment. The horses needed to be fed, watered, and groomed daily. The stables had to be cleaned and the manure disposed of, plus the stalls needed to be mulched with hay. The carriages

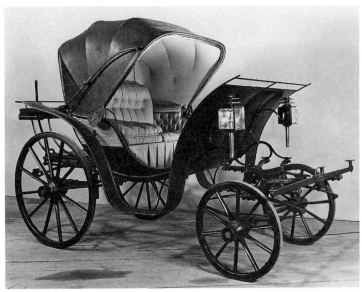

A George IV phaeton. Photo courtesy of the Shelburne Museum, Shelburne, Vermont.

required constant cleaning and maintenance, as did the harnesses and other tack. In urban areas, unless the owner loved horses and had the space, he or she typically rented space and services at the local livery stable.

Only the very wealthy maintained their own stable facilities and staff. It was not unusual for them to own a number of carriages, possess more than a dozen horses, and employ a stable staff of eight to ten, which included coachmen, grooms, and stable boys. Owners who could afford them insisted on owning pairs of horses that were matched in size, color, breeding, and training.

Public Passenger Carriages

A number of lighter coaches and wagons were used to transport paying passengers over short distances. In resort areas and major cities, hotels and livery stables operated coaches to transport guests to and from the railroad station. Resort hotel coaches were very elegant with gold-leaf lettering and decoration. Frequently, there was a painted scene of the hotel on the door and

An 1875 omnibus made by the J. Stephenson Company of New York. The omnibus was 36 feet long and required a team of 10 horses. The driver sat on the outside on the front. Passengers entered and exited through the rear door. Photo courtesy of the Smithsonian Institution, Washington, D.C.

plush velvet or leather seats in the interior. These coaches could accommodate 12 passengers on the inside and 12 on top on the outside. If the coach was full, a separate wagon was used to transport luggage.

Various styles of smaller wagons in the resort areas became known as depot or station wagons, or station omnibuses. In some mountain resorts livery stables and hotels had more rugged open wagons that accommodated 12 to 40 passengers for sight-seeing excursions on primitive mountain roads.

In the urban areas a wide variety of vehicles provided short-distance transportation. These included the hackney coach, cab, and omnibus. The hackney coach was similar to a stagecoach, but it had a square body and seated only four to six passengers. Hackneys were used for city transportation as well as for short runs between towns.

The most popular cabs were known as hansoms, named after J. A. Hansom, an English architect who designed the vehicle in the early 1850s. The cab (a term derived by shortening the word "cabriolet") was a low-hung, two-wheeled, covered vehicle drawn by one horse. Two passengers could sit inside, and the driver perched on a high seat behind the body of the cab to give him a view of the horses and traffic. The reins ran through a bracket on the roof.

Vehicles designed to carry up to 30 passengers were first developed in France and England in the early 1800s and were called omnibuses. When initially used in America, they were called "accommodations," but later reverted to the European name. The first American omnibuses were built by Wade & Leverich in 1827 for use in New York City.

The omnibus was open with low sides and a fixed roof supported by pillars. The seats were made of wood and the entrance door was located either on the side or in the back. Later omnibuses had windows and roll-up curtains. Some had a spiral staircase that provided access to additional seats on the roof. The exterior side panels were brightly decorated with signs describing the bus route and displayed advertisements of local businesses.

Sleighs

The winter months in the northern part of the United States were ideal for travel by sleigh. Packed snow and ice leveled the usually rough and difficult roads, making winter travel more enjoyable. During the Carriage Age of the 1800s and early 1900s, people welcomed the first snowfall. In northern cities throughout the winter months, there were more sleighs on the streets that there were carriages and wagons.

Except for the very ornate ones, sleighs were inexpensive to build and required little maintenance. Some carriages were designed with interchangeable wheels and runners, called bobs, for year-round use, as were trade vehicles and public conveyances.

Sleighs varied in size from small, light, one-horse cutters to more elaborate versions that resembled carriages on runners and required a team of two to four horses. The earliest American sleighs were open, box-like vehicles on runners that could be converted to freight transport by removing the seats.

The one-horse cutter was the most popular sleigh for personal travel, and could be quite ornate and expensive. The Albany cutter manufactured by James Gould of Albany, New York, for example, featured sweeping lines and a rounded body. It was expensive because the curved wooden side panels had to be formed by steam bending.

Sleighs were decorated either with paint or decals of flora and fauna. In the latter part of the nineteenth century, carriage makers manufactured enclosed sleighs, which were equal in opulence to fine coaches.

Passengers in the sleighs kept warm with fur or fur-trimmed clothing and used heated soapstones or foot warmers containing coal, charcoal, or hot water to keep their feet warm. Muffs and heavy lap robes of fur, wool, or horsehair provided additional warmth. The driver's hands were protected by special gloves of either sealskin or heavy fabric with a fur lining.

A string of sleigh bells was attached to the harness or a leather band around the horse's middle or neck. Their sound announced the coming of a sleigh on otherwise quiet snow-packed roads. Sleighs continued in common use in rural areas of the north until the 1930s.

Demise of the Horse-Drawn Vehicle

While horse-drawn vehicles continued to be used in rural areas until well after World War II, the shift toward motorized trucks and automobiles started around 1905. By 1919 at the end of World War I, the use of automobiles had become noticeable and greatly accelerated in the 1920s.

Trade journals in 1919 were full of articles weighing the relative cost and efficiency of horse-drawn wagons versus engine-powered trucks. The general consensus at the time was that the horse-drawn wagon was more economical than the truck for distances up to 12 miles. During the 1920s the truck continued to eat into the wagon's domain. American Railway Express reported that in 1918 they operated 15,600 wagons and sleds, using 18,420 horses. In 1928 they reported that those numbers had fallen to 7,710 and 6,621, respectively. While losing ground rapidly, the horse was clearly a viable alternative to the gasoline engine well into the 1930s, even in the major cities. Gas rationing during World War II delayed the demise of the horse-drawn delivery wagon even further.

Bicycles

The introduction of the pedaled bicycle in America in 1866 provided the average urban wage earner, who could not afford to make use of public or private carriages, the freedom to move about other than on foot. This meant that the urban worker did not have to live within walking distance of the workplace.

Improvements in the bicycle came slowly, however. The fashionable high-wheel (often reaching 60 inches in diameter) bicycle of the mid-1880s fostered cycle touring and organized cycle racing, but was dangerous to use for the average citizen. The development in the 1890s of the bicycle with two equal-size wheels, called a "safety," along with the free-wheeling hub, accelerated the use of the bicycle by the urban population. The free-wheeling hub allowed the rear wheel to continue turning while the peddles remained stationary.

Travel by bicycle declined after World War II in favor of the automobile. Bicycles are still used, however, as a means of transportation in urban areas, and bicycling continues to be popular as a recreational sport.

Wagon and Carriage Museums

❖ *EL POMAR CARRIAGE HOUSE MUSEUM, Broadmoor Hotel, Colorado Springs, Colorado 80906. Tel: 719-634-7711, ext. 5353. Open Tuesday through Sunday 10-noon and 1-5, except major holidays. Admission free.*

The El Pomar Carriage House Museum was founded by Spencer Penrose, who also built the Broadmoor Hotel in Colorado Springs, Colorado. Penrose was involved in gold and silver mining in Colorado and collected carriages as a hobby. In 1935 Penrose constructed a building on the Broadmoor property to house his carriage collection, which now consists of 33 carriages, all equipped with harnesses.

The carriages were in pristine condition when acquired and only five of them had to be restored. Notable in the collection is an 1862 Cinderella used by Chester Arthur, the 21st U.S. president, and a Studebaker carriage with a rumble seat. A carriage used at the 1841 inauguration of William Henry Harrison as president is also featured. Another outstanding carriage in the collection is the gentlemen's drag, which accommodated six passengers. There are no commercial wagons in the collection; however, there is a Conestoga wagon and an 1850 stagecoach.

In addition to the carriages, the collection houses two antique cars, a 1906 two-cylinder Renault and a 1928 V-8 Cadillac, both of which belonged to Spencer Penrose. Since Penrose's death, the museum has been operated by the El Pomar Foundation established by Penrose.

❖ *STUDEBAKER NATIONAL MUSEUM, 525 South Main Street, South Bend, Indiana 46601. Tel: 219-284-9714. Open Monday through Saturday 10-5, Sunday noon-5. Admission $3.50, senior and student discounts.*

The Studebaker National Museum contains the original company collection of carriages, wagons, and automobiles manufactured by the Studebaker Company from 1856 to 1963. It contains more than 100 carriages, wagons, cars, and trucks. The museum's archives house business records, ledgers, photographs, and advertising pertaining to the Studebaker Company. The archives are available for research by appointment.

The Studebaker Company was started as a blacksmith shop by Henry and Clement Studebaker in South Bend, Indiana. Since their father had been a blacksmith and wagon builder, they soon added wagon-building to their business. The brothers manufactured and sold their first wagon in 1852 for $18.

During the Civil War the Studebaker brothers built wagons for the federal army. After the war farm wagons as well as buggies, carriages, and commercial wagons were made at the growing factory. Over the years three other brothers joined the company, and Henry Studebaker left to become a farmer. In 1868 the company became known as Studebaker Brothers Manufacturing Company. By 1900 Studebaker employed 3,000 workers, many of whom were immigrants from Germany, Poland, and other European countries. The company was the largest wagon manufacturer in the world.

The Studebaker vehicle collection started as a corporate collection more than a hundred years ago. The horse-drawn vehicles in the collection include Studebaker-built carriages belonging to Presidents William Henry Harrison, Ulysses S. Grant, and William McKinley. The collection also includes the carriage in which Abraham Lincoln rode to Ford's Theater on the night of his assassination.

The earliest wagon on display is an 1830 Conestoga, reportedly built by the brothers' father, John Studebaker. There is also an 1876 Centennial wagon, an 1893 Columbian wagon made of rosewood, and a 1920 farm wagon, which was the last wagon made by the Studebaker Company.

❖ *OWLS HEAD TRANSPORTATION MUSEUM, State Route 73, Rockland, Maine 04854. Tel: 207-594-4418. Open daily 10-5 from May to October, weekdays 10-5 rest of year. Admission $4, senior and student discounts.*

The Owls Head Transportation Museum was established as a non-profit foundation in 1974 under the leadership of James S. Rockefeller Jr., and Stephan Lang. Rockefeller, a member of the famous Rockefeller family, is a boat builder and had lived in the Owls Head area for many years. The museum is devoted to all types of transportation vehicles, with the carriage collection numbering approximately 15 horse-drawn vehicles.

In the collection there is an original 1898 Bronson wagon, a variation of the Brewster Express wagon. It was used for transportation to and from sporting events, as well as for seating at the event. There is also a six-passenger utility-box wagon, which was used for general transportation to carry passengers to picnics, hunts, or the railroad station. It also carried freight.

Included in the transportation exhibit is a collection of American bicycles dating from 1885. There is a Columbia 54-inch "Ordinary" Highwheeler, which dominated cycling in the mid-1880s. Also included is a rare example of a bicycle with a small front wheel and a large rear wheel.

A 1920 six-passenger surrey. The surrey, which had many variations, came into existence in the early 1870s. It quickly became a popular family carriage ranging in price from $53 to about $600. Photo courtesy of the Owls Head Transportation Museum, Rockland, Maine, photographer Henry Austin Clark, Jr.

❖ *GRANGER HOMESTEAD SOCIETY AND CARRIAGE MUSEUM, 295 North Main Street, Canandaigua, New York 14424. Tel: 716-394-1472. Open Tuesday through Saturday 10-5, Sunday 1-5, June through August; Tuesday through Saturday 10-4, May and September through mid-October. Admission $3, senior and school-age discounts.*

The Granger Homestead Society and Carriage Museum collection of horse-drawn vehicles was started by Joseph Cribb, a local attorney and judge, who donated them to the museum. The vehicles have not been restored in order to show their original colors and adornment.

One of the earliest vehicles on display is a first-decade nineteenth-century sleigh that belonged to Oliver Phelps, who pioneered the western part of New York State. There is also a pre-Civil War, drop-front phaeton, which belonged to a dentist in Danville, New York. A Studebaker coupé, a Brewster quarter coach, and a park drag are also on display.

The most interesting commercial horse-drawn vehicle is the traveling store wagon of the late 1800s. Virtually a dry goods store on wheels, it had small compartments on the inside for the storage of various items. Accountings were written on the walls of the wagon, and they are still visible. Other commercial wagons in the collection include a butcher wagon and a Cuttingham hearse.

The runabout was also known as a road wagon. There were many varieties of these carriages in the late nineteenth century. Photo courtesy of the Carriage Museum, The Granger Homestead Society, Inc., Canandaigua, New York.

❖ GENESEE COUNTRY VILLAGE, *1 and 1/4 miles west of State Route 36 on West George Street (Flint Hill Road), Mumford, New York 14511. Tel: 716-538-6822. Open weekdays 10-4, weekends and holidays 10-5 mid-May to mid-October; closed Mondays in May, June, September, and October. Admission $9, senior and children discounts.*

Genesee Country Village was started by Jack Wehle, chairman of the board of Genesee Brewing Company. It consists of more than 55 farm and village structures and re-creates life in the nineteenth century in upstate New York. There are craft and cooking demonstrations and working operations such as printing, pottery making, and blacksmithing, as well as a horse-drawn vehicle collection.

In the 1950s before the village was constructed, Mrs. Wehle, an avid horse enthusiast and breeder of race and show horses, had started collecting racing sulkies and some carriages. The collection has now grown to 50 vehicles.

Most of the carriage collection consists of late nineteenth-century elegant private coaches and a variety of racing sulkies. One of the most elaborate coaches was manufactured by the James Cunningham Company of Rochester, New York. Also included in the collection is a large park cutter (sleigh), a Hansom cab from the 1890s, and an omnibus. One of the original beer wagons used by the Genesee Brewing Company is on display. It is equipped with hitches for a team of 12 horses.

❖ CARRIAGE MUSEUM, *Museums at Stony Brook, 1208 Route 25A, Stony Brook, New York 11790. Tel: 516-751-0066. Open Wednesday through Saturday 10-5, Sunday noon-5, except major holidays. Admission $4, senior and student discounts.*

The Carriage Museum is part of The Museums at Stony Brook, New York. This Long Island museum complex also encompasses an art museum and a living history museum. The carriage museum is one of the largest in the United States and comprises 250 carriages and 10,000 non-vehicular artifacts. The complex also houses a library of more than 1,000 books related to carriages.

This remarkable collection of horse-drawn vehicles was started by Ward Melville, president of the Melville Shoe Corporation, who wanted to use artifacts for public education. One of the outstanding pieces in the collection is a late eighteenth-century phaeton belonging to General Gainesfoot, a Revolutionary War hero from Albany, New York. Another is a 1908 cabriolet built by the Brewster Company for Alfred G. Vanderbilt for the sum of $1,250.

One of the most colorful and unique

vehicles in the collection is a Gypsy wagon. In the mid-1800s Gypsies immigrated to North America from England and many established residences in New England. This is one of the few Gypsy wagons to survive, since the Gypsy custom was to burn all possessions of an individual after death. Another unusual carriage is a Grace Darling omnibus which was built about 1880 by Concord Carriage Builders of Concord, New Hampshire. Drawn by two or four horses, this 23-foot-long omnibus was used primarily in New England for excursions.

Other outstanding vehicles on display are a basket wagon, several private road coaches, and a variety of phaetons, rockaways, and buggies. There is also a large array of sleighs and a number of pieces of horse-drawn fire-fighting equipment. The hose carriage was capable of carrying up to 900 feet of hose. The huge pumper weighs 9,240 pounds and was capable of pumping 900 gallons of water per minute. Both units were manufactured in the 1870s.

❖ *BOYERTON MUSEUM OF HISTORIC VEHICLES, 28 Warwick Street, Boyerton, Pennsylvania 19512. Tel: 215-367-2090. Open Tuesday through Friday 8:30-4, Saturday and Sunday 10:30-4. Admission $2.50, senior and school-age discounts.*

The Boyerton Museum of Historic Vehicles was established by Paul Hafer, who operated the Boyerton Body Works, which produced custom-built truck bodies. Before the age of automobiles, the Boyerton Body Works manufactured horse-drawn carriages. One of the purposes of the museum is to show transportation vehicles that were primarily manufactured in Berks County, Pennsylvania, including horse-drawn vehicles, bicycles, motorcycles, and cars and trucks. The carriage collection consists of 50 vehicles, many of which have been restored. The carriages, although graceful in design, do not have a great deal of fancy embellishments since most of them belonged to Pennsylvania Dutch families, who preferred plain things.

Included in the varied collection of wagons and carriages are several commercial vehicles, such as a dump-bottom, high-lift coal wagon, a creamery wagon, and a butcher's wagon. There is a doctor's carriage with a storage compartment underneath the seat to keep medicines dry, and a 1905 horse-drawn sleigh. The multi-passenger vehicles include a 1910 Pleasure Trap with hydraulic brakes and an eight-passenger "Tally-Ho" used for sporting events. Runabouts and buggies are prominently displayed. Some of the nation's earliest fire-fighting equipment is also in the collection, as is a collection of early bicycles.

❖ *GRUBER WAGON WORKS, Berks County Heritage Center, 5 miles northwest of Reading via State Route 183 and Red Bridge Road, Reading, Pennsylvania. Tel: 215-374-8839. Open Tuesday through Saturday and on Monday holidays 10-4, Sunday noon-5, May 1 to November 1. Admission $2.50, senior and school-age discounts.*

The Gruber Wagon Works, which was in operation for a century starting in the 1870s, comprises the majority of the exhibit. Although the plant is no longer in operation, it is open to the public, and there are guided tours. The various stations throughout the plant exhibit the stages of wagon construction. Many of the 19,000 artifacts from the original building are included in the exhibits. "The plant looks like it did in 1915, and the atmosphere is as if the workers had just left for lunch," said Cathy Wegener, director of Interpretive Services at the museum. Today, it is the nation's finest example of rural wagon manufacturing.

The Gruber Wagon Works, started by Franklin H. Gruber in the 1870s, primarily produced farm wagons. Gruber started his business by repairing agricultural implements and building wagons at his farm shop. As the business grew, mass-production methods were employed, and Gruber's four sons joined the business.

Following World War I, as the popularity of the automobile increased, wagon building declined. Gruber and his sons started making wooden truck bodies but continued to produce and repair wagons on a small scale until the plant closed in 1972. Seven of the wagons made at the Gruber Wagon Works are on display.

On December 22, 1977, the Gruber Wagon Works was declared a National Historic Landmark, although it had been moved to the Heritage Center from its actual location five miles away in the previous year.

Included in the Berks County Historical Center complex is a Canal Center, which chronicles canals in the vicinity of Reading, Pennsylvania.

Conestoga wagons were used primarily to haul freight in colonial America. The dory-shaped wagon body prevented loads from shifting on the trail. Photo courtesy of the Car & Carriage Caravan, Luray Caverns, Virginia.

❖ *IRON MISSION STATE PARK, 585 North Main Street, Cedar City, Utah 84720. Tel: 801-586-9290. Open daily 9-7, Memorial Day to Labor Day; daily 9-5 rest of year, except major holidays. Admission $1, school-age discounts.*

The horse-drawn vehicle collection is part of the Iron Mission State Park managed by the Utah State Division of Parks and Recreation. The park commemorates the settlement of the area in 1851 by a group of Mormons, who came to develop a newly discovered iron ore deposit.

Begun by Gronway Parry in 1911, the horse-drawn vehicle collection consists of carriages and wagons from Utah farms and towns. Parry amassed his collection over a period of 20 years, and in 1973 gave it to the state.

Included in the collection are a Stanhope phaeton, a Studebaker white-top wagon, and a bullet-scarred overland stagecoach from Butch Cassidy's era in the Four Corner-area of Utah. Other horse-drawn vehicles include a Brewster coupé, an old milk wagon, a hearse, and an open sleigh. There are also several industrial vehicles on display, such as a water-sprinkling wagon and a dump-belly wagon.

❖ *SHELBURNE MUSEUM, on U.S. Route 7, Shelburne, Vermont 05482. Tel: 802-985-3346. Open daily 9-5, mid-May through mid-October. Admission $15 adults and $7 children.*

The Shelburne Museum, which houses a wide collection of Americana, consists of 37 structures and covers 45 acres. When Dr. William Seward Webb and his wife Lila Vanderbilt Webb established their summer residence in Shelburne, Vermont, they had a gentlemen's stable and various carriages for their personal use. The carriage collection eventually became the property of their daughter Electra Havemeyer Webb, who established the Shelburne Museum to house her many-faceted collections.

The horse-drawn vehicle collection now includes more than 200 pieces categorized into four major areas. According to Robert Shaw, curator of the carriage division, these consist of carriages used by the gentlemen of the 1800s, horse-drawn vehicles constructed by important New York and New England carriage manufacturers, carriages used in small communities, and commercial vehicles. The horse-drawn vehicles have not been restored to show what the vehicles were like at the time they were used.

The Liberty coach with room for passengers on the inside and outside. Photo courtesy of the Shelburne Museum, Shelburne, Vermont.

One of the outstanding pieces in the collection is a George IV phaeton built in 1882 by the Brewster Manufacturing Company for Dr. Webb. This phaeton model, originally created for the king of England, was a very graceful vehicle with room for a footman in the back.

The museum also houses a Buxton Rheumatic Care Wagon. It was used by D.H. Buxton of Maine in the late 1890s to sell his cure-all medicine. There is also a Liberty road coach with seating inside and on top. It was driven by James Hazen Hyde, a well-known coach driver at the time, in a 1901 race from New York to Philadelphia. He made the trip in record time—19 hours and 35 minutes.

❖ *OLD WADE HOUSE AND WISCONSIN CARRIAGE MUSEUM, W7747 Plank Road, Greenbush, Wisconsin 53026. Tel: 414-526-3271. Open daily 9-5, May through October. Admission $4, senior and school-age discounts.*

The Wisconsin Carriage Museum is part of the Wade House Complex operated by the State of Wisconsin Historical Society. The carriage collection was started in 1948 by Wesley W. Jung Sr., a Sheboygan businessman. In 1968 the museum was constructed to house the Jung collection, which features many of the carriages and wagons built by the Wesley Jung Company of Sheboygan, Wisconsin.

The collection contains more than 120 horse- and hand-drawn vehicles from 1870 to 1915. Included is a large variety of wagons ranging from hay wagons and manure wagons used on the farm to commercial vehicles, such as butchers' carts, grocery wagons, a coal wagon, a street sprinkler, a mail delivery wagon, and a haberdasher's wagon. Some of the wagons could be converted to sleighs by adding bobs for use in the snow months in Wisconsin. Included in the collection are many personal transportation vehicles from elegant carriages of the wealthy to the common buckboard wagon.

There is also a separate section containing a myriad of fire-fighting equipment, both horse- and hand-drawn.

LOCK AND CANAL BOAT, WASHINGTON, D.C. by Charles A. Corwin, oil, 20 x 30 inches, courtesy of Taggart & Jorgensen Gallery, Washington, D.C.

Canals

Interest in connecting rivers and lakes by means of man-made waterways developed early in the American colonies. In 1673 Louis Joliet, having explored the Mississippi River basin, proposed a canal to connect Lake Michigan to the Mississippi River via the Des Plaines and Illinois rivers. This was the route subsequently used for the Illinois and Michigan Canal when it was finally built in 1848. Also in the late 1600s, William Penn proposed a canal from Philadelphia on the Schuylkill River to the Pittsburgh region on the Monongahela River. This formidable project was not undertaken until the 1830s. In Massachusetts, specific proposals to build the Cape Cod Canal were advanced as early as 1676, but it did not become a reality until 1914.

Until the late 1700s travel by water in America occurred on natural waterways. While river travel assisted greatly in opening new territories and in facilitating trade, it had its drawbacks. Many of the upland rivers frequently became unnavigable due to insufficient water levels during summer months and excessive runoff from heavy storms during almost any month of the year. These conditions prevailed even on such large rivers as the Ohio and the Missouri. Travel downstream could be fast, but often dangerous. Travel upstream was slow, arduous, and on swift rivers and streams, impossible. Rivermen traveling down large rivers frequently used log rafts that were broken up at the destination and sold for lumber. The boatmen returned home on foot.

The slower-moving streams near the tidewater regions could be traversed against the current by use of sail, pole, or paddle. Sails were used, for example, to move upstream on the Hudson, Potomac, and Delaware rivers. Poling or paddling were preferred on moderately fast-moving rivers such as the Connecticut and most rivers of the West.

Portage trails were built to bypass unnavigable stretches of water and cross terrain between navigable bodies of water. Portages were practical where boats no larger than canoes were used, but as settlements developed and trade increased, boats became larger and portaging more difficult. Several of the earliest canals were built to replace portages around falls and rapids on otherwise navigable rivers.

Early canal projects focused on eliminating circuitous journeys between population centers or enabling local products and materials to be brought to an urban center from outlying areas. One of the earliest examples of the former is the Dismal Swamp Canal between Elizabeth City, North Carolina, and Norfolk, Virginia, built in 1805. An example of the latter type, the Middlesex Canal in Massachusetts, was constructed between Lowell and Boston in 1803.

As commerce and travel developed between the coastal states and the western frontier, major commercial centers along the Atlantic Coast—Boston, New York, Philadelphia, Baltimore, and Richmond—vied to become the principal water gateway to the west. Even merchants as far south as the Carolinas hoped to establish a canal system to the west.

All but New York City faced almost insurmountable difficulties, however. The merchants of Boston, who possessed the most developed harbor on the eastern seaboard at the time, attempted to obtain state financing for a canal that would link up with the Erie Canal at Albany. The state legislature refused to support it, however, because of the prohibitive cost of building a lengthy tunnel through the Green Mountains. Philadelphia and the cities to the south faced an even greater mountainous barrier, the Alleghenies.

The Canal Era of American transportation began to take hold around 1800. Between then and 1850, approximately 4,000 miles of canals were built in the United States. Few were built after 1850 as, by then, the railroads had begun to take over the major transportation tasks of the expanding nation. Most of the canals were built in New York, Pennsylvania, and Ohio,

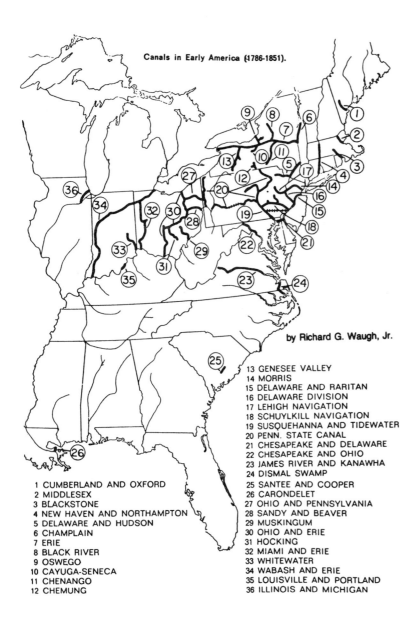

Canals in Early America (1786-1851).

by Richard G. Waugh, Jr.

Map of early American canals. Courtesy of the American Canal and Transportation Center, York, Pennsylvania.

1 CUMBERLAND AND OXFORD
2 MIDDLESEX
3 BLACKSTONE
4 NEW HAVEN AND NORTHAMPTON
5 DELAWARE AND HUDSON
6 CHAMPLAIN
7 ERIE
8 BLACK RIVER
9 OSWEGO
10 CAYUGA-SENECA
11 CHENANGO
12 CHEMUNG
13 GENESEE VALLEY
14 MORRIS
15 DELAWARE AND RARITAN
16 DELAWARE DIVISION
17 LEHIGH NAVIGATION
18 SCHUYLKILL NAVIGATION
19 SUSQUEHANNA AND TIDEWATER
20 PENN. STATE CANAL
21 CHESAPEAKE AND DELAWARE
22 CHESAPEAKE AND OHIO
23 JAMES RIVER AND KANAWHA
24 DISMAL SWAMP
25 SANTEE AND COOPER
26 CARONDELET
27 OHIO AND PENNSYLVANIA
28 SANDY AND BEAVER
29 MUSKINGUM
30 OHIO AND ERIE
31 HOCKING
32 MIAMI AND ERIE
33 WHITEWATER
34 WABASH AND ERIE
35 LOUISVILLE AND PORTLAND
36 ILLINOIS AND MICHIGAN

although the longest, the Wabash and Erie Canal, was located mainly in Indiana. Except in Virginia, few canals were built in the South, which seriously impeded the region's movement of troops and supplies during the Civil War.

Middlesex Canal

One of the earliest major canals built in America was the Middlesex Canal in Massachusetts. The canal, which extended from Boston to Lowell, received its charter from the commonwealth of Massachusetts in 1794 and opened for business in 1803. Lowell was blessed with an abundance of potential waterpower to operate mills but, until the canal was built, lacked the means to obtain raw materials and ship finished products to market. The Middlesex Canal enabled Lowell to become one of the first industrial centers in America.

The canal finally became profitable in the 1820s, with boats bringing lumber, marble,

Canal boats on the James and Kanawha Canal entering Richmond. Courtesy of the American Canal and Transportation Center, York, Pennsylvania.

agricultural products, and finished textiles to Boston and returning to Lowell with cotton for the textile mills. Its life proved short, however, as the Boston and Lowell Railroad began operating in parallel with the canal in 1835. During its life the Middlesex Canal generated a legacy that gives it importance beyond the local region. The builders of the canal developed a number of engineering innovations that were used by builders of the Erie and other canals. These included techniques for building locks and other structures out of massive pieces of stone; for creating an effective hydraulic cement (cement able to harden under water); and for sealing the unlined dirt sides of a canal.

Patowmack Canal

The first significant effort to start building a canal to the Ohio River took place in Maryland. Called the Patowmack Canal, it was built around the falls on the Potomac River near Washington, D.C. The venture, which was headed by George Washington, started in 1786 and was completed in 1802, three years after Washington's death. It became the forerunner of the Chesapeake and Ohio Canal.

James River and Kanawha Canal

In Virginia, wealthy landowners who owned vast tracts of land west of the Alleghenies, including George Washington, hoped to make Richmond on the James River the canal gateway for commerce to the Ohio River and western lands. They planned to build a canal to the upper reaches of the James River, then over the mountains and down the Kanawha River to the Ohio River. The first stage, for which a charter had been issued in 1784, was construction of a canal with locks around the rapids on the James River at Richmond.

While their plans were never fully realized, the James River Canal did ultimately reach the eastern slopes of the Alleghenies 15 miles west of Lynchburg, Virginia, with an extension to Lexington. The canal operated until 1880 and for many years was one of the most profitable ventures in Virginia. It ultimately became part of a transportation link to the west when a trail (later a road) was built over the Alleghenies to the Kanawha River. That river drained the western slopes of the Alleghenies into the Ohio River and had been made navigable up to Charleston, West Virginia.

Loading boats with coal in Cumberland, Maryland, for transport on the C&O Canal. Photo courtesy of the C&O Canal National Historical Park, Sharpsburg, Maryland.

Chesapeake and Ohio Canal

The Chesapeake and Ohio Canal Company was organized in 1828 to resurrect and expand on the earlier attempt to build a canal across the Alleghenies from the Potomac River to the Ohio River. Work went slowly and costs escalated far beyond the original estimates. The canal did not reach Cumberland, Maryland, a distance of 185 miles, until 1850, which put it ten years behind schedule. By then the canal had to compete with newly built railroads, and investors had long since given up any plans to extend the canal over the Alleghenies.

Construction of the canal from the tidewater at Georgetown in the District of Columbia to Cumberland proved to be much more of an engineering feat than its designers and builders had anticipated. While the canal rose only 605 feet over the 185 miles, it required 74 locks plus 11 aqueducts across major tributaries to the Potomac. One of the aqueducts was 438 feet long and required seven arches, each 54 feet high. By the time construction was completed to Cumberland, the company was seriously in debt and unable to push further west.

The excessive cost overrun was caused mainly by the building of the 3,000-foot Paw Paw Tunnel, a major engineering accomplishment at the time. The tunnel through solid rock was located approximately 25 miles downriver from Cumberland. Its purpose was to avoid a four-and-one-half-mile double bend of the river near the town of Paw Paw, West Virginia.

The canal continued to operate for almost 75 years, bringing coal, flour, and other farm goods to Washington, D.C. It was finally shut down after a major flood occurred on the Potomac in 1924. The National Park Service acquired the canal in 1937 from its then-owner, the Baltimore and Ohio Railroad. Many features of the canal can still be seen and parts are kept in operation for excursion purposes.

Erie Canal

The Erie Canal was built between 1817 and 1825. It ran 363 miles from the Hudson River at Albany to Lake Erie at Buffalo. It opened up an efficient means of transportation for goods and people between New York City and the far reaches of the Great Lakes. The Erie Canal is considered the most profitable canal ever built in the United States, having paid back its investors within a few years and then continuing to pay excellent dividends for many years.

Unlike the National Road, which was being built in the same time period, the federal government refused to help finance the Erie Canal. In 1806, when President Thomas

Looking down one of the two flights of locks on the Erie Canal at Lockport, New York. Historic print courtesy of the American Canal and Transportation Center, York, Pennsylvania.

Jefferson was asked to help get federal financial support for the canal (soon after he had signed the bill to help finance the National Road), he is reported to have replied, "General Washington's canal of a few miles on the Potomac has languished for many years because of the small sum of $200,000 . . . and you talk of making a canal 350 miles long through a wilderness! It is little short of madness to think about it."

In spite of this lack of interest from the federal government, the state of New York quickly obtained construction funds from private investors by guaranteeing their investments. The success of Wall Street brokers in handling the investments in the Erie Canal helped establish Wall Street and New York City, generally, as the commercial center of the country. Much of the credit for the creation of the canal is given to the untiring efforts of Governor De Witt Clinton, who has been called the "Father of the Erie Canal." While the canal was being built, however, it was known as "Clinton's Folly."

In building the canal the engineers faced a number of challenges. Until this project, the 28-mile-long Middlesex Canal was the longest in America. Machines had to be designed to mix large amounts of mortar and to uproot huge tree stumps. Techniques for building aqueducts across major rivers had to be developed. Work on the canal in the swamps near Syracuse had to be scheduled only during winter months when the ground was frozen, a decision made after 1,000 workmen died from malaria in the summer of 1819. The most difficult feat was blasting locks out of the Niagara Escarpment at Lockport, New York, in order to reach Lake Erie.

The opening of the Erie Canal on October 26, 1825, was a major event in New York State and the day was declared a state holiday. Governor Clinton brought a bucket of water from Lake Erie on the first canal boat to traverse the entire length of the canal and dumped it in New York Harbor, decreeing the ceremony as the "wedding of the water."

The Erie Canal's biggest contribution to the development of the nation was the opening of the Old Northwest Territory to immigrants from Europe, bringing thousands of settlers from New York to Indiana, Illinois, and Michigan. Settlers in the territory were no longer isolated from the rest of the nation as it opened eastern markets for farm products of the territory. Travel time between Buffalo and New York City decreased from 21 days to only 6, while freight rates dropped from $100 per ton to $5 per ton. Corn could be brought directly to New York rather than over treacherous trails on pack animals in the form of whiskey.

The Erie Canal enabled the small village of Rochester, New York, to grow into the principal flour-milling center in the Northeast. Buffalo ceased to be a remote outpost and started growing into a major city. Albany became a major inland port with more than 50 passenger- and cargo-canal boats leaving for the west daily. By 1872 the Erie Canal was handling six million tons of freight annually.

Chesapeake and Delaware Canal

The Chesapeake and Delaware Canal, which opened in 1829, is only 15 miles long, but it shortened the water route from Baltimore to Wilmington, Delaware, and Philadelphia by almost 200 miles. It also gave Baltimore direct access to the sea. As a result, the canal became an important commercial artery among the Middle Atlantic states during the 1800s.

The construction of the canal had an unusually long period of gestation. It was first proposed in 1661 by a Dutch surveyor named Augustine Herman, but nothing came of his suggestion. Another survey and set of recom-

mendations were made a century later, in the 1760s, but the colonies were still not ready for such an ambitious advance in intercolony commerce. Finally in 1788 Benjamin Franklin took an interest in the project, and he was able to bring about negotiations among the three states of Delaware, Maryland, and Pennsylvania. These led to the formation of the Chesapeake and Delaware Canal Company in 1799.

Work finally got underway in 1804, but the venture almost immediately ran into financial problems. Construction commenced again in 1823, although by then a new route had been selected and work had to start over. The canal was finally completed and opened for business in 1829, almost 170 years after it was first proposed.

As traffic built up on the canal, a shortage of water developed in the locks at Chesapeake City, Maryland. To replenish the water required for the locks, a huge wooden waterwheel, 38 feet in diameter and 10 feet across, was installed. Driven by a stationary steam engine, the wheel lifted 20,000 gallons of water per minute to an elevation of 15 feet.

Another engineering challenge was the need for a bridge across the canal at its summit. The construction of the canal had severed the Delaware State Road, which was the main north-south artery traversing the state. As a result the state built a wooden-arch, covered bridge with granite abutments. The single arch spanned a total of 247 feet, making it one of the longest wooden-arch bridges on the East Coast at the time.

The Delaware and Chesapeake Canal is still an important waterway as it continues to provide the Port of Baltimore access to the sea and serves as a link in the Atlantic Intracoastal Waterway. The federal government acquired the canal in 1919 and in 1927 made it a sea-level canal that could handle ocean-going ships. Today

A canal on a viaduct over a creek from a drawing by Storm. Courtesy of the Smithsonian Institution, Washington, D.C.

the canal is 450 feet wide and has a depth of 35 feet. Each year approximately 17 million tons of shipping pass through it, involving almost 2,000 large ships and 20,000 smaller commercial and pleasure craft—making the Delaware and Chesapeake Canal one of the busiest canals in the world.

Pennsylvania's "The Main Line"

With the opening of the Erie Canal in 1825, the merchants and community leaders in Philadelphia became concerned that they would lose out to New York City as the key shipping point to the west. They had instigated the construction of the Pennsylvania Road from Philadelphia to the Ohio River at Pittsburgh that opened in 1820. It was clear, however, that the Erie and Ohio canals provided a faster and more-efficient, although longer, route to the developing west and would draw traffic away from Philadelphia.

Consequently, in 1826 the state legislature passed an act commissioning what was called the State Road of Public Works, which included a combination of railroads, canals, and inclined planes between Philadelphia and Pittsburgh. It was undoubtedly the most complex transportation system built in the world at the time. When completed the project became known in Pennsylvania as "The Main Line."

The Main Line project consisted of four separate stages. The first involved a horse-powered railroad from Philadelphia to Columbia on the Susquehanna River, a distance of 81.6 miles, at which point the passengers were transferred to canal boats. The railroad included two inclined planes: one to climb out of the Schuykill River valley at Philadelphia and one to descend into the Susquehanna River valley at Columbia.

The second stage of the project was the Pennsylvania (Middle Division) Canal. It ran from Columbia along the Susquehanna and Juniata River valleys to Hollidaysburg, a distance of 128 miles involving a vertical rise of 500 feet through approximately 40 locks. When the canal boats reached Hollidaysburg, passengers were

transferred to the third stage, the Allegheny Portage Railroad for the trip to Johnstown.

The portage railroad opened in 1832. As originally built, it was a complex, two-track system that included ten inclined planes, four aqueducts, a 900-foot tunnel, and two sets of tracks. The rise from Hollidaysburg to the summit measured 1,398 feet in ten miles of track, while the decline to Johnstown totaled 1,172 vertical feet in 26 miles. At the top of each incline two sets of 30-horsepower stationary steam engines and ropes handled the ascending and descending trains on each track. Upon arriving in Johnstown, passengers were again required to transfer to canal boats.

The final stage of the Main Line was the Western Division Canal from Johnstown to Pittsburgh, a distance of 104 miles and a vertical drop of approximately 465 feet. It consisted of 152 bridges, 16 aqueducts, 66 locks, and a 1,000-foot tunnel. Since the canal frequently suffered from water shortages, a dam was built on the Conemaugh River to feed water into the canal. It was this dam that broke in 1889, causing the famous Johnstown Flood.

Sectional boats were used on the Main Line to carry freight directly from Philadelphia to Pittsburgh without the need to transfer the cargo between rail cars and canal boats at each stage. The boats were built in several sections, which could be separated while being carried by rail and then quickly reattached when traveling in the canal. The boat sections were carried through the streets of Philadelphia and Pittsburgh on rail cars to the points of loading and unloading, much like today's piggyback rail cars.

The Main Line operated for several decades, but as railroads proliferated, the commonwealth encountered increasingly larger deficits and finally offered the system for sale in 1854. The inclined planes proved to be one of the most expensive segments of the system, and the state was forced to build a New Portage rail line in 1855 to eliminate the planes. The system was finally purchased by the Pennsylvania Railroad in 1857. The railroad used the New Portage line to cross the Alleghenies until they could complete their own tracks with a lesser grade the following year. The latter involved the famous Horseshoe Curve west of Altoona.

Lehigh Canal

The Lehigh Canal was one of the most profitable canals in the early 1800s. It ran for 72 miles along the Lehigh River from White Haven, Pennsylvania, down to Easton, Pennsylvania, where it joined the state's Delaware Division Canal, which paralleled the Delaware River to Bristol, Pennsylvania, near Philadelphia. The Lehigh Canal was built and operated by the Lehigh Coal and Navigation Company which was formed by an enterprising Quaker named Josiah White. The original authorization was for a downstream-only operation, with the coal boats being dismantled and sold at the end of each run in Philadelphia. Two-way operation was initiated in 1829.

White developed anthracite coal mines near Mauch Chunk (now Jim Thorpe), Pennsylvania, which was the initial upper terminus of his canal. To bring the anthracite to his canal boats at Mauch Chunk from adjacent Summit Hill, White built an 18-mile gravity railroad. He later extended the canal north to White Haven for the purpose of bringing anthracite from the Susquehanna River valley around Wilkes-Barre, Pennsylvania, to Philadelphia. The canal brought manufactured goods from Philadelphia to Wilkes-Barre on the return trips.

The "Switchback Railroad" from Summit Hill to Mauch Chunk on the Lehigh River was the highest incline built in the United States. It was 18 miles in length and involved two inclines: one of 664 feet over a distance of 2,322 feet, and another of 462 feet over a distance of 2,070 feet. Cars traveled by gravity from the top of each incline. Thousands of tourists came each summer to ride this scenic roller coaster until it shut down in 1932.

Boats in the weigh lock on the Lehigh Canal operated by Lehigh Coal and Navigation Company. Photo courtesy of the American Canal and Transportation Center, York, Pennsylvania.

White, a talented inventor, also designed and built a 25-mile railroad between Wilkes-Barre and White Haven. He used three inclined planes and an 1,800-foot tunnel to lift the loaded cars to the summit, then a gravity railroad to transport them down to White Haven. The inclined planes were also reported to have been among the highest-rising set of planes in the world at the time. The locks on the canal from Mauch Chunk to White Haven involved lifts of 30 feet, which were the highest rises of any locks in America.

White operated several factories and was one of the first users of anthracite in America. He developed a much-copied forced-draft technique to burn what was called "black rock."

Delaware and Hudson Canal

The Delaware and Hudson Canal was another interesting privately financed canal used mainly for transporting anthracite coal. It was conceived and organized in 1823 by two Swiss-born entrepreneurs from Philadelphia, William and Maurice Wurts. They proposed to bring badly needed hard coal to New York City from the Carbondale region of northeastern Pennsylvania by constructing a canal northeast from Honesdale, Pennsylvania, to the Hudson River at what is now Kingston, New York.

The two brothers were able to obtain capital from a group of financiers in New York and began construction in 1825. The canal went into operation in 1828 and continued to operate for 70 years until put out of business by rail competition in 1898. In the peak year of 1872, the Delaware and Hudson Canal carried almost three million tons of coal to New York City.

A railroad was built to bring the coal 16 miles from Carbondale to the upper terminus of the canal at Honesdale, Pennsylvania. This required the construction of eight inclines to raise the cars 950 feet over the Moosic Mountains. From Honesdale the 108-mile-long canal brought barges loaded with up to 130 tons of hard coal to a point on the Hudson River near Kingston. There the barges entered the Hudson River and continued down to New York City. The entire trip took from six to ten days, depending on traffic and water levels.

The canal required 108 locks to make the drop of 967 feet between Honesdale and the Hudson River. The Delaware and Hudson Canal crossed the Delaware and several smaller rivers. In the original design, the Delaware River, as well as several smaller streams, were dammed to permit slack-water crossings. These dams created problems for riverboat traffic, particularly on the heavily used Delaware River, and overhead aqueducts were subsequently built to separate canal and river traffic. The company hired John Roebling, who later built the Brooklyn Bridge, to design and build four aqueducts, the most ambitious of which was a 600-foot span across the Delaware River.

Inclined planes of the Morris Canal. Photo courtesy of the American Canal and Transportation Center, York, Pennsylvania.

Morris Canal

New Jersey's Morris Canal connected the Delaware River at Phillipsburg, New Jersey, with the tidewater at Newark, New Jersey. In its 102-mile length the Morris Canal overcame a total elevation change of 1,675 feet, which required 24 locks and 23 inclined railways. Each plane was powered by water passing through a unique underground turbine connected to a drum on the surface that operated the track cable.

Built between 1824 and 1831, the Morris Canal was the highest climbing canal ever constructed. The original purpose of the canal was to bring anthracite coal from the Lehigh Valley of Pennsylvania to the Newark-New York region. Phillipsburg is across the Delaware River from the terminus of the Lehigh Canal at Easton, Pennsylvania, and the upper terminus of the state-owned Delaware Division Canal. Unfortunately the Morris Canal was designed too narrow to accommodate many of the large coal-carrying barges. It did, however, help revive New Jersey's iron industry and provided a means of capitalizing on New Jersey's sources of construction materials. A typical transit time through the canal was five days. During the canal's peak year of 1866, it handled 900,000 tons of materiel and products.

Boats were carried in cradles on the inclines. The cradles and specially-designed boats were built in two sections, hinged in the middle. The hinges enabled the boats to pass over the hump at the top of each incline as they entered the water at the upper level. The Morris Canal was replaced by a railroad in 1888, although parts of it continued to operate until 1924.

Delaware and Raritan Canal

The Delaware and Raritan Canal was another important artificial waterway in New Jersey. Completed in 1834, it ran from Trenton on the Delaware River to New Brunswick at the mouth of the Raritan River in New York Harbor. The canal became a significant avenue of commerce because, unlike the Morris Canal, it was built to handle the large coal barges from the coal regions of Pennsylvania. The canal was 42 miles long, required 13 locks to accommodate the 116-foot change in elevation, and was 80 feet wide by 8 feet deep.

While the canal proved successful, it did not reach its ultimate potential as political pressures within the state forced its merger with the Camden and Amboy Railroad in 1831. In spite of this conflict of interest, the canal operated continuously from 1834 to 1932. During this period it served primarily through-traffic originating in Pennsylvania destined for the New York-Newark region, generating only a small amount of local traffic. In the peak year of 1866, the Delaware and Raritan Canal handled almost three million tons of cargo, 83 percent of which was coal. In later years the banks of the canal were lined with rocks to enable use of steam-powered tugs and other small vessels.

Map of historic Ohio canals. Courtesy of the American Canal and Transportation Center, York, Pennsylvania.

Canals of Ohio

As the Erie Canal was being built, businessmen and farmers in Ohio foresaw that they would benefit from the New York canal. Before the Erie Canal was completed, therefore, they persuaded the Ohio legislature to authorize construction of two north-south canals to link the Great Lakes with the Ohio River. One extended from Lake Erie at Cleveland to Portsmouth on the Ohio River in the eastern part of the state. It was officially designated as the Ohio and Erie Canal, although locally referred to as the Grand Canal. The other ran from Toledo at the west end of Lake Erie to Cincinnati on the Ohio River and ultimately became the Miami and Erie Canal. Unlike the privately-financed Erie Canal, both of the Ohio canals were financed and operated by the state of Ohio.

Ground was broken for both Ohio canals simultaneously in July 1825, with both Governor Jeremiah Morrow of Ohio and Governor De Witt Clinton of New York in attendance. The 308-mile Ohio and Erie Canal was rushed to completion by 1832. To overcome a total elevation change of 1,206 feet, it required 151 locks, and to cross various streams and rivers, engineers had to build 14 aqueducts.

Construction on the Miami and Erie Canal started at Cincinnati and proceeded north slowly in stages, each stage providing the income to finance construction of the next. The project did not reach Toledo until 1845. When completed, it was 249 miles in length and traversed a total rise and fall of 890 feet, which required the construction of 105 locks.

To provide water for these two canals, five artificial lakes were constructed that covered a total of 32,000 acres. These lakes still exist and have provided the bases for a series of state parks.

Illinois and Michigan Canal

As settlements and trade moved west, the need for an improved water connection between Lake Michigan and the Mississippi River became more acute. The bottleneck was the 90-plus mile portage between the eastward-flowing Chicago River, which fed Lake Michigan, and the southwestward-flowing Illinois River, which joined the Mississippi above St. Louis, Missouri. As noted earlier, such a canal was first proposed by Louis Joliet in 1673.

The Illinois legislature initially granted a charter for the Illinois and Michigan Canal in 1825, but the charter was recalled the following year. Nine years later, in 1835, the legislature authorized the canal to be built by a state commission. Due to several financial crises encountered by the state, the canal was not completed until 1848. When opened for traffic, the Illinois and Michigan Canal was 60 feet wide at the top, 36 feet wide at the base, and 6 feet deep. Each of the 16 locks were 110 feet long and 18 feet wide. The design was unusually large for canals at the

time. Its designer, William Gooding, wanted to avoid the bottlenecks caused on the original Erie Canal due to its inadequate size.

Once open, the canal became an immediate success. It contributed immensely to the growth and importance of Chicago as a trade and travel hub. The value of the canal was dramatized several days after the canal opened when a riverboat, the *General Thorton*, arrived in Chicago from New Orleans with a load of sugar destined for Buffalo, New York.

The rapid growth of Chicago created sanitation problems in the Chicago River and Lake Michigan. The city decided to flush the sewage out of Lake Michigan by reversing the flow of the Chicago River and using the canal to carry the waste to the Illinois River at Joliet. Since the summit between Lake Michigan and the valley of the Des Plaines River was only eight feet above the lake, it was decided to deepen the canal sufficiently to allow the Chicago River to flow west. This project was authorized in 1865 and was completed in 1871. Between 1892 and 1901 a much larger canal, the Chicago Sanitation and Ship Canal, was built paralleling the route of the original Illinois and Michigan Canal. Following World War I, the canal was further widened and deepened to create the Illinois Waterway, which opened in 1933.

Birth of Civil Engineering

The design and construction of the Erie Canal is considered to be the genesis of the civil engineering profession, the term "civil" being used to distinguish it from "military" engineering. The engineers who had worked on the Erie Canal became much in demand throughout the canal-building states. Many of the earth-moving and other techniques developed during construction were used to build canals throughout the world during the remainder of the 1800s, and even in the construction of the Panama Canal in the early 1900s. In 1882, Judge Benjamin Wright, the chief engineer for the Erie Canal, received an award from the American Society of

Civil Engineers (ASCE) and was given the title "Father of American Engineering."

Canal building was the first major technical challenge faced by the fledgling American construction industry. Hundreds of construction and engineering problems requiring innovative solutions had to be overcome, such as how to remove stumps, move massive amounts of earth and rock, construct lengthy feeder dams and canals, and bridge major rivers. Canal engineers pioneered the design of inclined portage railways, canal tunnels and bridges, novel lock designs, and improved surveying techniques. Accurate surveying was important because, unlike a river, the current in a canal must be kept to a minimum—both to conserve water, which was almost always in short supply, and to allow "up-boats" to make efficient headway.

An example of what engineers faced in providing adequate water is found in the construction of the Union Canal in Pennsylvania, which connected Reading, Pennsylvania, on the Schuylkill River to Middletown, Pennsylvania, on the Susquehanna River. The 75-mile-long canal reached a summit of 495 feet at Lebanon, Pennsylvania. Along the way, it passed through extensive limestone deposits, which were porous, requiring that the canal be constantly replenished. Engineers built a dam 22 miles north of Lebanon and a feeder-line to the summit. The gravity-flow of the feeder brought the water to a point four miles from the summit and 85 feet below it. The engineers designed a huge pumping station, called the "Water Works," which involved four steam engines; two immense water wheels, each 40 feet in diameter and 10 feet across; and a three-foot diameter wooden piping system. The Water Works raised the water 95 feet to a four-mile ditch that fed the canal.

Ironically, canal-building helped in the introduction of the railroad. The challenge of constructing canals across mountain ranges and out of river valleys was overcome by the invention of the inclined railroad. The engineering techniques involved were imported from England and made a significant contribution to American railroading technology.

In the second half of the nineteenth century, railroads replaced canals as the primary means of transport in America. The cost of building and maintaining canals was the major factor in their demise. As the number of miles of canals expanded, finding sufficient sources of water to keep them navigable became difficult. Further, railroads could be built in locations where canals were impractical, and they were less costly to build and maintain. Railroad trains could travel significantly faster than horse- or mule-drawn canal boats, which were limited to about four to six miles per hour. Further, railroads were able to operate during the winter when canals froze over.

Canal Boats

Being accustomed to today's high-speed travel and instant communications, we would find life on the canal in the mid-1800s similar to being in a slow-motion movie. Speed was limited by the pace of the mules or horses used to tow the boat. Much of the time, it was a silent journey, broken only by the sounds of nature and the hooves of the tow animals.

The speed at which canal boats were permitted to travel was limited by law in most states, both to prevent accidents and to prevent bow waves from destroying the dirt banks of the canals. Most boats were pulled by one or two mules. Horses were somewhat faster than mules, although not as sturdy, and were usually used by passenger and mail boats where speed was more critical. Powered tugboats were not permitted on any but the largest canals.

There were four types of boats operating on American canals during the 1800s: packet, line, state, and freight. The fastest was the packet boat, which could typically carry 50 to 75 passengers and maintained a fixed schedule. The line boats carried a combination of passengers and freight. They were slower than packet boats, provided a lower class of accommodations, and charged less per mile. They offered less service as they usually had a crew of only four—captain, bowsman, steersman, and driver. State boats were mainly used for canal maintenance. The majority of the boats on most canals were freight boats, which varied widely in shape and size, depending on the type of cargo.

Freight carriers typically carried between 25 and 90 tons of cargo, although coal barges could carry up to 150 tons. During the later years, in particular, they dominated traffic on most canals. Of the 4,200 boats operating on the Erie Canal in 1847, for example, 3,520 were freighters, 620 line boats, and only 60 were packets. Operators of freight boats and their families usually lived on the boat, some during winter months.

Dinner on board a canal packet boat. Sketch courtesy of the American Canal and Transportation Center, York, Pennsylvania.

Traveling on a Packet Boat

Life on the packet boat was both crowded and boring. The largest packets were approximately 80 feet long and 10 to 12 feet wide. A long cabin ran the length of the ship, with the women's cabin in the front and the men's cabin, which also served as a common room, in the center. These were usually followed by the galley and the crew's quarters. A stall for extra horses would be located at either the bow or the stern. The ladies' cabin typically held eight to twelve passengers and was separated from the gentlemen's section by a curtain in the smaller boats, or by a cargo section in the larger ones. The gentlemen's room was the largest and could accommodate fifteen to twenty passengers. It was designed to be large enough to seat all passengers for meals. During the day, the tables were against the wall, then moved to the center at meal times and at night. On some boats, there was a separate cabin for meals and daytime lounging.

Meals were served three times a day and generally consisted of the same food. According to Charles Dickens, who wrote about his experiences traveling on the Pennsylvania Main Line in 1842, meals invariably consisted of a combination of tea, coffee, bread, smoked (although sometimes fresh) fish, liver, steak, chops, sausage, potatoes, pickles, and black puddings.

After supper, the passengers were sent on deck while the tiers of bunks (three high) were prepared for sleeping. The bunks consisted of a board hinged to the wall that was only slightly more than one foot wide and on which a thin mattress and blanket were laid. Day and night, the cabins were crowded as many kept their carry bags with them. When the weather was pleasant, passengers could relax on the small deck or the roof of the cabin. It was necessary to stay alert, however; when the steersman yelled, "low bridge," passengers were expected to respond quickly by stooping or, if a particularly low bridge, by lying on the deck. During inclement weather the cabins became unbearably crowded and filled with a variety of odors ranging from kitchen odors to those of the spare animals on board.

The crowded quarters meant that there was little passengers could do for recreation other than to chat with fellow passengers, many of whom, apparently, proved not to be talkative. These would frequently just sit and sleep with their heads on the tables since there was no place to lie down except on the roof. Male passengers occasionally debarked and walked along the levy.

The crew of a packet consisted of a steersman, usually the captain; a driver on shore with the animals; several cabin stewards; and a cook. Frequently a spare team of extra mules or horses was also kept on board. The driver was responsible for capturing any poultry that strayed from neighboring farms. He also picked fruit from orchards adjacent to the canal.

Canal Locks

Except on the very large canals, locks were typically 90 feet long by 15 feet wide to accommodate boats that were 60 to 80 feet long by 12 to 14 feet wide. The locks were operated by two to three tenders, depending on the size of the lock and the amount of traffic, although locks on smaller canals were frequently operated by the boat crew. Lock tenders typically worked a 12- to 15-hour day. The larger locks were staffed with two crews, a night crew and a day crew.

Fights occasionally ensued between boat crews traveling in opposite directions as to who was entitled to pass through the lock first, particularly where the locks were unattended. In general down-boats had priority over up-boats. Packets had precedence over line or freight boats, both at the locks and on the canal. Establishing priorities was necessary because boats could be lined up for over a mile on both sides of a lock on a busy canal.

Transition to Modern Waterways

Expansion of America's canal system essentially stopped in the 1850s in the sense that net mileage of canals no longer increased each year. In spite of the expansion of railroads during the remainder of the 1800s, however, canal traffic

Inland waterways in the eastern part of the United States. Except in New York State, most are maintained by the U.S. Army Corps of Engineers. Courtesy of the American Canal and Transportation Center, York, Pennsylvania.

in terms of total tonnage continued to increase into the 1880s. Passenger traffic was the first to abandon the canals in favor of the railroad. Shipments of high-valued manufactured goods were next. Bulk products, such as coal, sand, gravel, and other building materials, were the last to go. Supported by traffic from these low-valued commodities, some of the historic canals continued to operate until the 1920s.

Starting in the 1880s, the federal government, through the U.S. Army Corps of Engineers, took an interest in improving inland waterways for large barge and even ship traffic. Canals such as the Chesapeake and Delaware in Maryland were widened to accept ocean-going ships. The modern New York Ship Canal evolved from the Erie Canal, as did the Illinois Waterway from the Illinois and Michigan Canal. Dams and locks on major rivers such as the Mississippi and the Ohio were enlarged to handle huge tows of barges and ore transports. Construction of improvements to the nation's waterways continues.

Today, there are 25 navigable river systems in the United States, ranging in length from 72 miles on the Allegheny River to 2,460 miles on the Mississippi River. In addition to these navigable rivers, the Corps of Engineers has constructed the 234-mile Tenn-Tom Waterway (1972-1984) from the Tennessee River to the Tombigbee River, and the Illinois Waterway (1933). It also maintains the Intracoastal Waterway, totaling 2,242 miles.

Locks on the Mississippi and Ohio Rivers

The Mississippi River has been one of the major waterways of America since it was discovered by the Spanish explorer, Hernando de Soto, near the site of modern Memphis, Tennessee, in 1541. For several hundred years the French and Spanish fought over control of the river, a conflict that lasted until the United States negotiated the Louisiana Purchase in 1803. Settlers who moved into the Ohio River valley made use of the Ohio and Mississippi rivers as a means of transportation to New Orleans and the Caribbean.

The Ohio River has been made navigable for large, modern barge tows from Pittsburgh to its entrance into the Mississippi River at Cairo, Illinois, a distance of 981 miles. The construction of locks on the Ohio River started with the Portland Canal around the falls at Louisville, Kentucky, in 1830. This permitted stern-wheeled riverboats to navigate from New Orleans all the way to Pittsburgh.

In the 1880s several innovative locks were built on the Ohio River, having the unique width of 110 feet and length of 600 feet. The unusual width was necessitated by the practice on the Ohio River of towing barges four abreast. It took until 1929 before the Ohio River became completely canalized, a system that required 46 dams and locks. In 1955 a modernization program was started to reduce the number of locks to 19 and doubling the length of the locks to 1,200 feet. This program is still underway.

When the Illinois and Michigan Canal opened in 1848, Chicago and Great Lakes shipping was given access to the lower Mississippi River and the Caribbean via the Illinois and Mississippi Rivers. In the 1920s, the federal government built a modern deepwater canal, now called the Illinois Waterway, which is able to handle large power-driven riverboats. Many historians consider the construction of the Illinois and Michigan Canal to be as important to the economic development of the central United States as the Erie Canal had been in the 1830s.

Navigation (as well as flood control) on the Mississippi River became an important political issue in the 1870s. It was not until the 1930s, however, that comprehensive navigational improvements were made when construction started on a system of 28 dams and locks on the upper Mississippi between Minneapolis and the mouth of the Illinois River. On the lower Mississippi between Memphis, Tennessee, and Baton Rouge, Louisiana, work on 16 cutoffs was undertaken to reduce the navigational distance between the two cities by 170 miles.

Another important waterway that has been developed to handle modern shipping is St. Marys River, which connects Lake Superior and Lake Huron. To overcome the 23-foot drop in the river's 60-mile length, five locks have been constructed to allow ore ships and other large vessels to travel between the two lakes. The first canal and locks were built by the British in 1797 to eliminate the portage around the rapids. This canal was destroyed by American troops during the War of 1812. Forty years later, a second canal was built, this time by the state of Michigan with federal support.

Traffic through the Soo Locks became so heavy by 1870 that the U.S. Army Corps of Engineers took over the locks from the state and expanded them. In 1895 the Canadian government opened a separate set of locks on its side of the river. Today, the Soo Locks system is reported to handle the largest annual tonnage of any lock system in the world—mostly iron ore, coal, and grain.

Canal Museums

Historic Canals and Locks

❖ *ILLINOIS AND MICHIGAN CANAL MUSEUM, 803 South State Street, Lockport, Illinois 60441. Tel: 815-838-5080. Open daily 1-4:30, closed holidays and mid-December to January 2. Pioneer Settlement is open from mid-April through September. Admission free.*

The museum is located in the original headquarters building of the Illinois and Michigan Canal Commission, built in 1837. It features displays of artifacts, photographs, and documents concerning the history of the canal.

Also featured are exhibits on early life along the canal. These include the Pioneer Settlement, which many consider one of the best-preserved canal towns in the country. The Old Stone Annex contains tools, carriages, and other artifacts from the canal period, including a scale model of the *City of Pekin*, one of the largest boats to travel the canal.

❖ *GREAT FALLS TAVERN AND MUSEUM, CHESAPEAKE AND OHIO NATIONAL HISTORICAL PARK, 11710 MacArthur Boulevard, Great Falls, Maryland 20854. Tel: 301-443-0721. Open Wednesday through Sunday 9-5, April through October; Saturday and Sunday, rest of year; closed major holidays. Admission free.*

❖ *HANCOCK VISITOR CENTER, 326 East Main Street, Hancock, Maryland 21750. Tel: 301-678-5463. Telephone for open times and days. Admission free.*

View of the C&O Canal from Round Top Mountain, Hancock, Maryland. Photo courtesy of the C&O Canal National Historical Park, Sharpsburg, Maryland.

*On the C&O Canal.
Photo courtesy of the
C&O Canal National
Historical Park,
Sharpsburg, Maryland.*

❖ *CUMBERLAND VISITOR CENTER, One Canal Street, Cumberland, Maryland 21502. Tel: 301-722-8226. Telephone for open times and days. Admission free.*

The Chesapeake and Ohio Canal Park follows the Maryland bank of the Potomac River and extends from Georgetown in the District of Columbia to Cumberland, Maryland. Founded by Congress in 1854, it is operated by the National Park Service. The museum is housed in an old Chesapeake and Ohio Canal Company hotel built in 1830, now referred to as the Great Falls Tavern. Additional information about the canal can be obtained at two other visitor centers: one in Cumberland, Maryland, and the other at Hancock, Maryland. Boat trips on the canal are available from the Tavern in Great Falls and from Georgetown in the District of Columbia.

The museum in the Great Falls Tavern provides exhibits on the history of the canal, including a brief film titled *The C&O Canal.* The Cumberland visitor center is located in an old railroad station built in 1810 by the Western Maryland Railroad Company (now part of the CSX). The National Park Service plans to "rewater" a section of the canal near Hancock and expand the exhibits at the Hancock visitor center. They are planning a similar rewatering near Williamsport, Maryland, which is located at approximately the midpoint of the original canal. Canal boat rides will be available at both locations when these projects are completed.

❖ *CHESAPEAKE AND DELAWARE CANAL MUSEUM, Chesapeake City, Maryland. Tel: 301-885-5621. Open Monday through Saturday 8-4:30, Sunday 10-6, Easter through October; closed Sundays and holidays. Admission free.*

The Chesapeake and Delaware Canal Museum at Chesapeake City, Maryland, shows the original pump house and models of the locks, as well as artifacts and photographs that help the visitor picture conditions on the canal in the 1800s. Of special interest is the 38-foot lift wheel used from 1852 to 1927 to lift water 17 feet at a rate of 20,000 gallons per minute. The steam engines that drove the water wheel have been in place since they replaced the original engines in 1851.

One of the original canal locks can still be seen at Delaware City, Maryland.

❖ *GRAND PORTAGE NATIONAL MONUMENT, U.S. 61, Grand Portage, Minnesota 55604. Tel: 218-387-2788. Open daily 8-5, mid-May to mid-October. Admission $1, seniors and students free.*

Grand Portage is located on Lake Superior, near the U.S.-Canadian border. It is 35 miles from Grand Marais where the headquarters of the national monument is located. Founded by French fur traders at the beginning of the portage to the string of lakes leading to the Lake of the Woods, Grand Portage was the first settlement in Minnesota.

The stockade and several of the original buildings have been replicated to show how the village looked at the peak of traffic over the portage, around 1800. The 9-mile portage trail used by fur trappers and traders can be followed to Fort Charlotte.

❖ *CANAL MUSEUM AT WATERLOO VILLAGE, Waterloo Road, Stanhope, New Jersey. Tel: 201-347-0900. Open Tuesday through Sunday 10-5, mid-April through December; closed major holidays. Admission $6.50, senior and under-16 discounts.*

Waterloo Village near Stanhope, New Jersey, contains remnants of one of the 23 inclines on the Morris Canal. Waterloo was originally called Andover Forge, which operated from 1760 to 1815. Following the closing of the iron mines and forge, the town atrophied for 15 years until the Morris Canal opened in 1831. The town soon renewed its vigor as it became a transshipment point on the canal. It continued to prosper until a railroad bypassed the town in 1901. The canal itself was finally demolished in 1927.

The Canal Museum was established in 1975 by the Canal Society of New Jersey and contains artifacts, photographs, paintings, and models interpreting the canals of New Jersey. Artifacts from the Morris Canal include a section of the wire rope used to haul boats up the inclined plane and a piece of the track. A portion of the canal adjacent to the museum has been rewatered. A nearby inclined plane is under restoration.

Founded in 1740, the Village of Waterloo has been restored with more than 28 buildings open for visitors. These include a working gristmill, a sawmill, a farmhouse, a tavern, and several houses. During the summer months costumed guides and artisans explain the workings of the village during the mid-1800s.

A water turbine used to power an inclined plane can still be seen at Lake Hopatcong State Park a few miles east of Waterloo. Lake Hopatcong, located at the summit of the Morris Canal, was the canal's main source of water. Slightly further east, at Ledgerwood, stand the remains of another inclined plane.

❖ *DELAWARE AND HUDSON CANAL MUSEUM, Mohonk Road, High Falls, New York 12440. Tel: 914-687-9311. Open Thursday through Saturday and Monday 11-5, Sunday 1-5, May 30 to Labor Day; Saturday 11-5, Sunday 1-5, May and September through October; closed November through April. Admission $1.*

The Delaware and Hudson Canal Museum is supported by the D and H Canal Historical Society, founded in 1966. The purpose of the society is to educate the public on the history and significance of the Delaware and Hudson Canal and to promote the restoration and maintenance of portions of the canal. The portion that has been preserved is at the town of High Falls, New York, which is approximately ten miles south of Kingston, New York. A self-guided tour allows visitors to inspect the construction of the locks, the tow paths, and the foundations of the aqueduct built to cross over Roundout Creek at High Falls.

The museum is adjacent to the five High Falls locks (designated as a national historic site in 1969). It contains working models of the gravity railroad and the canal locks. Using maps

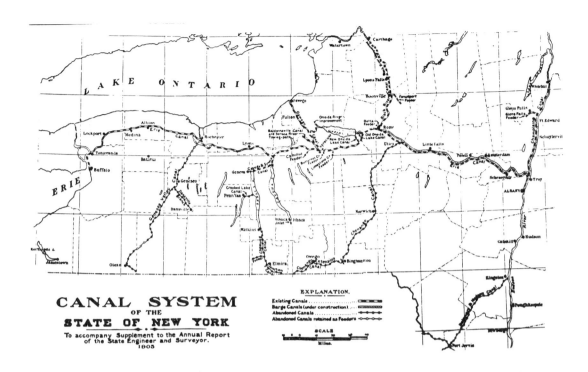

CANAL SYSTEM
OF THE
STATE OF NEW YORK
To accompany Supplement to the Annual Report
of the State Engineer and Surveyor.
1905

Historic Canals of New York State. Courtesy of the American Canal and Transportation Center, York, Pennsylvania.

and dioramas, the museum shows the entire operation of the canal. A cross-sectional view of the canal depicts the 108 locks and aqueducts, as well as the 22 reservoirs and 14 feeder streams used to maintain water in the canal. There are also dioramas showing the interior of a canal boat and how boats passed on the narrow canal.

The aqueduct across the Delaware River,

built by John Roebling in the 1850s, is still standing, although it was converted into a road around the turn of the century. Considered the oldest suspension bridge in America, it has been declared a National Historic Landmark and was purchased by the National Park Service in 1980. The bridge is located on the New York-Pennsylvania border near Port Jervis, New York.

❖ *NIAGARA COUNTY HISTORICAL SOCIETY, 215 Niagara Street, Lockport, New York 14094. Tel: 716-434-7433. Open Thursday through Sunday 1-5, closed major holidays. Admission free.*

The Niagara County Historical Society operates a museum in Lockport that contains a small exhibit on the Erie Canal. The museum consists of a complex of five buildings containing displays and artifacts dealing with the life of early settlers in the area and with the Indians of the region.

Lockport is located near the west end of the Erie Canal and is the location of one of the

most remarkable engineering feats on the canal, the climbing of the Niagara Escarpment. Engineers cut and blasted five steps of double locks out of solid rock, each step providing a lift of 12 feet.

A portion of the original Lockport locks on the Erie Canal can still be seen alongside the modern ones. There is a small unstaffed museum at the site of the old locks.

❖ *ERIE CANAL VILLAGE, State Route 49, Rome, New York 13440. Tel: 315-337-3999. Open daily 10-5, May 15 to September 17 (subject to change). Admission $6, senior and student discounts.*

Founded in 1973, Erie Canal Village is a restored canal village dating from the 1840s. It shows life along the canal in the mid-1800s and offers rides along a restored segment of the canal. The Canal Museum contains artifacts and displays that describe the history of the Erie Canal, including its political, social, and economic significance.

The buildings represented in the village include a tavern, church meeting hall, blacksmith shop, train station, school, and a Victorian-style house.

❖ *ERIE CANAL MUSEUM, Weighlock Building, 318 Erie Boulevard, Syracuse, New York 13202. Tel: 315-471-0593. Open Tuesday through Sunday 10-5, closed major holidays. Admission $1, under-12 discount.*

The Erie Canal Museum in Syracuse is located in the original canal-boat weighlock, built in 1850, and is the only weighlock still in existence. When in operation, it was capable of weighing canal boats up to 100 feet long, based on the amount of water displaced in the lock. The weighing of canal boats carrying freight was necessary because rates on many canals were based on the weight of the cargo. The weighlock was used by the state of New York until 1957, when it stopped basing rates on the weight of the boat's cargo.

The museum is associated with the Syracuse Urban Cultural Park. It contains a restored canal boat named the *Frank Thomson* and a number of exhibits about the Erie Canal. The museum also offers rides along a restored segment of the canal.

❖ *ROSCOE VILLAGE, 381 Hill Street, Coshocton, Ohio 43812. Tel: 614-622-9310. Open daily 10-5, May through December; 11-5, rest of year; closed major holidays. Admission to village free; tour of exhibit buildings $6, student discount.*

Founded in 1968, Roscoe Village is a re-creation of a canal village as it looked during the heyday of canal transportation around 1850. Coshocton is located on the former Ohio and Erie (Grand) Canal, which connected Lake Erie at Cleveland to the Ohio River at Portsmouth. The village contains more than 30 homes, shops, and businesses that were present in a canal town of the mid-1800s. Many of the buildings contain artifacts and furnishings of the period, a number of which are related to the canal and its operations.

There are two sets of locks near Roscoe Village: a set of double locks and one of triple locks. The restored triple locks are considered to be the best remaining example of locks in Ohio.

❖ *ALLEGHENY PORTAGE RAILROAD NATIONAL HISTORICAL SITE, Old U.S. 22 and Gallitzin Road, Cresson, Pennsylvania 16630. Tel: 818-886-8176. Open daily 8:30-6, Memorial Day to Labor Day; 8:30-5 rest of year. Admission free.*

The Allegheny Portage Railroad National Historical Site west of Altoona, near Cresson, Pennsylvania, is the only significant remaining artifact of the portage railway. The site contains the remnants of the roadbed and the foundation of the engine house that once stood at the top of the summit incline. The old Lemon House Tavern, which was a wayhouse for food and drink on the portage line, still stands adjacent to the roadbed at the summit. A recently built museum nearby shows the history and operation of the canal and the portage railroad. The new and enlarged museum opened on the site in the spring of 1992.

Inclined plane number 6 on the Allegheny Portage Road. The sectional boats were drawn up and down these planes by cable, powered by a stationary steam engine on top. Photo courtesy of the American Canal and Transportation Center, York, Pennsylvania.

❖ *THE CANAL MUSEUM, HUGH MOORE PARK, 200 South Delaware Drive, Easton, Pennsylvania 18044. Tel: 717-636-2070. Open daily 10-4, Monday through Saturday; Sunday 1-5; closed major holidays. Admission $1.50, under-13 discount.*

Easton, Pennsylvania, was an important canal center during the 1800s. It was located at the junction of three canals, the privately-owned Lehigh and Morris canals, and the commonwealth of Pennsylvania-owned Delaware Division Canal. The latter canal paralleled the Delaware River for 60 miles from Easton down to Trenton, New Jersey, (entrance to the Delaware and Hudson Canal), and further south to Bristol, Pennsylvania, near Philadelphia.

Hugh Moore Park was founded by the city of Easton to preserve the city's canal and industrial heritage. The park includes approximately six miles of the Lehigh Canal, and canal rides are offered during the summer months. The Canal Museum, which contains exhibits about the canal and industrial history of Easton, was started in 1970 as a joint project between the Hugh Moore Park staff and the Pennsylvania Canal Society. The park also includes the Locktender's House Museum, where costumed guides show visitors through various period rooms and explain how the locktender and his family lived during the 1800s.

❖ *DELAWARE CANAL, Delaware Canal State Park, Upper Black Eddy, Pennsylvania 18972. Tel: 215-982-5560. Many of the sites in the park are open 24 hours every day, others only from sunup to sundown. Phone for schedules at specific sites. Admission free.*

Originally named Roosevelt State Park (after President Theodore Roosevelt) when it was founded in 1940, the Delaware Canal State Park is a 60-mile long linear park that includes the full length of the original Delaware Division Canal, which extended from Easton, Pennsylvania, to Bristol, near Philadelphia. The Delaware Canal is the only remaining continuously intact remnant of the American canal system of the mid-1800s. With the exception of the last 0.7 miles at Bristol, where the tidewater locks have been removed, the canal retains all of its original engineering and operational features.

The canal has become a favorite of canal enthusiasts, as well as a popular recreational facility. In summer months a mule-drawn barge run is operated from New Hope, Pennsylvania. All but a very few of the canal's 24 locks can still be inspected, as can the remains of the seven aqueducts. The headquarters of the park is located at Lock 19.

A packet passing a freight boat on the Pennsylvania State Canal. Copy of a painting from a print in the Chaney Collection, Smithsonian Institution, Washington, D.C.

Modern Canal Locks

❖ *ILLINOIS WATERWAY VISITOR CENTER, Starved Rock Lock and Dam, Utica, Illinois. Tel: 815-667-4054. Open daily 9-8, Memorial Day to Labor Day; 9-5, Labor Day to mid-December and March to Labor Day. Admission free.*

The Illinois Waterway is the modern version of the Illinois and Michigan Canal. It was undertaken by the U.S. Army Corps of Engineers in the 1920s and was completed in 1930.

The visitor center at the Starved Rock Lock and Dam provides excellent views of the locks in operation. The center also has displays that explain the operation of the locks and a slide show about the history of the waterway.

❖ *LOCKS AND DAM #15, MISSISSIPPI RIVER VISITOR CENTER, Rodman Avenue, Arsenal Island, Rock Island, Illinois 61201. Tel: 309-788-6412. Open daily 9-5, early March to late May; 9-9, late May to late September; 9-5, late September to early December; closed rest of year. Admission free.*

The Visitor Center provides models and other displays showing how the transportation system on the Mississippi River functions. It includes a computer-operated model of the river to explain the impact of different levels of flow in the river. There are excellent viewing opportunities to watch the operation of the locks.

❖ *KEOKUK LOCK AND DAM #19, Keokuk, Iowa 52362. Tel: 319-524-6363. Open for tours Monday through Friday, Memorial Day to Labor Day; by appointment rest of year. Phone ahead for schedule. Admission free.*

Tours of hydroelectric plant and facilities are made regularly five times each weekday.

❖ *THE SOO LOCKS, Tower of History, Sault Ste. Marie, Michigan 49783. Tel: 906-635-3050. Open daily 9-9, July through August; 10-6, May 15 through June 30 and September 1 to mid-October; closed mid-October to mid-May. Admission $2.75, senior and student discounts.*

❖ *SOO LOCKS BOAT TOURS, 515 and 1157 East Portage Avenue, Sault Ste. Marie, Michigan. Tel: 906-632-6301. Daily 9 -7, mid-May to mid-October. Admission $11, student discount.*

The site contains several viewing platforms, including a Corps of Engineers Visitor Center, and the Tower of History, which offers exhibits on the region and excellent views of the locks and the city.

❖ *WATERWAYS EXPERIMENTAL STATION, Halls Ferry Road, Vicksburg, Mississippi 39180. Tel: 601-634-2502. Visitor Center open Monday to Friday 10-2; self-guided tour available Monday to Friday 7:45-4:15; laboratory tours available by appointment. Admission free.*

The U.S. Army Corps of Engineers' Waterways Experimental Station carries out research on the environmental impact of man-made structures on existing waterways, particularly the Mississippi River. The station offers demonstrations of these impacts by use of an operating model as part of regular tours of the laboratory.

❖ *BERTRUM SNELL AND DWIGHT D. EISENHOWER LOCKS, ST. LAWRENCE SEAWAY, Robert Moses State Park, Massena, New York. Tel: 315-769-8663. Open daily. Admission free.*

These two locks on the St. Lawrence Seaway, which helped open up the Great Lakes to sea-going vessels, overcome a drop in elevation of 90 feet. They can be viewed from within the Robert Moses State Park and from a viewing site on State Route 131 just north of Massena.

❖ *THE DALLES DAM AND LOCKS, The Dalles, Oregon 97058. Tel: 503-296-4868. Check in advance for tour schedule. Admission free.*

The Dalles Dam and Locks are located 180 miles upstream from the mouth of the river. Tours of the facilities, including the powerhouse, dam, locks, and fish ladder, are offered.

❖ *MCNARY LOCK AND DAM, Umatilla, Oregon. Tel: 503-922-3211. Check in advance for tour schedule. Admission free.*

The McNary Lock and Dam at Umatilla, Oregon, which are 104 miles upstream from The Dalles, also provide an excellent means of observing lock operations on the Columbia River. The Visitor Center at McNary offers a history of the locks and an explanation of their operation. The fish ladder can be observed through a fish-viewing window.

❖ *LAKE WASHINGTON SHIP CANAL AND HIRAM M. CHITTENDON LOCKS, Seattle, Washington. Tel: 206-783-7059. Open daily 10-7, June 15 to September 15; Thursday to Monday 11-5, rest of year. Admission free.*
The Lake Washington Ship Canal connects Puget Sound with Lake Washington and is one of the most-used canals in the country. The Visitor Center describes the history and operation of the canal. Trout and salmon ladders can be observed from the viewing platform.

*BOSTON HARBOR FROM CONSTITUTION WHARF by Robert Salmon, oil, 26 ¾ x 40 ¾ inches,
courtesy of the United States Naval Academy Museum, Annapolis, Maryland.*

Maritime

From its creation, America has been a maritime nation. It was discovered and settled via the ocean. The sea has been America's medium for international trade, a source of essential food, and protective buffer from potential enemies. Many of its important battles have been fought on water. Shipbuilding and coastal fishing in New England became the first industries in the New World.

With the growth of New England's fishing industry, its excellent harbors, and abundance of timber, the region's shipbuilding industry sprang up within a decade after the Pilgrims landed in 1620. By the late 1600s, Portsmouth, New Hampshire; Boston and New Bedford, Massachusetts; and Bath and Belfast, Maine; had become major shipbuilding centers. During the 1600s shipyards in these cities concentrated on building small, broad-hulled fishing boats, as well as slimmer sloops and schooners for coastal trade. The first large ship built in America, a 44-gun, three-masted square-rigger commissioned by the Royal Navy, was built in Portsmouth, New Hampshire, in 1690.

During the 1700s American shipyards continued to focus on small craft, primarily sloops and schooners. These one- and two-masted sailing ships with lengths of less than 60 feet had in-line sails and were ideal for coastal trading and fishing. They required only small crews, sailed well in all types of weather, were fast, and had shallow drafts. Their speed made them the favorite vessels of American smugglers and privateers.

American shipbuilders did construct larger, square-rigged ships during the 1700s for extended trading voyages to the Indian and South Atlantic Oceans. American traders preferred the smaller West Indiaman of less than 600 tons to the larger East Indiaman, which could approach 1,000 tons, favored by Europeans. American shipyards began to build larger ships following the Revolutionary War. The 204-foot U.S. Navy frigates *Constitution*, *Constellation*, and *United States* were built in 1797 and had gross weights of 2,200 tons.

During the 1700s the English looked increasingly to the American colonists for their ships as the 200-year-old trees needed to construct seagoing ships had become scarce in England. It took several acres of ancient oaks to build the largest wooden sailing ship of the line. By the start of the Revolutionary War, one-third of the ships under British registry had been contributed by American shipyards. Many of these ships were owned and sailed by American colonists, since British maritime law did not distinguish between colonists and British citizens until the start of the Revolution.

While England encouraged the colonies to engage in maritime trading, it placed severe restrictions on foreign merchants who attempted to trade with the colonies. The Navigation Acts, originally created by the British Crown in the fifteenth and sixteenth centuries to protect English coastal shipping, were strengthened in the late seventeenth century to prevent direct foreign trade with the colonies. Trade between the colonies and foreign countries had to be transshipped through English ports and carried in English ships.

During the infancy of America's maritime fleet, England treated American-built ships with American crews as if they were English ships with English crews. Boston traders were treated as equals to their London counterparts. As a result, Boston became the third-largest trading port in the British Empire, after London and Bristol, England.

This arrangement worked well as long as the colonies served as suppliers of raw materials to the British factories. Colonies were even given subsidies to encourage the production of items needed by the British navy such as ship's masts, hemp, and naval stores, as well as consumer items desired in England such as silk and indigo.

The USS Constitution *on a visit to San Diego, February 2, 1933. Photo courtesy of the National Archives, Washington, D.C.*

As the American colonies began to develop their own manufacturing industries, however, England attempted to put restrictions on colonial merchants engaging in foreign trade. The British Parliament passed laws prohibiting the colonies from manufacturing goods in competition with those being produced by English factories, such as woolen cloth (1699), hats (1732), and wrought iron (1750).

New England traders were not content to abide by the British restrictions. Profits on foreign trade were too high to ignore for long. A 100 percent profit on the cost of a single voyage was not unusual. By the mid-1700s the key ports of New England had become centers of world trade, notwithstanding the restrictions placed on such trade by the English Crown.

Triangular Trade

Unlike Southern colonies, northern colonies had little in raw materials to export to England. On the other hand, they were eager to obtain English manufactured goods such as furniture, textiles, tools, guns, and ceramics. Export of the few items they did have to offer—

fish, cereals, and meat—was forbidden as they competed with England's own food industries. Unable to acquire English currency through direct trade, the northern colonies developed complex indirect trading schemes.

Triangular trading first developed in the 1640s, when American merchant ships started carrying fish, tobacco, and lumber to Spanish and other Mediterranean ports, where they were exchanged for wine and European manufactured goods. These were then taken to the West Indies, where they were traded for much-needed sugar and molasses.

Triangular trading grew slowly until after 1700, when American ships became major factors in the slave trade. They had been participating since the 1650s but their involvement was restricted by the monopoly the British Crown gave to the Royal African Company.

The first leg of the triangular slave trade took rum, flour, pots, clothing, and other manufactured items to Africa, where they were traded for slaves. The second leg, called the "middle passage," involved transporting the slaves to the British West Indies, where they were sold. The proceeds from selling the slaves were then used to buy sugar and molasses for the New England rum industry. The wages and profits derived from the manufacture of rum and related products were then used by the colonists to buy English goods. Immense fortunes were accumulated from the triangular trade which later became an important source of capital for the creation of New England's industrial base.

American involvement in the slave trade grew steadily until the Revolutionary War. England attempted to stop colonial participation by passing the Molasses Act in 1733 and the Sugar Act in 1764, which American merchants largely ignored. In 1770, Rhode Island alone was home port to 150 ships engaged in slave traffic. Congress finally outlawed the importation of slaves in 1808, but the smuggling of slaves from islands in the Caribbean by American privateers continued until the Civil War.

Following the Revolutionary War, the American merchant marine grew and prospered. England and France were preoccupied with protracted warfare throughout the world. Since American merchants were able to present themselves as being neutral, they were welcomed at most foreign ports. Except for the disruption of the War of 1812, the American merchant marine continued to grow until the 1850s. By then, steam power was rapidly replacing sails, and the American overseas merchant marine was starting to decline in significance. It became almost dormant until World War I, when it was revived by government subsidies to transport troops across the Atlantic.

Golden Years of American Maritime

Following the War of 1812 American shipping entered its period of dominance. American shipowners were the first to develop the transatlantic packet, providing scheduled departure times from Boston or New York and arrival times in England or France. Previously, ships departed when they received a full cargo or passenger complement. The first packet fleet was created by an American company, the Black Ball Line. It was followed by other American packet lines with such picturesque names as the Red Star Line, the Swallow Tail Line, the Patriotic Line, and the Dramatic Line. (The latter named its ships after famous names of the theater such as *Shakespeare*.)

These square-rigged sailing ships ushered in the birth of modern passenger travel. Ship captains took pride in meeting or bettering their schedules. Initially, transatlantic crossings took 25 to 40 days, depending on the weather and wind directions. In 1824 a westbound record of 15 days and 14 hours was set by Captain Philip Fox in the 352-ton *Emerald*. Soon thereafter Captain Pitkin Page achieved an eastbound record of 13 days and 14 hours.

In spite of records and advertising claims, crossing times were still dependent on the weather and the wind. For every 15-day crossing there was a 70-day one caused by storms or lack of wind. More than one packet simply disappeared while crossing, assumed to be lost in a storm at sea while under full sail. Conditions aboard transatlantic packets were primitive and frequently not sanitary. Immigrant packets would arrive in New York or Boston reporting that ten percent of their 600 to 1,000 passengers had died, and were frequently buried at sea.

By the 1840s the sailing packets were losing business to the steam packets. In a last desperate effort to prolong the life of the sailing ship, American ship designers searched for ways to add speed. They made such changes as narrowing the hulls and adding more sails. Out of these innovations developed the clipper ships, which became known as the "greyhounds of the sea." While these sleek, yacht-like ships evolved over a period of years, maritime historians consider the *Rainbow*, which was built in New York in 1845, as the first of the "extreme" clippers.

Other historians credit the *Ann McKim*, a rakish 143-foot, square-rigged schooner built in Baltimore in 1832, as the first clipper. The Baltimore clipper originated as a sloop around 1812. Because of its speed, it was quickly adopted by American privateers and smugglers and later by slave runners. The square-rigged

Baltimore clippers were generally smaller than the great clippers of the 1850s, measuring 150-200 feet long with a gross weight of 250-500 tons. By comparison, the great clippers measured 250-300 feet long and had gross weights in the range of 1,500-2,500 tons.

The narrow lines of the great clippers limited the amount of cargo they could carry. They were, therefore, economical only for premium cargoes where speed over long distances was required. The clippers were used mainly in the China tea trade and to carry prospectors to the gold fields of California and Australia. Speed was crucial in the China tea trade because tea lost its flavor during extended periods at sea. Most important to ship owners, the first tea of a new season to arrive in London, Boston, or New York could be sold for up to double the normal price.

In 1846 the *Sea Witch* sailed from Hong Kong to New York in 74 days and 14 hours, a sailing record that still stands. In 1854 the *Flying Cloud* took only 89 days and 8 hours to reach San Francisco from New York. The return-trip record of 76 days and 7 hours was achieved by the *Comet* in 1853-4. The westbound voyage to California was always slower than the eastbound return because of the perennial head winds the ships faced as they fought their way north after rounding Cape Horn.

American clipper ships captured the English tea trade during the 1850s, after the English Parliament repealed the Navigation Acts in 1849. American ships could now carry tea and other goods from China directly into English ports. Ultimately the English developed their own version of the clipper ship and were able to compete more or less on an equal basis. By then, however, the sailing ship was clearly doomed to play a secondary role to the steamship. The clipper and other sailing ships were increasingly relegated to carrying less-valuable cargo such as lumber and other bulk cargoes, as well as European immigrants bound for America and Australia.

Steam Power

While Englishman James Watt built the first practical steam engine in 1765, the first successful steam-powered boat, a sternwheeler, called the *Charlotte Dundas*, was not demonstrated until 1802. Financed by Lord Dundas, the governor of the Forth and Clyde Canal in Scotland, and built by William Symington, a Scottish engineer, the *Charlotte Dundas* was able to tow two 70-ton barges for 20 miles at a speed of 3 knots. The ship was taken out of service on the canal after several weeks when canal-boat owners complained that her wake was damaging the banks of the canal.

One of the passengers on the *Charlotte Dundas* during her brief period of service was an American inventor, Robert Fulton, who was working in Paris at the time. Upon returning to Paris, Fulton convinced the French navy to finance construction of his own version of the Scottish vessel. While Fulton's first attempt sank under the weight of the boiler and engine, his second effort in August 1803 was successful. Apparently receiving little further encouragement from the French navy, Fulton returned to America to pursue his ideas.

In New York Fulton obtained financial support for his experiments from Robert Livingston, a wealthy businessman who owned an estate on the Hudson River named Clermont. Fulton acquired a steam engine from the British firm founded by James Watt and installed it in a 133-foot, wooden-hulled ship, connecting the engine to two side-mounted, 15-foot paddle wheels. In 1807 Fulton successfully steamed up the Hudson River from New York to Albany and back in 62 hours, for an average speed of 3.9 knots. Traditionally, historians have referred to Fulton's steamboat as the *Clermont* but extensive research in recent years has revealed that the ship was actually named the *North River Steamboat*.

Fulton and Livingston operated the *North River Steamboat* on the Hudson River (frequently referred to at the time as the North River) for seven years and subsequently built larger boats to handle the throngs of passengers

Side-wheel steam packet Illinois, *circa 1852, Law Line, engraving by Endicott & Co. Courtesy of the Smithsonian Institution, Washington, D.C.*

desiring to ride this new mode of transportation. The two men convinced the New York state legislature to give them a monopoly to operate steamboats on the waters of the state. This meant that shipowners wishing to provide steamship services in New York were required to obtain a license from the Fulton-Livingston enterprise. In 1824 this monopoly position was substantially weakened by a milestone case before the Supreme Court (Gibbons v. Ogden), which gave federal regulations of commerce precedence over those of the states.

Fulton's second steam-powered vessel, the *Phoenix*, was built to provide a similar service on the Delaware River. Since Fulton had to "sail" the *Phoenix* down the coast of New Jersey to reach the mouth of the Delaware River, maritime historians credit her with being the first steam-powered ship to navigate at sea.

The first ship equipped with steam power to cross the Atlantic was the American-built *Savannah*. Built in New York in 1818, the *Savannah* spent most of her life as a sailing packet along the Atlantic coast. In 1821, however, equipped with a steam engine connected to retractable side-mounted paddles, she achieved immortality by being the first ship to use steam in crossing the Atlantic. Carrying 60 tons of coal to fuel the engines, the *Savannah* actually made use of steam power for only 80 hours of the total crossing time of 29 days, relying on sails for most of the voyage.

While American shipowners quickly adopted steam to power ships on the nation's inland waterways, they exhibited little interest in developing its use to replace sail power on ocean-going ships. British shipowners were more aggressive in adopting steam power.

In 1838 two British shipping companies competed for the honor of being the first to cross the Atlantic relying solely on steam. On April 23, 1838, the *Sirius*, a steamship designed for service between London and Ireland and owned by the British and American Steamship Company, entered New York harbor to be received by cheering crowds. Within hours another British steamship, the *Great Western*, owned by the Great Western Railway Company, also steamed into New York harbor. The smaller *Sirius* had left Ireland 18 days before while the *Great Western*, a larger ship designed specifically for transatlantic service, required only 15 days.

While the voyage of the *Sirius* was primarily a publicity stunt, the *Great Western*'s voyage was the inaugural voyage of regular commercial steamship service between Europe and America.

British shipowners followed this inaugural voyage with a series of further innovations. Within two years, a Nova Scotian named Samuel Cunard had started regular steamship service between Liverpool, England, and Boston. In 1845 the British designer of the *Great Western*, Isambard Kingdom Brunel, designed and built the 322-foot *Great Britain*, the first iron-hulled ship to enter transatlantic service. Cunard launched the last of the side-wheelers, a 400-foot liner named the *Scotia*, in 1863. The twin-screw propeller was introduced soon thereafter.

The U.S. Congress subsidized an American steamship company called the Collins Line in the 1840s in an attempt to overcome British competition, but to no avail. The Collins Line went bankrupt by the time of the Civil War after consuming millions of federal dollars. Until the 1920s transatlantic service remained in the hands of the British, French, and Germans.

While American shipowners were unable to compete with their European counterparts in transatlantic service, they faced no obstacles in the development of a domestic merchant marine. In 1817 Congress aided American shipowners engaged in domestic trade by prohibiting foreign ships from carrying cargo between domestic ports. While coastal shipping continued to rely heavily on sail power until the late 1800s, Fulton's invention provided the means to expand commerce on the major rivers of the American Midwest.

Cornelius Vanderbilt

The most successful of the early coastal shipowners was Cornelius Vanderbilt (1794-1877). Born on Staten Island, Vanderbilt left school at the age of eleven to work for his father. Within five years he was operating a sail-powered ferry service between Staten Island and New York City. By 1815 he had acquired a fleet of schooners that served ports on the Atlantic Coast from Boston to Charleston, South Carolina. At the age of twenty-four Vanderbilt sold his sailing fleet to become captain of a steam ferry operated by Thomas Gibbons (the same Gibbons involved in the Gibbons v. Ogden Supreme Court case). Vanderbilt soon became manager of Gibbons' fleet, and in 1829 started his own fleet of steamships serving coastal ports.

By 1844 Vanderbilt had become a millionaire and been awarded the honorary title of "Commodore" by his peers. When gold was discovered in California in 1848, Vanderbilt initiated steamship service to Nicaragua and built roads across the Isthmus of Panama to connect with shipping lines on the Pacific Coast. By 1853 his wealth had grown to exceed $10 million. A year later he entered the transatlantic competition against Cunard, suffering one of his few setbacks. Vanderbilt then turned to establishing a railroad empire.

Riverboats

The first steamboat to navigate the Mississippi River was the *New Orleans*, which

Landing and waterfront on a Western river. Collection of the author.

The Robert E. Lee *on the Mississippi River. Photo courtesy of the Smithsonian Institution, Washington, D.C.*

was based on a Robert Fulton design and launched in Pittsburgh in 1811. The 300-ton, 2-masted side-wheeler sailed down the Ohio and Mississippi rivers to New Orleans where it took on its first cargo and headed back upstream. While the *New Orleans* continued in service for a number of years, it was soon found that the Fulton design, which was intended for deep-current river and ocean travel, required too much draft for the relatively broad and shallow rivers of the Midwest. Riverboat designers moved the machinery from below decks to the main deck, flattened the hull, and repositioned the paddle wheels to the stern to improve maneuverability. By 1820 the modern sternwheeler could be seen regularly on the Mississippi as well as its tributaries, the Missouri and Ohio rivers.

By 1834 there were 230 steamboats plying the Mississippi and its tributaries. Twelve years later 1,190 steamboats were engaged in river travel. This steamboat fleet equaled that of the entire British merchant marine at the time. It carried ten million tons of freight in 1846—double the amount of all U.S. foreign trade in that year. At one time 40 tributaries to the Mississippi River were being regularly navigated by sternwheelers.

While the Mississippi and Ohio rivers were the most heavily traveled, the Missouri River provided critical access to the developing West. Shallow-bottom riverboats carrying up to 400 tons of freight and passengers traveled up the meandering Missouri River for considerable distance. During spring runoffs, they were able to reach Fort Benton, Montana. The river was full of snags (submerged trees) and shallow sand bars that continually needed removal. More than 400 steamboats sank on the Missouri River during the 1800s due to collisions with underwater obstructions. Old-timers described the Missouri River as being "one inch deep and a mile wide" and claimed that boats plying the river had to have sufficiently shallow draft to be able to "sail on the mist."

The race for speed soon became an almost overriding objective among riverboat captains. In 1815 the upstream voyage from New Orleans to Louisville, Kentucky, usually took 25 days. By the early 1850s riverboats were making the journey in five days. A famous race from New Orleans to St. Louis, Missouri, took place in June, 1870, between the *Robert E. Lee* and the *Natchez*. The *Robert E. Lee* set an up-river record for the 1,250-mile trip that has never been beaten, 3 days and 18 hours, with an average speed of 14 knots. The *Natchez*, which made several additional stops along the way, arrived six hours later.

By the start of the Civil War, railroads had begun to kill off riverboat traffic. Rail lines

The Annie M. Ash, *a four-masted schooner, is shown loading iron ore at docks in Two Harbors, Minnesota, in 1884. The 200-foot schooner was built in 1883 and typified the larger sailing craft on the Great Lakes in the 1870s and '80s. She carried about 12,000 tons of cargo. Photo courtesy of the Canal Park Marine Museum, Duluth, Minnesota.*

already paralleled the Mississippi River from Minneapolis, Minnesota, to New Orleans. A railroad had reached St. Joseph on the Missouri River in western Missouri, and another bypassed the Ohio River from Pittsburgh, Pennsylvania, the head of navigation, to Memphis, Tennessee, on the Mississippi.

While the heyday of steamboats on American rivers declined in the 1860s, it continued on the Great Lakes. Railroads could not compete with the large ore and grain haulers for traffic from the western regions of Lake Superior to Lake Erie, even though the lakes were navigable for only four months each year. Passenger ships brought immigrants to Milwaukee, Wisconsin, Chicago, and other major cities on the western rim of the Great Lakes from ports on Lake Erie. Even today, huge ore carriers carry more tonnage through the Soo Locks connecting Lake Superior and Lake Huron than is carried through any similar waterway in the world.

Pacific Trade

Cut off from trade with British possessions in the Caribbean following the Revolution-

ary War, New England merchants sought out the China trade. The first Far Eastern venture was undertaken in 1785 by the *Empress of China*, which was based in New York. It proved so successful that merchants in other ports along the Atlantic Coast from Philadelphia to Maine entered the Far East trade. Most of these early voyages followed an eastern route around the Cape of Good Hope, across the Indian Ocean, and through the Dutch East Indies. Eastbound cargoes were mainly silver dollars and American-grown ginseng, which the Chinese believed had recuperative powers. The ships brought back tea, chinaware, silks, and a durable textile called nankeen.

In 1787 Captains John Kendricks in the *Columbia* and Robert Gray in the *Lady Washington* sailed from Boston around Cape Horn to the Pacific Northwest and Alaska, thereby bringing the importance of that region to the attention of the nation. They took clothing, hardware, and trinkets, which they exchanged with the Indians for otter furs. These they took to Canton, the only Chinese port open to foreigners, where they exchanged the pelts for tea and other goods. Other American merchants soon followed their lead. When the supply of Alaskan otters became exhausted, merchants directed their ships to hunt seals off the coast of Chile and around the islands of the South Pacific. They also brought back sandalwood from South Pacific islands and the Hawaiian Islands.

The China trade involved long and arduous voyages lasting several years. The trade was usually quite profitable, however, and existed for more than 50 years. With the exception of that with Japan, trade with China and other Asian countries continued to grow. By the 1850s American interests in the region were so well established that in 1853, and again in 1854, the American government sent Commodore Matthew Calbraigh Perry on his successful mission to open trade negotiations with Japan. His specific instructions were to open Japan to

American trade, to arrange for protection of American sailors shipwrecked in Japanese waters, and to obtain water, fuel, and provisions for American whaling and trading ships on their extended voyages.

Whaling

Until the discovery of petroleum and the invention of electricity in the late 1800s, the whale was the major source of oil for lighting and lubrication, fats (spermaceti) for making candles, and bony stiffening material (baleen) for clothing. Nations throughout the world had been hunting whales as far back as history can record. American involvement, however, commenced in the 1700s and underwent rapid growth prior to the Revolutionary War. While interrupted by the war, the American whaling fleet continued to expand well into the 1800s. The profession of whaling was so absorbing that many American whalers transferred to British whaling ships during the war in order to remain in the trade.

American whalers first started hunting for whales off Newfoundland and southwestern Greenland. By 1770 they had ventured south of the equator. While the first whaler to round Cape Horn (in 1799) was of British registry, it was manned by American sailors, and an American gunner's mate is reported to have killed the first whale in the Pacific. American whaling ships soon followed, and whaling in the Pacific Ocean became an American monopoly for almost a century. An American ship, lost in the fog, drifted through the Bering Strait in 1846 and discovered the rich whaling grounds of the Arctic seas. By that year, there were 700 American whalers operating in the Pacific whaling grounds.

During the height of whaling, New Bedford, Massachusetts, became the most important whaling port in the world. Other major New England whaling ports included Nantucket and Edgartown (Martha's Vineyard), Massachusetts; New London, Connecticut; and Sag Harbor (Long Island), New York. By the mid-1800s, many New England shipowners were basing their ships in Hawaii and San Francisco,

thereby reducing the length of voyages from four or five years down to less than one year. Unfortunately, using San Francisco as a home port caused the whaling shipowners to lose many crewmen and ships when gold was discovered in California in 1848. San Francisco went on, however, to become a major whaling port. Local investors began constructing their own whaling ships and in the 1890s built rendering plants along San Francisco Bay.

Steamships were introduced into the whaling trade around 1880. By then, however, the industry was dying. Petroleum, which had been discovered in Titusville, Pennsylvania, in 1859, had taken over much of the market served by whale oil. The industry kept going until the 1920s, when the last American whaling ship put to sea. The schooner *John R. Manta* sailed out of New Bedford in 1925, providing this epitaph to the saga of the American whaling fleet.

U.S. Coast Guard

Soon after the creation of the new nation, Congress realized it needed a means of collecting duties from foreign ships. In 1790 it created the Revenue Marine, which later became the Revenue Cutter Service. The function of this service was to enforce quarantine laws, to protect the coast from pirates and privateers, and to extract customs and tariffs from maritime commerce and smugglers. In 1915 Congress changed the name of the Revenue Cutter Service to the Coast Guard and transferred the U.S. Life-Saving Service to it. The Lighthouse Service was transferred to the Coast Guard in 1939; the Department of Commerce's Bureau of Marine Inspection and Navigation, in 1942.

The Coast Guard reported to the Treasury Department until 1967, when it was transferred to the newly created Department of Transportation. In times of war or other national emergencies, the Coast Guard becomes part of the U.S. Navy. The present mission of the Coast Guard is promoting marine safety, enforcing maritime law, rendering assistance to vessels in distress, saving life and property, and maintaining

Nineteenth and twentieth century U.S. Coast Guard ships. Photo courtesy of the Smithsonian Institution, Washington, D.C.

extensive merchant marine safety programs. Specific duties of the Coast Guard include ice patrol in the North Atlantic and the Bering Sea, ice-breaking services on the Great Lakes, removal of obstructions to navigation such as oil spills and derelicts, and providing medical aid to deep-sea fishermen and Alaskan natives.

The Coast Guard currently operates close to 200 ships and more than 100 fixed and rotary wing aircraft. It has a total complement of approximately 30,000 men and women.

Seaports

While America's maritime might was created by aggressive and talented seamen, merchants, and naval leaders who were willing to take risks, little would have come of their efforts if the nation had not been blessed with ample harbors. Protected harbors of sufficient size to accommodate large numbers of ships and extensive port facilities exist on all three of the nation's coastlines. Each port developed a character of its own, depending on the cargoes flowing through it. The New England ports, for example, developed into fish-handling ports as early colonists turned to the sea for their livelihood, while southern ports focused on cotton and tobacco.

Salem, Massachusetts

Salem, Massachusetts, was one of the first seaports in America to develop a shipbuilding industry, which started within two decades of the founding of the town in 1626. During the Revolutionary War many traders and sea captains in Salem made fortunes off privateering. Following the war they became traders and continued to accrue wealth from ships sailed by others.

Newport, Rhode Island

Newport, which lies at the mouth of Narragansett Bay, was founded in 1639 and quickly became a major shipbuilding center. As a port it rivaled New York and Boston until the Revolutionary War. Newport has an exceptional naval heritage. During the early 1900s Narragansett Bay served as the principal anchorage for the U.S. Navy's Atlantic Fleet. Two brothers, Oliver Hazard Perry and Matthew Calbraigh Perry were natives of Newport. Oliver Hazard Perry is noted for his defeat of the British fleet on Lake Erie, while his brother is mainly known for his successful trade negotiations with the Japanese.

Mystic Seaport, Connecticut

Mystic, Connecticut, is a New England seaport that owes its origin to shipbuilding. Although a latecomer to the industry—its first ship was launched in 1784—Mystic's small harbor supported five shipyards by the 1840s. During its shipbuilding era, which lasted until World War I, the Mystic shipyards built more than 500 ships. Among them was the clipper ship *Andrew Jackson*, which shares the record with the more-famous *Flying Cloud* for the fastest time between New York and San Francisco.

New York Harbor

New York Harbor has provided a gateway to the nation for trade and European immigrants since it was first settled by the Dutch in 1625. Its importance became established with the construction of the Erie Canal, which, combined with the Hudson River, provided access to the Old Northwest Territory and the Great Lakes. Out of its role as a trading center, New York City became the most important cultural and financial center of the nation.

Industry began to cluster around this busy port, and it quickly became the shipping point for America's growing export of manufactured products. It also served as the point of embarkation for the thousands who joined the Gold Rush to California.

The focal point for all this activity in the 1800s was the East River at the lower end of Manhattan. A complex beehive of supporting activities built up around the docks at the foot of Fulton Street, where Robert Fulton operated a ferry to Brooklyn. As ships became larger, particularly as steam-driven ships took over ocean transport, the deeper-draft docks along the Hudson River began to expand. Docks also sprang up on Staten Island and the New Jersey shore of the Hudson River. The Port of New York took shape by the turn of the century to manage this complex of waterways and facilities. The maritime importance of the section of New York surrounding South Street, Front Street, and Fulton Street has faded, but its role in the maritime heritage of the nation has remained.

BROOKLYN BRIDGE by George Schreiber, oil, 31 ½ x 44 inches, courtesy of Michael Rosenfeld Gallery, New York, New York.

Oyster fleet in Baltimore Harbor, circa 1890. Photo courtesy of the Smithsonian Institution, Washington, D.C.

Baltimore, Maryland

Founded in 1729 at the mouth of the Patapsco River, a tributary to Chesapeake Bay, Baltimore quickly became a major seaport for the export of tobacco and grain, followed later by coal and iron. With the availability of water power, the port also became a center for flour milling and shipbuilding. The Baltimore clippers built at the city's shipyards proved instrumental in helping to win the War of 1812.

Opening of the Chesapeake and Delaware Canal in 1829 gave Baltimore almost direct access to the sea and to ports on the Delaware River. In the 1870s and 1880s Baltimore's role as an international port grew when it became a major terminus for midwestern and eastern railroads bringing coal and grain, as well as manufactured goods, for export.

Philadelphia on the Delaware River

Philadelphia, although 100 miles inland from the sea, also became a major port in the early days of the nation. Founded in 1682 by William Penn, the city quickly became the largest English-speaking city after London, in part because of its excellent harbor facilities. Throughout the next 250 years Philadelphia continued to contribute to the maritime development of the country and was a major shipbuilding center through World War II.

Chesapeake Bay and James River

One of the finest deep harbors in the world lies at the mouth of the James River where it joins Chesapeake Bay as it flows into the Atlantic. Chesapeake Bay and its contributing rivers—the Susquehanna, Potomac, Patapsco, Severn, Patuxent, Rappahannock, York, and James—have played a significant role in the development of the nation.

It was on the James River that the first permanent English settlement was founded at Jamestown in 1607, and it was near the mouth of the James that the final battle of the Revolutionary War was fought at Yorktown. The *Merrimack* and the *Monitor* fought their famous battle during the Civil War in Hampton Roads, as the mouth of the James is called. Today, Hampton Roads is the site of the nation's major naval complex.

The Mississippi Queen *is considered the grandest river steamboat ever built. It is still used for luxury cruises. Photo courtesy of the Smithsonian Institution, Washington, D.C.*

Savannah, Georgia

Savannah, Georgia, was founded in 1733 as the first settlement in the Georgia Colony, which was the thirteenth and last English colony established in America. It quickly became a major port city for the export of tobacco and cotton to England. The first ship equipped with steam-driven paddle wheels to cross the Atlantic sailed from Savannah in 1819. During the Revolution the British used the city and its port as headquarters for their southern campaign. Union forces blockaded the port during the Civil War. Cotton continued to make Savannah a major port until the end of the 1800s.

New Orleans, Louisiana

The city of New Orleans was founded on the Mississippi River in 1718 by French colonists and quickly became the French capital of the Louisiana region. Even though located 100 miles upriver from the mouth of the Mississippi, New Orleans developed rapidly into the most important seaport on the river and served as the foreign trade gateway for the American heartland. By the late 1700s, agricultural products of the Midwest were being transshipped

from riverboats and barges to ocean-going vessels destined for the East Coast, Europe, and South America.

The Port of New Orleans is located along the New Orleans riverfront on the Mississippi River and on the nearby Industrial Canal built to connect the river to Lake Pontchartrain. Today, the Port of New Orleans handles more imported iron and steel than any other port in the country. It has become an important transshipping point for Japanese imports of steel and automotive parts destined for American assembly plants. More than 60 percent of the exports through the port consist of agricultural products, with grain being the predominant crop.

Galveston, Texas

The history of the Port of Galveston is one of the most dramatic of all American seaports. Galveston Island was originally settled in 1817 as a fiefdom of Jean Lafitte, the celebrated pirate who operated in the Gulf of Mexico. Lafitte was ousted in 1821, and in 1825 the Mexican congress designated Galveston as the official port and customs entry point for the region. When the Republic of Texas was created in 1836, Galveston became the new republic's center of commerce and culture, and its major port. It remained in this role through the Civil War and into the 1880s.

Following the Civil War the Port of Galveston grew rapidly. Regular steamship service was initiated between Galveston and all major East Coast and Gulf cities. As late as the 1870s, 95 percent of all merchandise moving into and out of Texas came through the Port of Galveston. By the end of the 1800s, Galveston was the largest cotton-shipping port in the world.

The hurricane that hit Galveston in 1900, one of the country's worst disasters, demolished the city as a major port. By the time Galveston recovered during World War I, the Port of Houston had become competitive and had captured the state's emerging oil and chemical trade. Galveston continues, however, to be a major shipping point for Texas wheat and cotton.

Houston, Texas

When Houston was established in 1836, its connection to the Gulf of Mexico, 50 miles away, was a meandering backwater at the upper end of Galveston Bay called Buffalo Bayou. Ships of even modest size could not turn around upon reaching Houston and were forced to back six miles down the 15-mile bayou to Constitution Bend (named after the first steamboat to reach Houston) before finding room to turn.

In spite of the inadequacies of the waterway, within a few years regular steamboat service was in operation between Houston and Galveston. Due to sandbars and other obstacles only ships with shallow drafts could maneuver the waterway, and it soon became clogged with unlucky derelicts. It was not until after the Civil War that major improvements were made to the waterway.

By the 1880s, Houston had become a major railhead for cotton from the interior. At Houston the cotton was compressed into bales and loaded on barges destined for Galveston, where they were loaded on seagoing ships. Public pressure developed to deepen the channel so that

ocean-going vessels could reach Houston, thereby avoiding the wharfage and transfer charges at Galveston. Finally, in 1914, dredging of a Houston Ship Channel to a depth of 25 feet was completed from the mouth of Galveston Bay to the turning basin at Constitution Bend, and the first ocean-going vessel, *Satilla* out of New York, tied up at the Houston wharf.

Just prior to World War I, the Texas oil industry began to boom, and by the end of the war, Houston had become a major shipping point for petroleum products. The petrochemical industry emerged in the 1920s, causing further expansion of the Port of Houston.

San Diego, California

San Diego was discovered in 1542 by a Spanish military explorer, Juan Rodríguez Cabrillo, who immediately claimed all of what is now California for the Spanish Crown. A permanent settlement was not established at San Diego until 1769, when a fort was built by Gaspar de Portolá, Spanish governor of Baja (Lower) California.

Following California's acquisition by the United States in 1848, San Diego grew slowly relative to Los Angeles, which became Southern California's center of commerce. The city of San Diego and its port facilities grew rapidly in the early 1940s, when the U.S. Navy established San Diego as its major base on the West Coast. Today, naval activities, an active tuna fleet, and pleasure boating comprise the major maritime activities of the harbor.

Los Angeles Harbor

When first visited by Spanish explorer Cabrillo in 1542, what is now the busiest seaport in the United States was merely a series of sandbars and tidal flats. Protected from ocean storms by the Palos Verdes Peninsula, which juts into the Pacific Ocean to the west, the location subsequently proved to offer the best harbor site on the California coast between San Diego and San Francisco.

Following Cabrillo's visit little happened to disturb the natural environment of the harbor until the second half of the 1700s. By then the Spanish Jesuits had established the missions of San Gabriel Arcángel (1771) and San Juan Capistrano (1776), 25 miles inland and 40 miles down the coast, respectively, from San Pedro. The secular village of *El Pueblo de Nuestra Senõra la Reina de Los Angeles de Porciuncula* (the Village of our Lady the Queen of Angels of Porciuncula, as Los Angeles was first christened) was founded in 1781 a few miles from the San Gabriel mission. As the population of the region grew, the Spanish found it increasingly difficult to prevent foreign ships from landing at the remote harbor of San Pedro. Consequently, an active smuggling trade in cattle hides developed.

Sailing schooners in a Western harbor, circa 1880. Sketch collection of the author.

When Mexico took control of California in 1822, trade restrictions were eliminated, and legitimate traffic through the harbor expanded rapidly—mostly in hides for shipment around Cape Horn to the New England shoe industry. Since there was no currency in the region and the hide trade was so vigorous, the hides became known as "California bank notes."

While trade through the harbor increased, harbor facilities were not improved. Loading and unloading cargo was sufficiently arduous that Richard Dana felt compelled to describe these tasks in his famous novel, *Two Years Before the Mast.* Finally, in 1848 a wharf was constructed at San Pedro, a warehouse was built, and both passenger-stage and freight-wagon service to Los Angeles was instituted.

Competition developed among transport companies. Unable to develop suitable wharf facilities at San Pedro, Phineas Banning relocated five miles further inland on the estuary and founded a new town that he named Wilmington after his birthplace in Delaware. Being closer to Los Angeles, Wilmington dominated harbor traffic until after the Civil War. In 1869 Banning built the first railroad in Southern California to connect his wharf to the city of Los Angeles.

The rate of improvements to the harbor became increasingly rapid after the Civil War. In the early 1870s federal funds were provided to deepen the channel and build the first breakwater. Dock facilities expanded as the city of Los Angeles grew and lumber became a major import. In 1906 the city of Los Angeles annexed a strip of land one mile wide and 16 miles long that extended from Los Angeles to the city limits of San Pedro and Wilmington. Los Angeles then offered a very favorable merger proposal to the cities of San Pedro and Wilmington, which, after much anguish and debate, the two cities accepted. The consolidation took place in 1909 with a formal ceremony attended by President William Howard Taft.

The combined ports of Los Angeles and adjacent Long Beach now handle more than twice as much trade, in terms of dollar value, as either of their nearest competitors, New York/New Jersey and Seattle/Tacoma.

Early San Francisco wharves, circa 1880. Sketch collection of the author.

San Francisco Bay

One of the outstanding harbors of North America, San Francisco Bay, lay undiscovered until a land-based expedition led by Gaspar de Portolá happened upon it in 1769. Juan Rodríguez Cabrillo in 1542, Sir Francis Drake in 1579, and a number of other English, Spanish, and Portuguese explorers of the sixteenth, seventeenth, and eighteenth centuries had sailed by the Golden Gate without knowing of the marvelous harbor that lay behind it. In 1776 the Spanish established an outpost in the bay at what was then referred to as Yerba Buena. The presidio and mission remained neglected and isolated until 1835, when New England whalers and hide traders began to use the bay as a base for their Pacific operations.

An unofficial expedition of U.S. Marines commanded by John Charles Frémont secured San Francisco Bay for American rule in 1846. The city's name was changed from Yerba Buena to San Francisco the following year. The discovery of gold near Sacramento in January 1848 transformed San Francisco into one of the world's most active ports and famous cities. Since then, San Francisco has remained as one of

America's leading naval ports and trading gateways in the Pacific Basin.

Portland, Oregon

Portland, located 105 miles from the ocean at the confluence of the Willamette and Columbia rivers, was first established by the Chinook Indians as a stopover point on their travels through the region. The Indian campsite subsequently became a convenient base for early white explorers. A town was established in 1844 by two New Englanders, Amos Lovejoy and Francis Pettygrove.

Portland soon became a trading center and a transshipment point from riverboats to ocean-going vessels when the California Gold Rush opened a market for Oregon timber and agricultural products. Once established, Portland became a major shipping point for inland products to overseas markets such as Hawaii, China, Australia, and Europe. Together with Tacoma and Seattle, Portland provided the shortest connection from the West Coast to Far Eastern ports.

As seagoing ships became larger and required deeper drafts, Portland was in danger of being cut off from ocean shipping due to the shallow depth of the Columbia River at low water. Consequently, in 1891 the Oregon legislature created a Port of Portland Commission and authorized it to dredge and maintain a 25-foot-deep ship channel from Portland to the Pacific Ocean. The Port of Portland continues to maintain the ship channel, in cooperation with the U.S. Army Corps of Engineers, and the depth has been increased to 40 feet. Upriver from Portland, the Columbia and Snake rivers have been developed into a major inland waterway reaching all the way to Lewiston, Idaho—a distance of 465 miles from the Pacific Ocean.

Today, the Port of Portland, along with a number of nearby ports on both the Washington and Oregon sides of the Columbia River, provides the largest shipping point on the West Coast for grain to the Far East. Because of its connection to three transcontinental railroads, Portland has become a major automobile receiving point from Japanese and Korean automakers and is one of the nation's largest container ports.

Ports of Puget Sound

Covering 650 square miles and indented with numerous bays and inlets, Puget Sound is one of the largest harbors in the world. It was first explored in detail by Captain George Vancouver of the British Royal Navy in 1792 during a period when British and American interests were vying for control of the region.

Even before Vancouver's arrival, British merchantmen, working from a harbor on Vancouver Island, had developed an active trade with China of otter and beaver furs, as well as sailing ship spars and masts. By the 1830s the English Hudson's Bay Company had a trading post in Puget Sound from which they operated the first steamship in the Pacific Ocean, the *Beaver.*

Puget Sound became part of the United States with the settlement of English and American interests in the region in 1846. This settlement occurred just in time for the region to capitalize on California's expanding need for lumber following the discovery of gold in 1848. During the 1850s a number of sawmills were built on the bays and inlets around Puget Sound. One such mill was established in 1852 by a Swedish immigrant named Nicholas DeLin on Commencement Bay, toward the southern end of the sound. Commencement Bay proved to be an excellent harbor for ocean-going ships, and the mill provided the basis of a growing settlement that subsequently grew into the city of Tacoma.

A settlement in Elliott Bay, which became the city of Seattle, started at about the same time, although its first wharf was not built

View of the Seattle harbor from a sailing ship, circa 1870. Engraving collection of the author.

until the late 1850s. Being closer to the open sea than Tacoma, Elliott Bay became a popular transshipment point. Here the fleet of modest steamships that served the hundreds of small settlements on Puget Sound (termed the "Mosquito Fleet") transferred their cargo to the deepwater ships destined for California, Hawaii, and the Far East. The principal cargoes included fish, timber, and newly discovered coal. With the introduction of coal-fired steamships, Seattle became the major coaling port on the West Coast.

Puget Sound ports benefited, relative to Portland, when the Northern Pacific built a railroad line from eastern Washington direct to Tacoma and Seattle in 1884. By 1895 Puget Sound was being served by four transcontinental railroads. Two years later, gold was discovered in Alaska, and Seattle quickly became one of the busiest West Coast ports. The opening of the Panama Canal in 1914 increased trade through both ports almost immediately, which soon brought governance of port facilities into public hands. Today the value of total imports and exports of the Puget Sound ports of Seattle and Tacoma equal those of New York/New Jersey, and are exceeded only by the ports of Los Angeles/Long Beach on the West Coast.

Maritime Museums

❖ *LOS ANGELES MARITIME MUSEUM, Foot of Sixth Street, Berth 84, San Pedro, California 90731. Tel: 310-548-7618. Open Tuesday to Sunday 10-5; closed major holidays. Admission free, donations of $1 suggested.*

Los Angeles opened its maritime museum in 1979. Housed in the Art Deco-style former San Pedro Municipal Ferry Terminal built in 1941, it is the largest maritime museum on the West Coast. The museum contains exhibits describing the history of San Pedro and the Port of Los Angeles through photographs and local maritime memorabilia.

The museum also features a collection of 700 ship models, believed to be one of the largest collections in the world. Visitors can listen to radio communications within the port concerning ship movements as well as view port activities from the upper deck of the old terminal building.

❖ *ALLEN KNIGHT MARITIME MUSEUM, 550 Calle Principal, Monterey, California 93942. Tel: 408-375-2553. Open Tuesday to Friday 1-4, Saturday and Sunday 2-4. Admission free.*

Founded in 1971, this small museum provides exhibits on the maritime history of the Spanish capital of California, based on the private collection of local maritime enthusiast, Allen Knight. Exhibits include ship models, photographs, and articles used by local mariners during the period when Monterey was an active fishing and whaling port. Included among the ship models in the museum is one of the first Spanish ships to explore the West Coast.

❖ *SAN DIEGO MARITIME MUSEUM, 1492 North Harbor Drive, San Diego, California 92101. Tel: 619-234-9153. Open daily 9-8. Admission $5, over-65 and student discounts.*

The San Diego Maritime Museum was founded in 1927 to save the three-masted bark, *Star of India*. The ship was restored and opened to the public in 1948. Since then, the museum has acquired two additional ships: the ferry boat, *Berkeley*, and the steam yacht, *Medea*. The museum exhibits are located on the three ships and deal with Pacific maritime history, the U.S. Navy's contribution to San Diego, and oceanography.

The *Star of India* was built in England in 1863 with the original name of *Euterpe*. The iron-hulled square-rigger initially carried travelers, immigrants, and cargo between England and India, New Zealand, and Australia. In her 60 years of service, she made 21 trips around the world. Alaska Packers bought *Euterpe* in 1901 and made her part of its fleet of salmon-fishing mother ships, changing her name to *Star of India* in 1906. She was retired from service in 1923 and lay dormant in San Diego until her restoration in the 1950s.

The 289-foot, 1,945-ton ferryboat *Berkeley*, built in 1896, was the first successful propeller-driven, double-ended ferryboat built on the Pacific Coast. Operated by the Southern Pacific Railroad on San Francisco Bay, she remained in service until 1958. After sitting idle for 15 years, the *Berkeley* was acquired by the San Diego Museum in 1973. Most of the museum's exhibits, its ship-model shop, and research library are located on the *Berkeley*.

Built in the early 1900s and recently restored, the *Medea* is one of the few large steam yachts still in operation.

The Balclutha. *Photo courtesy of the San Francisco Maritime National Historic Park, San Francisco, California, I. F. Dunn collection.*

❖ *SAN FRANCISCO MARITIME NATIONAL HISTORICAL PARK, Fort Mason, San Francisco, California 94109. Tel: 415-556-6435 and 556-3002. Museum open Wednesday to Sunday 10-5. Hyde Street Pier open daily 10-7, mid-June to mid-September; 10-5, rest of year. Admission to museum free. Hyde Street Pier $2, students and over-65 free.*

Headquartered at Fort Mason, the Maritime National Historical Park comprises three facilities: a museum on Beach Street at the foot of Polk Street, six nineteenth- and early twentieth-century ships docked at Hyde Street Pier, and the J. Porter Shaw Library at Fort Mason.

The museum provides an excellent review of West Coast maritime history, beginning around 1840. There are displays describing maritime activities during the California Gold Rush, experiences in rounding Cape Horn on the clipper ships bound for California, the whaling era, coastal shipping, and the San Francisco fishing fleet. The museum contains several ship models, including steamships built in the twentieth century.

The ships docked at Hyde Street Pier include the three-masted, squared-rigged *Balclutha*, built in 1886; a three-masted sailing schooner, the *C.A. Thayer*; an 1890 side-wheel ferryboat which served on San Francisco Bay for many years, the *Eureka*; a seagoing tug built in New Jersey in 1907 named the *Hercules*; an English-built, side-wheeled tug named *Eppleton Hall*; and a sailing scow schooner, the *Alma*, used on San Francisco Bay to haul lumber and other bulk commodities. The *Eureka* was once the largest passenger ferry in the world.

In addition to the ships at Hyde Street Pier, the WW II liberty ship *Jeremiah O'Brien* is docked at Pier Three in Fort Mason; and the 1915 steam schooner *Wapama* is across the Golden Gate at the Bay Model Visitor Center in Sausalito (*Wapama* tours by special appointment). The piers at Fort Mason were the embarkation point for hundreds of thousands of American troops sent to the Pacific theater during World War II.

❖ *MYSTIC SEAPORT MUSEUM, 50 Greenmanville Avenue, Mystic, Connecticut 06355-0990. Tel: 203-572-0711. Open daily 9-5, early April to late October; 10-4 rest of year; closed Christmas. Admission $14, student discount.*

Mystic Seaport Museum was established in 1929 to preserve the heritage of American shipbuilding and of American maritime heritage generally. This reconstructed shipbuilding town containing 30 buildings is located on a 17-acre site on the Mystic River. Included in this living museum are historic homes, shops, and a shipyard. The ground floor of the Stillman Building contains exhibits on the maritime history of New England. The second floor displays collections of ship models, scrimshaw, and other mariners' handiwork. Sixty separate exhibits are located throughout the museum complex.

The museum also has more than 400 watercraft, representing all types of vessels used on the New England coast. A number of ships built in the 1800s have been brought to Mystic, refurbished in the shipyard, and are open to the public. These include the last surviving wooden whaling ship, the *Charles W. Morgan* ; a fishing schooner, the *L.A. Dunton* ; and the three-masted, iron-hulled training ship, the *Joseph Conrad. Charles W. Morgan* is a 113-foot bark built in 1841 that engaged in the whaling trade for more than 80 years, longer than any whaling ship on record.

The viewing gallery at the DuPont Preservation Shipyard at Mystic Seaport provides visitors an opportunity to observe preservation work in progress.

❖ *U.S. COAST GUARD MUSEUM, U.S. Coast Guard Academy, 15 Mohegan Avenue, New London, Connecticut 06320-4195. Tel: 203-444-8270. Open daily 9-5, May though October; Monday to Friday 8-4, rest of year. Admission free.*

The Coast Guard Museum in Waesche Hall includes exhibits on the predecessor services to the Coast Guard: the Revenue Cutter Service, the Lighthouse Service, and the Life-Saving Service. The visitor's pavilion provides a multi-media presentation on life at the academy.

The three-masted training bark, *Eagle*, is open to visitors on weekends from noon to 5 when it is in port. The ship was built in 1936 in Hamburg, Germany, as a training ship for German naval cadets and given the name *Horst Wessel.* It was claimed by the United States as a war prize at the end of World War II and commissioned into the Coast Guard in 1946 with the name *Eagle.*

❖ *THE SHIPS OF SEA MARITIME MUSEUM, 503 East River Street and 504 East Bay Street, Savannah, Georgia 31401. Tel: 912-232-1511. Open daily 10-5; closed major holidays. Admission $3, under-13 and student group discounts.*

Founded in 1966, the Ships of Sea Maritime Museum commemorates Savannah's heritage as a major seaport during the early development of the tidewater region of the South. The museum is located on the riverfront plaza in a restored, four-story warehouse, which originally stored cotton, lumber, and resin waiting to be loaded aboard ships. The museum contains ship models, scrimshaw, figureheads, and an extensive exhibit of ships in bottles. There is also an exhibit titled, "Savannah in the Great Age of Sail."

The collection of 65 ship models ranges in time from Viking ships to modern nuclear-powered vessels, and in size from a few inches to eight feet. In addition to the *NS Savannah*, there are models of three other ships named after the city; the oldest, the 350-ton, 110-foot *USS Savannah*, became the first ship to cross the Atlantic equipped with steam-driven paddle wheels, in 1819. The next oldest, the 44-gun U.S. frigate *Savannah*, was launched in 1842 and was the flagship of the Pacific fleet at the time California joined the nation. The newest and largest ship honoring Savannah is the 10,000-ton cruiser, *USS Savannah*, which was launched in 1937 and decommissioned in 1959.

Other interesting ship models include John Paul Jones' flagship, the *Bon Homme Richard*, and the famous clipper ship, *Flying Cloud*. The nine-foot model of *Flying Cloud* in full sail shows why this ship designed by America's most famous shipbuilder, Donald McKay of Boston, set a number of speed records.

❖ *HAWAII MARITIME CENTER, Pier 7, Honolulu, Oahu, Hawaii 96804. Tel: 808-523-6151. Open daily 9-8, except Christmas. Admission $6, student discount.*

The Hawaii Maritime Museum is located in the 27,000-square foot Kalakaua Boat House on the Honolulu waterfront. It offers 35 exhibits on the history of the port of Honolulu, and the maritime history of Hawaii, starting with its discovery by Polynesian voyagers. The displays cover early trade, Hawaii's involvement in the whaling industry, commercial fishing, and Hawaiian culture as related to the sea.

Moored to the pier as part of the Hawaii Maritime Center is the square-rigged, four-masted sailing ship, *Falls of Clyde*. Built in Glasgow, Scotland, in 1878, the wrought-iron-hulled cargo ship is 266 feet long and fully loaded had a displacement of 1,807 tons. She was purchased by Captain William Matson in 1898, prior to his forming the Matson Navigation Company, making it one of the firm's first ships. Rigged as a bark, *Falls of Clyde* made more than 60 voyages to the mainland in the sugar trade before being sold to an oil company in 1907 and converted into a tanker. The ship was acquired by the Bernice P. Bishop Museum in Honolulu in 1968 and restored to her original rigging. She became a National Historic Landmark in 1973.

❖ *FRED W. WOODWARD RIVERBOAT MUSEUM, Second Street and Ice Harbor, Dubuque, Iowa 52001. Tel: 319-557-9545. Open daily 10-6:30, May through October; Tuesday to Sunday 10-4, rest of year. Admission $4, student, family, and winter discounts.*

The Woodward Riverboat Museum displays 300 years of Mississippi River history, including riverboating and fur trading. Adjacent to the museum is the river dredge *William M.* *Black*. Built in 1934, it is one of the last of the side-wheel, steam-powered riverboats and was used mainly to remove sand and gravel from Mississippi River channels.

❖ *KEOKUK RIVER MUSEUM, Foot of Johnson Street, Victory Park, Keokuk, Iowa 52632. Tel: 319-524-4765. Open daily 9-5, April through October 9-5. Admission $1.50, grade-school student discount.*

The museum is located on the *George M. Verity*, a 160-foot steam-powered, sternwheeled barge tug. Built after World War I and retired in 1960, she is one of only a few river towboats of her type. The ship is in good condition and can be toured throughout.

Nearby is the Keokuk Lock and Dam, one of the major shipping locks on the Mississippi River.

❖ *MAINE MARITIME MUSEUM, 243 Washington Street, Bath, Maine 04530. Tel: 207-443-1316. Open daily 9:30-5. Admission $5, under-16, senior, and family discounts.*

Created in 1963, the Maine Maritime Museum encompasses two historic shipyards on the Kennebec River. Its indoor museum focuses on Maine's maritime history, ranging from local shipbuilding and fishing to deep-sea trading vessels. It contains 250 ship models, 200 marine paintings, and assorted scrimshaw and navigation instruments. Also included are displays on life at sea during the sailing-ship era.

The shipyards cover a 10-acre site on which are several shops used in the construction of wooden sailing ships, including a mill and joiner shop, a paint and treenail shop, a pitch oven, a caulking shed, and a mold loft. An apprentice shop is used to demonstrate and teach the techniques of building wooden ships. A separate building contains exhibits on Maine fishing and lobstering. The *Sherman Zwicker*, a 142-foot, two-masted, Grand Banks fishing schooner built just prior to World War II, is anchored at the museum's dock.

Bath has been a major shipbuilding center since the 1600s. The first sea-going vessel built in America, called the *Virginia*, was built at Bath by English fishermen around 1607. It is reported to have been a small (30-ton, 50-foot) single-masted sailing ship called a pinnace, and was used for fishing and fur trading along the coast during summer months. Not wishing to brave the harsh winters in America, the fishermen sailed the *Virginia* across the Atlantic to England and returned in it the following spring.

❖ *PENOBSCOT MARINE MUSEUM, Church Street, Searsport, Maine 04974. Tel: 207-548-2529. Open Monday to Saturday 9:30-5 and Sunday 1-5, mid-May through mid-October. Admission $4, senior and student discounts.*

Located on Penobscot Bay, the Penobscot Marine Museum was founded in 1936 to collect and preserve materials associated with Maine's maritime history. The museum consists of seven historic buildings containing 50 ship models and 450 paintings, plus a number of documents, gathered from the homes of local sea captains. A diorama recreates the Searsport harbor and shipyard as it looked in the nineteenth century. There is also a special exhibit on Penobscot Bay's contribution to Maine shipbuilding with particular focus on the square-rigged "down-easters."

❖ *RADCLIFFE MARITIME MUSEUM, Maryland Historical Society, 201 West Monument Street, Baltimore, Maryland 21201. Tel: 410-685-3750. Open Tuesday to Friday 10-4:30, Saturday 9-4:30, year-round; Sunday 1-5, October through April. Admission $2.50, over-65 and under-13 discounts.*

The Radcliffe Maritime Museum, housed in the Maryland Historical Society headquarters building, provides displays on the maritime history of Maryland with particular focus on the upper Chesapeake Bay.

The museum includes models of the *Ark* and the *Dove,* two small ships that brought the original colonists recruited by Cecil Calvert, Lord Baltimore, to the shores of Maryland in 1633. Also on display are models and paintings of the famous Baltimore clipper, a schooner used by Baltimore privateers during the War of 1812; its smaller sister, the Baltimore pilot boat; coastal traders; various Chesapeake fishing boats; and early steamboats, such as the 1813 *Chesapeake.*

The museum displays a number of photographs depicting the development of the Port of Baltimore, plus re-creations of a boat shed, sail loft, ship chandlery, and other facilities associated with harbor activity.

❖ *CHESAPEAKE BAY MARITIME MUSEUM, Navy Point, St. Michaels, Maryland 21663. Tel: 301-745-2916. Open daily 10-5, May through October; 10-4, November, December, and mid-March through April; Saturday and Sundays 10-4, January through mid-March. Admission $5, senior and student discounts.*

The Chesapeake Bay Maritime Museum, which occupies 17 acres, was founded in 1965 to maintain an appreciation for the maritime heritage of the Chesapeake Bay. A boat-building shop lets visitors observe the traditional techniques used in the construction of small boats.

The four theme buildings containing 48,000 square feet of exhibit space focus on the history of Chesapeake Bay, the Hooper Strait Lighthouse, waterfowling (decoys, guns, and mounted birds), and a small-boat collection. The latter features 80 small craft, including a skipjack, crab dredger, and a bugeye. Exhibits include the gear used by fishermen on the Chesapeake Bay and the history of steam- and gas-powered watercraft on the bay.

Skipjack under full sail in the Chesapeake Bay. Photo courtesy of the Chesapeake Bay Maritime Museum, St. Michaels, Maryland.

❖ *CALVERT MARINE MUSEUM, State Route 2 at Solomon's Island Road, Solomons, Maryland 20688. Tel: 301-326-2042. Open daily 10-5, May through September; Monday to Friday 10-4:30, Saturday and Sunday noon-4:30, October through April; closed major holidays. Admission $3, senior, under-13, and family discounts.*

The Calvert Marine Museum was founded in 1970 to study the interaction between man and the marine environment in the Chesapeake Bay and the Patuxent River estuary. The complex includes an exhibit building, a small-craft building, and the restored Drum Point Lighthouse, built in 1893.

Several exhibits relate the maritime history of the region, focusing primarily on the crab, oyster, and fishing industry of the region, including boat building. Small craft on display include a clamboat, a draketail, several yawls, a skipjack, and an oyster "bayboat."

❖ *NEW BEDFORD WHALING MUSEUM, 18 Johnny Cake Hill, New Bedford, Massachusetts 02740. Tel: 508-997-0046. Open Monday to Saturday 9-5 and Sunday 1-5; closed major holidays. Admission $3.50, over-59 and under-15 discounts.*

Founded in 1903, the New Bedford Whaling Museum is one of the largest whaling museums in the world. It offers excellent displays of the nation's whaling heritage, particularly during the sailing ship era. A half-section of

a fully rigged whaling ship provides an opportunity to observe conditions and activities aboard a whaler. A film on whaling is presented twice each day during July and August.

❖ *MAYFLOWER II, State Pier, Plymouth, Massachusetts 02360. Tel: 508-746-1622. Open daily 9-6:30, July through August; 9-5, April, June, and September through November. Admission $5.50; under-13 discount. Combination ticket with Plimoth Village admission, $10.*

Mayflower II is an accurate reproduction of a typical ship of the period. The original *Mayflower* was sold for scrap shortly after returning to England in the early 1620s. The *Mayflower* was primarily a cargo ship, carrying wine,

grain, and other food items. Guides explain the activities of the crew and passengers during the arduous voyage to the New World. The ship is part of Plimoth Plantation, located three miles south of Plymouth.

❖ *PEABODY MUSEUM OF SALEM, 161 Essex Street, Salem, Massachusetts 01970. Tel: 508-745-9500. Open Monday to Saturday 10-5, Sundays noon to 5; closed major holidays. Admission $5, over-65 and student discounts.*

The Peabody Museum is the nation's oldest maritime museum, dating back to the formation of the East India Marine Society in 1799, which was formed to provide support for the families of Salem seamen lost at sea. Other objectives of the society were to collect navigational information and establish a museum displaying "natural and artificial curiosities, particularly such as are to be found beyond the Cape of Good Hope and Cape Horn." The society's reputation was greatly enhanced by the membership of the navigational scientist Nathaniel Bowditch (1773-1838), who first published his *American Practical Navigator* in 1802.

In 1867 the society changed its name to the Peabody Academy of Science when the need to display exotic curiosities diminished and an English philanthropist, George Peabody, provided funds to keep it going. The museum shifted its emphasis to maritime history in 1905, when it opened the Marine Room. It then started to display ship models, portraits of ships and sea captains, and sea-going artifacts. The museum's current name, Peabody Maritime Museum of Salem, was adopted in 1915. Today, the museum is considered one of the finest maritime museums in the world.

The museum consists of four separate collections: maritime history, artifacts from Asia and the Far East, natural history, and Asian art. The maritime collection consists of ship models, marine art, figureheads, and navigational tools. The museum also maintains an excellent library of more than 100,000 maritime-related items.

❖ *DOSSIN GREAT LAKES MUSEUM, 100 Strand Drive, Belle Isle, Detroit, Michigan 48207. Tel: 313-267-6440. Open Wednesday to Sunday 10-4; closed holidays. Admission free, suggested donation $1.*

Opened in 1960, the Dossin Great Lakes Museum is a branch of the Detroit Historical Society. The museum contains exhibits describing the history of Great Lakes shipping, including an extensive collection of photographs and files on Great Lakes ships. The most dramatic feature of the museum is the reassembled smoking room from the 1912 lake steamer, *City of Detroit III*, one of the largest side-wheelers ever built on the Great Lakes. The Gothic Room, named for its Gothic style, contains nearly eight tons of massive carved-oak arches. A striking stained glass window from the ship highlights one end of the room. The museum also features the first hydroplane to exceed 100 mph, the *Miss Pepsi*, which was raced by the Dossin family from 1949 to 1955.

The museum contains the largest and most complete set of Great Lakes ship models in existence. They show the evolution of ships on the Great Lakes from the birch-bark canoe to the modern 1,000-foot bulk-cargo carriers. Among the most significant of these ship models are the first sailing ship on the Great Lakes, the first steamship on the lakes, the first iron-hulled ore ship, the only five-masted schooner on the lakes, a whaleback, and a palatial side-wheeler.

❖ *SS KEEWATIN, Harbor Village, Union Street and Blue Star Highway, Douglas, Michigan 49406. Tel: 616-857-2151 or 2107. Open daily 10-4:30, Memorial Day weekend to Labor Day. Admission $3, under-13 discount.*

This 350-foot-long, turn-of-the-century, coal-burning steam passenger ship was built in Scotland. She was in service on the upper Great Lakes for almost 60 years. The ship has been preserved to show life on a Great Lakes steamer. Harbor Village also contains several other smaller ships used on the Great Lakes, including a fishing schooner and a tugboat.

The steamboat Sylvester *on the Great Lakes. Photo courtesy of the Smithsonian Institution, Washington, D.C.*

❖ *MUSEUM SHIP—SS VALLEY CAMP, corner of Johnson and Water Streets, Sault Ste. Marie, Michigan 49783. Tel: 906-632-3658. Open daily 10-6, mid-May through June and September to mid-October; daily 9-9, July and August. Admission $5.25, over-65 and student discounts.*

The *Valley Camp*, a 550-foot Great Lakes ore freighter, was in service between Lake Superior and Lake Erie until her retirement in 1967. Visitors can tour most of the ship, including the wheelhouse, crew's and officers' cabins, and engine rooms. The holds feature exhibits of navigational aids, several aquariums of Great Lakes marine life, models of other Great Lakes cargo ships (including a 32-foot model of another ore carrier), and a maritime Hall of Fame.

A centerpiece of the museum is an exhibit on the loss of the 729-foot ore carrier, the *Edmund Fitzgerald,* that broke apart and sank in 1975 during a violent storm on Lake Superior and artifacts from an ore carrier, the *SS Cayuga,* that sank in the Straits of Mackinac in 1895.

❖ *MICHIGAN MARITIME MUSEUM, Dyckman Avenue at the bridge, South Haven, Michigan 49090. Tel: 616-637-8078. Open Tuesday to Sunday 10-5, May through October; Tuesday to Saturday 10-4, rest of year; closed major holidays. Admission $1.50, over-62 and under-13 discounts.*

Founded in 1976, the Michigan Maritime Museum focuses on the cultural interaction of man and the natural environment in the Great Lakes region, beginning with the Native Americans. In 1990 the Michigan legislature merged the privately held Michigan Maritime Museum into the Michigan Bureau of History.

The museum contains ships and models of ships used on the Great Lakes, as well as artifacts pertaining to the maritime history of the lakes. An exhibit on the U.S. Life-Saving Service is contained in a station built by the service in 1900. The museum also maintains a special collection of historical documents, photographs, films, and taped oral histories in its Marialyce Canonie Great Lakes Research Library.

❖ *SHIPWRECK HISTORIC MUSEUM AND LIGHTHOUSE, Whitefish Point, Michigan. Tel: 906-492-3436. Open daily 10-6, Memorial Day to mid-October. Admission $3.50, children and family discounts.*

Located on the grounds of historic Whitefish Point lighthouse and Coast Guard station on the Michigan Upper Peninsula, the museum describes the numerous shipwrecks that have occurred in Lake Superior on and around Whitefish Point. Experts have estimated that

6,000 ships and thousands of lives have been lost in the Great Lakes. The museum provides exhibits and a film describing 12 of the major disasters, including underwater video showing the remains of sunken ships. There are also exhibits on the lighthouse, Coast Guard lifesaving activities, and undersea-exploration efforts used to identify and document sunken ships.

The Roger Blough, *an 858-foot ore freighter, is one of today's modern lake carriers. She is shown loading grain in Two Harbors, Minnesota. The ship is 105 feet wide and displaces 45,000 tons. Photo courtesy of the Canal Park Marine Museum, Duluth, Minnesota.*

❖ *CANAL PARK MARINE MUSEUM, 600 Lake Avenue South, Duluth, Minnesota 55802. Tel: 218-727-2497. Open daily 10-9, Memorial Day to Labor Day; daily 10-6, April to Memorial Day and Labor Day to December 10, closed rest of year. Admission free.*

The Canal Park Marine Museum is located on the Duluth Ship Canal, which connects the Port of Duluth-Superior with Lake Superior. Founded and operated by the U.S. Army Corps of Engineers in 1973, the museum focuses on the improvements the Corps has made to navigation and the harbors on the Great Lakes. The museum has an excellent exhibit on the evolution of ore-carrier loading and unloading systems. A series of 45 scale models shows the evolution of Great Lakes shipping.

❖ *MUSEUM OF MISSOURI RIVER HISTORY, Brownville State Recreation Area, Brownville, Nebraska 68321. Tel: 402-825-3341. Open daily 10-5:30, mid-May to mid-September; Saturday and Sunday 10-5:30, mid-April to mid-May and mid-September to mid-October. Admission $1, under-12 discount.*

The museum is located on the bank of the Missouri River in the *Captain Meriwether Lewis,* a dry-docked, steel-hulled, side-wheeled river dredge. The 268-foot long, steam-powered dredge was built in 1932 at Point Pleasant, West Virginia, for the U.S. Army Corps of Engineers, and cleared channels on the Missouri River until 1969. In 1976 the Corps of Engineers gave the *Captain Meriwether Lewis* to the Nebraska State Historical Society, which moved her to the present site the following year. The ship was declared a National Historic Landmark in 1989.

The museum contains displays on the river's history starting with the indigenous Indians and white fur-traders. Visitors may tour the boat and view the dredging equipment, engine room, giant wooden paddlewheels, pilot house, and crew quarters.

❖ *THE ANTIQUE BOAT MUSEUM, 750 Mary Street, Clayton, New York 13624. Tel: 315-686-4104. Open daily 9-4, mid-May to mid-October. Admission $4, senior and student discounts.*

Called the Thousand Islands Shipyard Museum when it was founded in 1964, the Antique Boat Museum has expanded its scope to become one of the leading small boat museums in the country. Its purpose is to preserve and interpret the freshwater nautical history of small boats and related artifacts. The collection of 150 freshwater boats is one of the largest in the world, ranging from Indian dugout and birch-bark canoes to high-speed racing boats. Included are craft owned by former U.S. Presidents Ulysses S. Grant and James A. Garfield, both of whom summered in the Thousand Islands area.

There are also exhibits on boat-building techniques, ice boats, and a collection of 200 outboard and inboard engines. Also included are thousands of nautical artifacts and an extensive library of photographs and publications. Early each August the museum sponsors an antique boat show and regatta, both of which have received national attention. During summer months the museum's boat-building school conducts classes on traditional wooden boat-building and restoration techniques.

❖ *AMERICAN MERCHANT MARINE MUSEUM, U.S. Merchant Marine Academy, Steamboat Road, Kings Point, New York 11024. Tel: 516-773-5000. Open Tuesday and Wednesday 11-3 and Saturday and Sunday 1-4:30; closed month of July. Admission free.*

The museum was created in 1978 to publicize the role the Merchant Marine has played in the development of the nation. The Merchant Marine Academy was established in 1943, during World War II, to train merchant marine officers in nautical and naval sciences and in ship management. Graduates receive a bachelor of science degree and a commission in the naval reserve.

Exhibits in the museum focus on merchant marine developments since World War I. There are approximately 40 ship models, a collection of antique navigation instruments, and a display on tugboats. The museum includes an exhibit on the history of the academy and a National Maritime Hall of Fame.

❖ *SOUTH STREET SEAPORT MUSEUM, 207 Front Street, New York, New York 10038. Tel: 212-699-9400. Open daily 10-5; closed major holidays. Admission $6, over-65 and under-13 discounts.*

In 1967 the city and State of New York, plus the federal government, put together sufficient resources to form a non-profit maritime museum organization that created the South Street Seaport Museum. The site selected for the museum on the East River in lower Manhattan was the center of the Port of New York during the sailing days of the late eighteenth through nineteenth centuries. This historic 12-block area centers on South and Fulton Streets. The latter was named after Robert Fulton, who docked his steamboats in the vicinity in the early 1800s.

The area contains the historic Fulton Fish Market and a number of restored buildings dating from sailing ship days that house commercial businesses as well as an indoor museum describing the development of the port and city.

The Melville Library houses an extensive collection of books and other publications dealing with New York maritime history.

A number of turn-of-the-century sailing and steam-powered ships are anchored at the foot of Fulton Street for public viewing. The most significant of these is the 350-foot, four-masted, iron-hulled bark, *Peking*. Built in 1911, she is the second-largest sailing ship still in existence. During her 20-year commercial life, the *Peking* was used in the nitrate trade between Europe and Chile. In 1931 she became a training ship and remained in that role until acquired by the museum in 1975. Other sailing ships berthed at the museum include the three-masted, iron-hulled square-rigger, *Wavertree*, built in 1885, and a nineteenth century schooner, *Pioneer*.

❖ NORTH CAROLINA MARITIME MUSEUM, 315 Front Street, Beaufort, North Carolina 28516. Tel: 919-728-7317. Open Monday to Friday 9-5, Saturday 10-5, and Sunday 1-5; closed major holidays. Admission free.

The museum, founded in 1975, focuses on the natural and maritime history of the North Carolina coast, including the history and development of North Carolina small craft. Exhibits cover privateering, coastal shipping, and the U.S. Life-Saving Service.

The museum contains collections of small craft, ship models, and mounted specimens of birds and fish indigenous to North Carolina.

The collection of 75 ship models ranges from small sailing skiffs to large square-rigged sailing vessels. There is also an extensive collection of duck-hunting boats and decoys. Natural science exhibits include saltwater aquariums and collections of North Carolina seashells. The museum has recently reconstructed its boat-repair facility, where visitors can observe traditional boat-building techniques.

❖ OHIO RIVER MUSEUM AND W. P. SNYDER, JR., 601 Front Street, Marietta, Ohio 45750. Tel: 614-373-3750. Open daily Monday to Saturday 9:30-5, Sunday noon-5, May through October; Wednesday to Saturday 9:30-5, Sunday noon-5, March, April, and November; closed rest of year and major holidays. Admission $3, senior and under-13 discounts.

The Ohio River Museum contains artifacts and models of riverboats from the 1800s and a movie presentation on river transportation.

The *W.P. Snyder, Jr.* is a steam-powered towboat that was used to pull barges on the Ohio River in the late 1800s and early 1900s.

Onoka *was the Great Lakes' first iron-hulled bulk freighter. She was built at Cleveland in 1882, measured 287 feet in length, and carried 2,400 tons of cargo. The ship was the prototype ore/grain/coal freighter. She sank in 1915. Photo courtesy of the Canal Park Marine Museum, Duluth, Minnesota.*

❖ SS WILLIS B. BOYER MUSEUM SHIP, 26 Mint Street, Toledo, Ohio 43605-2032. Tel: 419-698-8252. Open Wednesday to Sunday noon-6, May through August; Saturday and Sunday noon-6, September. Admission $3.50, over-62 and under-12 discounts.

The *Willis B. Boyer,* a 617-foot Great Lakes freighter, was built in 1911 and remained active until 1980. The interior of the ship, one of the largest on the Great Lakes during its active life, has been maintained as it was when in operation. Guided tours include the engine room, fore and aft cabins, and pilothouse. A modest museum aboard the ship contains photographs of Great Lakes ships, half-hull models, and exhibits on the history of Great Lakes shipping.

❖ *COLUMBIA RIVER MARITIME MUSEUM, 1792 Columbia Drive, Astoria, Oregon 97103. Tel: 503-325-2323. Open daily 9:30 to 5, except major holidays. Admission $3, student and over-64 discounts.*

Founded in Astoria in 1962, the Columbia River Maritime Museum chronicles the maritime history of the Oregon-Washington coast and the Columbia River. Located at the mouth of the Columbia River, Astoria was built on the site of Fort Clatsop, where the Lewis and Clark expedition wintered in 1805-6.

The theme-oriented museum focuses on navigation and marine safety, fishing and whaling, the Columbia River, sailing vessels, steamships, and naval history. Each subject is described through exhibits of boats, ship models, historic photographs, and marine art.

The lightship *Columbia*, moored alongside the museum, is open for visitors. The ship was anchored off the mouth of the Columbia River for 30 years as a navigational aid.

❖ *OREGON MARITIME CENTER AND MUSEUM, 113 Southwest Front Avenue, Portland, Oregon 97204. Tel: 503-224-7724. Open Wednesday to Sunday 11-4, Memorial Day to Labor Day; Friday to Sunday 11-4, rest of year. Admission $2, over-62 and student discounts.*

The Oregon Maritime Museum contains artifacts and navigational instruments, ship models, and other materials that focus on marine activities on the Willamette and Columbia rivers. Of special interest is a collection of antique century sextants and octants, and models of ocean-going ships and riverboats used in the region. The museum recently acquired the stern-wheeled towboat *Portland*, which is in the process of being restored.

❖ *PHILADELPHIA MARITIME MUSEUM, 321 Chestnut Street, Philadelphia, Pennsylvania 19106. Tel: 215-925-5439. Open Tuesday to Saturday 10-5, Sunday 1-5; closed major holidays. Admission $2.50, senior and under-12 discounts.*

In 1962 a local attorney named J. Welles Henderson succeeded in bringing together sufficient resources and his own extensive maritime collection to open the Philadelphia Maritime Museum. In its 32,000 square feet of exhibit space, the museum displays a varied collection of maritime artifacts and paintings, plus a library of photographs, maps, charts, and manuscripts. The small-boat collection features craft used on the Delaware River and Bay.

The museum also maintains a small-boat repair and construction workshop, which is open to the public on Penn's Landing at the foot of Chestnut Street.

❖ *PATRIOTS POINT NAVAL AND MARITIME MUSEUM, 40 Patriots Point Road, Charleston, South Carolina. Tel: 803-884-2727. Open daily 9-6, April to September; daily 9-5, rest of year. Admission $8, military, over-62, and under-13 discounts.*

In addition to World War II naval ships—the aircraft carrier *USS Yorktown*, a submarine, and a destroyer—the museum includes the experimental nuclear merchant ship, *NS Savannah*, and the Coast Guard cutter *Ingham*. All ships are open for self-guided tours.

Launched in 1959, the *Savannah* was the world's first nuclear-powered merchant ship. She was named in honor of the first ship equipped with steam propulsion to cross the Atlantic, in 1812. Her first voyage under nuclear power occurred in 1962 and included passage through the Panama Canal and up the West Coast to the Seattle World's Fair. The vessel did not prove economical as a merchant ship and was retired to Patriots Point in 1970. By then the *Savannah* had cruised more than 450,000 miles on 27 voyages to various parts of the world.

❖ *MISSISSIPPI RIVER MUSEUM, Mud Island, 125 North Front Street, Memphis, Tennessee 38103. Tel: 901-576-7241. Open daily 10-8, late May to early September; daily 10-5, mid-April through May; closed rest of year. Admission $1 to park and $5 to museum, over-60 and under-13 discounts.*

The Mississippi River Museum, founded in 1978 by the city of Memphis, is located on Mud Island, a 52-acre waterfront theme park. In addition to the 18-gallery museum, the park also contains a half-mile long re-creation of 950 miles of the lower Mississippi River Valley designed to scale by the U.S. Army Corps of Engineers. The walk along the re-creation features 90 panels providing geographical and historical highlights.

The museum is divided into eight theme areas, each showing a specific aspect of the river's history. The tour starts with a description of the relationship between the river and the Native Americans, followed by the impact of early white explorers and settlers. Through a series of models, the next exhibits recount the history of river craft, from log rafts to steamboats, including the era of the packet boat. Within the packet-boat exhibit the visitor can tour a reproduction of the pilot house, main deck, and grand salon of a Mississippi River packet boat. The final segment of the exhibit describes the transition from steam-powered to diesel-powered barge towboats. The museum also provides exhibits on river disasters, the people who made their living on the river, and the role of the river during the Civil War.

❖ *TEXAS SEAPORT MUSEUM, Pier 21, foot of 22nd Street, Galveston, Texas 77550. Tel: 409-763-1877. Open daily 10-5, except major holidays. Admission $4, student and over-65 discounts.*

The most important artifact of the Texas Seaport Museum is the *Elissa*, a rehabilitated three-masted, iron-hulled bark. Launched in 1877 at Aberdeen, Scotland, *Elissa* was acquired by the Galveston Historical Foundation in 1976. The ship is now fully seaworthy, making regular voyages under sail. She has become recognized as one of America's outstanding "tall ships."

The museum focuses on the maritime history of Texas, with particular emphasis on the Port of Galveston during the period 1880 to 1920. Exhibits include a scale model of the port in 1883 that traces the movement of cargo and immigrants through the facility. Other exhibits show the influence of cotton on the port and life in Galveston during its heyday. Additional

The 1877 tall ship Elissa *at the Texas Seaport Museum on Galveston Island. Photo courtesy of the Texas Seaport Museum, Galveston, Texas.*

exhibits, located in the hold of the *Elissa*, depict life at sea and the workings of a sailing ship.

❖ *THE MARINERS' MUSEUM, 100 Museum Drive, Newport News, Virginia 23606. Tel: 804-595-0368. Open Monday to Saturday 9-5 and Sunday noon-5; closed Christmas. Admission $4, over-60 and student discounts.*

The Mariners' Museum at Newport News was founded in 1930 by Archer M. Huntington to preserve the maritime heritage of the region. It has since become one of the outstanding maritime museums in the country. The museum possesses excellent collections of scrimshaw, carved ship figureheads, maritime art, and various watercraft. The museum has recently opened a Chesapeake Bay wing, which features informative displays on the maritime history of the bay, with particular emphasis on fishing and shipbuilding.

The August Crabtree Collection of exceptionally detailed, hand-carved miniature ships traces the 3,000-year evolution of man's relationship to the sea. A separate exhibit of drawings and photographs focuses on the works of William Francis Gibbs, a noted ship designer who designed the *USS United States* and the World War II merchant vessel known as the Liberty Ship. One large gallery is devoted to steamship models.

❖ *DISCOVERY, GODSPEED, AND SUSAN CONSTANT, Jamestown Settlement, Route 31 South, Williamsburg, Virginia 23118. Tel: 804-253-4838. Open daily 9-5, except major holidays. Admission $7, under-13 discount.*

Jamestown Settlement was built in 1957 to dramatize the life experienced by the colonists in the first permanent English settlement in America. The complex includes full-scale reproductions of the sailing ships that brought the first settlers to the Virginia Colony in 1607.

Costumed interpreters describe life aboard the three ships during the four-and-one-half-month sea voyage. The Jamestown Settlement complex also includes a reproduction of James Fort in which the settlers lived and an indoor museum describing the history of the colony.

❖ *GRAYS HARBOR HISTORICAL SEAPORT, 813 Heron Street, Aberdeen, Washington. Tel: 206-532-8611. Open daily 9-5. Admission free to shipyard and museum, $3 to ship, senior and student discounts.*

Grays Harbor Historical Seaport is a shipyard museum project sponsored by the city of Aberdeen and the state of Washington in honor of New Englander Captain Robert Gray, who discovered the harbor while exploring the Northwest in 1790.

In 1989 a replica of Gray's brig *Lady Washington* was built and launched at the shipyard. She is actively sailed throughout the Pacific Northwest as the official "tall ship" of the state of Washington. *Lady Washington* is open for tours when in port and can also be visited when at other Northwest ports. A schedule of port calls is available from the Grays Harbor Seaport office. The ship is also available for charter.

The seaport complex is in the process of developing a maritime museum. The shipyard is currently building two 26-foot longboats of the type that accompanied Captain Gray on the *Lady Washington*.

❖ *MUSEUM OF HISTORY AND INDUSTRY, Puget Sound Maritime Historical Society, 2700 24th Avenue East, Seattle, Washington 98112. Tel: 206-324-1126. Open daily 10-5, except major holidays. Admission $3, over-65 and under-13 discounts.*

The collections of the Puget Sound Maritime Historical Society are housed in the Museum of History and Industry. Founded in 1948, the Maritime Historical Society collects materials related to the maritime history of Puget Sound and the Pacific Northwest. The Historical Society has no permanent staff, relying on that of the Museum of History and Industry to maintain and display its collections of maritime photographs, ship models, and artifacts. Exhibits focus on commercial shipping and fishing, sailing ships, and shipwrecks of the Northwest.

Tall ship Wanwona *berthed at the Northwest Seaport Museum, Seattle, Washington. Photo courtesy of the Northwest Seaport Museum, Seattle, Washington.*

❖ *NORTHWEST SEAPORT, 1002 Valley Street, Seattle, Washington 98109. Tel: 206-447-9800. Open daily. Admission free, although small fee for special tours and classes.*

Northwest Seaport is dedicated to the preservation and interpretation of the maritime heritage of Puget Sound and the Northwest Coast. It originated in 1963 with the formation of a local volunteers' organization, whose purpose was to save the three-masted schooner *Wanwona*, the last surviving vessel of its type in the Northwest.

In 1970 the organization expanded its scope and adopted its present name. It subsequently acquired three additional ships: the sea-going tug *Arthur Foss* (1889), the lightship *Relief* (1904), and the steam ferry *San Mateo* (1922). All three ships are National Historic Landmarks. Only the *Wanwona* and *Relief* are open to the public, the former daily and the latter on weekends, while the other two are under restoration.

Immediately adjacent to Northwest seaport is the Center for Wooden Boats. Founded in 1978, its objective is to retain the heritage of the construction and use of small rowing and sailing craft.

❖ *MANITOWOC MARITIME MUSEUM, 75 Maritime Drive, Manitowoc, Wisconsin 54220. Tel: 414-684-0218. Open daily 9-5, summer 9-8; closed major holidays. Admission $5.75 combination museum and submarine, $3.50 museum only; under-13 and family discounts.*

The Manitowoc Maritime Museum is one of the most diversified maritime museums on the Great Lakes. It provides a comprehensive review of the history of Great Lakes shipping. Displays include one on ship disasters on the Great Lakes. There is also an interesting display of carved wooden-ship models.

During World War II, Manitowoc shipyards built submarines for the U.S. Navy. The museum contains an exhibit on this shipbuilding program and provides an opportunity to tour a World War II submarine, the *USS Cobia*, which was built in Manitowoc during the war.

❖ *DOOR COUNTY MARITIME MUSEUM, Foot of Florida Street, Sturgeon Bay, Wisconsin 54235. Tel: 414-743-8139. Open daily 10-4, Memorial Day to mid-October. Admission free; donation of $1 (suggested).*

❖ *DOOR COUNTY MARITIME MUSEUM, 12950 Highway 42, Gills Rock, Wisconsin 54307. Tel: 414-854-2860. Open daily 10-4, July and August; Saturday and Sunday 10-4, mid-May through June and September through mid-October. Admission free, donation of $1 (suggested).*

The Door County museums have interesting exhibits on Great Lakes shipping, shipbuilding, and fishing in the area. Sturgeon Bay, one of the largest shipbuilding ports on the Great Lakes, is the focus of the Sturgeon Bay branch of the museum. It contains an exhibit on the canal that cuts through the Door Peninsula, connecting Sturgeon Bay and Lake Michigan. The canal eliminated a 100-mile voyage around the tip of the peninsula that was required to reach Green Bay from Lake Michigan. The Sturgeon Bay branch also features the 90-year old launch *Wanda*, an early Chris Craft speedboat.

Gills Rock, at the northern tip of Door Peninsula, was the site of many wrecks, and artifacts from a number are on display at this branch of the museum. There is also a collection of carved models of boats and ships commonly seen in the area, including sailing schooners and steamers.

❖ *SS METEOR MARITIME MUSEUM, Barker's Island, Superior, Wisconsin 54880. Tel: 715-392-5742 or 1083. Open daily 10-5, May through early September; Saturday and Sunday 10-5, September to mid-October; closed rest of year. Admission $3.25, senior and student discounts.*

Built in 1896 at a Superior, Wisconsin, shipyard and originally named the *Frank Rockefeller*, the *Meteor* was the thirty-sixth of 42 whalebacks designed and built specifically for use on the Great Lakes. It is the last of these cigar-shaped boats still in existence.

In 1972 the *Meteor* returned to Superior after a citizens committee raised the money needed to purchase the ship from Cleveland Tankers, Inc., her last operating owner, which retired her in 1969. The *Meteor* had originally been built as an iron-ore carrier. The 367-foot-long *Meteor* now contains a museum that describes the purpose of the whaleback design and its history. Also included are exhibits relating the shipbuilding history of Superior.

The flat-bottom, rounded-hull design of the whaleboat, which tapered to a point at both ends, provided stability in rough weather and more efficient headway. Designed by Captain Alexander McDougall, founder of the American Steel Barge Company in Superior, where most of

Like the Meteor, *the* John Ericson *whaleback was built at the American Steel Barge Company in Superior, Wisconsin. Photo courtesy of the Canal Park Marine Museum, Duluth, Minnesota.*

the whalebacks were built, the whaleback proved an effective cargo ship. Limited by its construction to a length of less than 400 feet and to a beam of 45 feet, the whalebacks were being overtaken by the increasingly larger, straight-sided cargo ships by the time the *Meteor* was constructed. In spite of their specialized design for use on the Great Lakes, whaleboats (also termed "pig" boats) saw service on both the Atlantic and Pacific oceans.

FAST FREIGHT SOUTH by Ron Flanary, oil painting from the series, Great Trains South. Courtesy of the artist.

Railroads

While the existence of waterways was instrumental in opening and settling the lands east of the Mississippi River in the early 1800s, lands west of the Mississippi could not have been developed without the railroads. It is not outside the realm of possibility that America might still be an agrarian economy today if railroads had not been invented.

Horse-powered railroads were introduced in America around 1800, the same time that canal fever started to spread through the eastern states. Until the 1840s, a period when canals where already reaching their peak, railroads developed slowly, lack of appropriate technology being the limiting factor. Ironically, canal engineers helped accelerate the development of railroads by adapting them to the portage of boats, cargoes, and passengers over mountainous terrain. The limiting railroad technologies during the early decades of the 1800s included practical steam locomotion, sound roadbed construction, and iron-making technology.

First Railroads

Use of animal-drawn carts riding in a stone or wooden groove goes back many centuries. Flanged wheels riding on raised rails were first used in the 1600s. The first recorded use of rail transportation in the United States occurred in Boston at a quarry in the base of Bunker Hill in 1795. Over the next three decades, a number of tramways were built throughout the East, all involving single horse-drawn carts with flanged wheels on wooden rails.

The first charter issued to operate a public railroad was granted by the commonwealth of Massachusetts in 1826 to the Granite Railway Company, located south of Boston near Quincy. The designer and superintendent of the Granite Railway Company, Gridley Bryant, was the inventor of the switch, crossover (frog), and the turntable, and is reported to be the first in

America to use iron strips on top of wooden sills to provide a more lasting rail for the horse-drawn carts. He later used granite rails and designed a unique carriage to haul the massive slabs of granite from the mine to the dock on the Neponset River.

The Granite Railway, and other public railways at the time, were operated like toll roads; that is, anybody could place his cart on the track with his own mule or horse and pay a toll for use of the track. Since there was no lay-by track, draymen heading in opposite directions had to settle who had the right of way, frequently by fisticuffs. Public use of the tracks continued until the introduction of the steam locomotive made it obvious that the railway companies had to own and operate their own locomotives and trains.

The first railroad to offer regular passenger service, albeit using horse-drawn carriages, was the Baltimore and Ohio Railroad (B&O), which inaugurated the service in May 1830.

Development of Steam

During the early 1800s, England took the leadership in the development of steam technology. The first successful steam locomotive is reported to have been built in 1804 for an iron foundry in Wales by a Cornishman named Richard Trevithick. It was not until 1813, when Englishman George Stephenson built a locomotive for an Welsh colliery, that steam railways began to catch on in England. Stephenson's fame in England spread, and he was soon asked to build the first public steam railroad in the world, the Stockton and Darlington, which initiated service in front of tens of thousands of curious onlookers on September 27, 1825.

America lagged behind England in the development of steam technology as the country was blessed with ample sources of water power. In fact, America made greater use of water power than any country in the world during the 1700s and 1800s. Its waterways enabled canals to be

The B&O steam locomotive No.13, Lafayette, *was originally built in 1837 by William Morris. It contained B&O's first horizontal-boilered engine. Photo of replica built in 1927, courtesy of the B&O Railroad Museum, Baltimore, Maryland.*

built and water was even used to power railway inclined planes that raised and lowered canal boats over difficult terrain. Steam-engine technology in America during the first quarter of the 1800s was applied mainly to stationary engines and to marine craft.

Having heavy investments in canals and steamships, the American financial community was slow to invest in railroad companies until the 1830s. By 1840, however, railroad expansion was well under way. During the 1830s, railroad mileage increased from 23 miles to 2,818 miles. By 1840, technologies of steam locomotion, rail and roadbed design, and iron-making had advanced sufficiently to cause railroad construction to spread like wildfire, which it continued to do for the following 60 years.

Early American Steam Railroads

New York financiers were far from the minds of the merchants of Charleston, South Carolina, when, in the late 1820s, they decided to build a railroad to Hamburg, South Carolina, a town on the east side of the Savannah River across from Augusta, Georgia. The railroad, named the South Carolina Canal and Railroad Company, hired Horatio Allen as its chief

engineer. Allen had previously been chief engineer of the Delaware and Hudson Canal Company, where, on August 8, 1829, he had experimented with the first steam locomotive operated on the American continent, the *Stourbridge Lion.*

The English-built *Stourbridge Lion* had proved too heavy for the light American trackage, so Allen contracted for the first steam locomotive made in the United States, which he named the *Best Friend of Charleston.* On Christmas Day 1830, Allen introduced the first scheduled steam train service in the United States. Pioneering had its drawbacks, unfortunately. The *Best Friend of Charleston* blew up the following year after the fireman tied down the safety valve to obtain more steam. This caused the first major railroad accident in America. The company survived the accident and went on to complete its track to Hamburg in 1833. Other railroads were subsequently built to extend rail travel from Charleston to Atlanta, then to Chattanooga, and finally to St. Louis and Memphis. Following the Civil War, these lines became the basis of the Southern Railroad.

The following year several steam railroads initiated passenger service, including the B&O, which, in July, substituted its newly-

Gwynn's Falls Bridge, Maryland, with B&O Engine No. 12 and train northbound, Chaney drawing circa 1880. Courtesy of the Smithsonian Institution, Washington, D.C.

acquired engine, the *York*, for horsepower on its 13-mile Baltimore to Ellicott Mills line; and the Mohawk and Hudson, which commenced service between Albany and Schenectady in August of 1831. The first locomotive acquired by the Mohawk and Hudson, which provided the genesis of the New York Central, was built in New York City and named the *DeWitt Clinton*, in honor of the governor of New York who created the Erie Canal.

Baltimore and Ohio Railroad

Most historians consider the B&O as the first railroad common carrier of both freight and passengers in America. It was incorporated in February 1827 and completed its first 13 miles of track from Baltimore to Ellicott Mills in May 1830. While initially using horses and mules to pull its carriages, the B&O was the first to experiment with a steam locomotive when it acquired the *Tom Thumb* in August 1830. Built in 1829 by a New York mechanic named Peter Cooper, the *Tom Thumb* was used mainly for experimental and demonstration purposes. Although historians say the event never happened, the story persists that in one trial run between Baltimore and Ellicott, the *Tom Thumb*

lost a race against a horse and carriage because a belt slipped off the firebox blower pulley.

The B&O operated the *York* for a number of years on the 80-mile line between Baltimore and Frederick, Maryland. By 1835, the B&O had seven locomotives, 44 passenger cars, and 1,078 "burden" cars. It had extended its tracks to Harpers Ferry on the Potomac River, and to Washington, D.C. The line to the Potomac at Harpers Ferry opened up the Baltimore market for farm products from western Maryland and the Shenandoah Valley in Virginia. The line between Baltimore and Washington immediately became successful, carrying an average of 200 passengers daily. Ultimately the B&O extended its system west to Cincinnati, Chicago, and St. Louis.

The B&O was only one of four pioneering railroads that pushed west toward Chicago and St. Louis. The others were the New York Central, which initially extended only from Albany to Buffalo; the Pennsylvania Railroad, which moved west from Philadelphia via Pittsburgh to Chicago; and the Erie Railroad, which started from the Hudson River and originally terminated in Dunkirk, New York, on Lake Erie.

The DeWitt Clinton, *one of the first locomotives on the New York Central Railway. Antique sketch courtesy of the author.*

New York Central System

The New York Central, like most of the early long-haul railroads, is actually an amalgamation of smaller town-to-town railroads. It was initially created in 1853 out of nine railroads connecting Albany and Buffalo, the oldest link being the Mohawk and Hudson Railroad Company (later renamed to the Albany and Schenectady Railroad), which was founded in 1826. The merger in 1853 brought about integrated service of through trains between the two cities. The connection from Albany to New York City was, for many years after the merger, via river steamer on the Hudson River.

Before the merger each segment of the Albany to Buffalo line operated separately, with freight and passengers changing trains at each connection. In Rochester, for example, the two terminals were several blocks apart, so taxis and wagons were used to connect the two. This arrangement persisted for a number of years at the insistence of the taxi and drayage companies in Rochester (similar situations existed in other cities throughout the country).

The New York Central faced another roadblock in those early years. The New York state legislature placed onerous restrictions on the railroad when granting the original charters. These restrictions included not allowing the railroad to carry freight, allowing it to carry freight only when the Erie Canal was frozen over, and requiring the railroad to reimburse the Erie Canal for any losses incurred because of the railroad. These restrictions were voted into law by the many state legislators who were investors in the Erie Canal. The situation for the railroads improved only after legislators started investing in railroads and the canal-investing legislators lost their influence.

The New York Central did not enter New York City until acquired by Commodore Cornelius Vanderbilt in 1867. His campaign started in 1862, when he began to acquire stock in the New York and Harlem Railroad, which extended from 23rd Street in New York City to Chatham, southeast of Albany. He later acquired control of the Hudson River Railroad, which ran along the eastern shore of the Hudson. Vanderbilt merged the two small lines and then proceeded to gain control of the New York Central.

The New York Central eventually reached Chicago in 1877, a year after the commodore's death. By then the commodore's son, William, had taken over control of the New York Central.

Pennsylvania Railroad

By 1838 it had become apparent to a group of businessmen in Philadelphia that the state-operated canal-rail system, popularly called the Main Line, was not able to compete with the

Erie Canal for western traffic. (See section on Canals for description of the Main Line system.) Consequently, in 1840, after forming a corporation named the Pennsylvania Railroad Company and surveying possible routes, they obtained a charter from the state to operate an all-rail system from Philadelphia to Pittsburgh. By 1849 the railroad had commenced operations on the first segment of track between Harrisburg and Lewistown. The following year, the track reached Hollidaysburg and linked up with the state-owned Allegheny Portage Railroad, and in 1852 track had been laid west from Johnstown to Pittsburgh.

Using the state-operated Philadelphia and Columbia Railroad as the eastern segment and the Allegheny Portage Railroad as the middle segment, the Pennsylvania Railroad ran its first train from Philadelphia to Pittsburgh in May 1854. In 1857 the Pennsylvania Railroad bought the Main Line system from the state. In the following year, the railroad built its own tracks across the Alleghenies at a lower elevation and shut down the Allegheny Portage, which had proven to be very expensive to operate.

Through acquisition of the majority stock in the Northern Central in 1861, the Pennsylvania Railroad gained access to Baltimore, towns in northern Pennsylvania, and as far north as Canandaigua, New York. Equally important, the Northern Central provided the Pennsylvania Railroad with a line leading to Washington, D.C., although because of resistance from the B&O, the Pennsylvania Railroad did not reach there until 1873. In 1869 the Pennsylvania Railroad acquired operating rights on the Pittsburgh, Fort Wayne & Chicago Railroad, which gave it access to Chicago eight years ahead of New York Central.

Like the New York Central, the Pennsylvania Railroad suffered from a lack of direct access to New York City. One of the early railroads built in the United States had been the Camden and Amboy, which was chartered in 1830 and started operations from Perth Amboy to Camden in 1834. Competition with the Camden and Amboy soon appeared in the form of the New Jersey Railroad, which started at the Hudson River and expanded south, first to Elizabeth in 1834 and then to New Brunswick in 1836. After 30 years of jockeying for position, the two railroads finally merged in 1867 under the name of the United Railroads of New Jersey.

The Pennsylvania Railroad acquired the United Railroads in 1871, which enabled it to reach New York Harbor. Since the United Railroads did not operate tracks under the Hudson River into Manhattan, the Pennsylvania Railroad had to rely on ferry service to transport cargo and passengers into the city. In 1910 the Pennsylvania Railroad finally built an electrified line to Manhattan under the Hudson River and constructed Pennsylvania Station between 31st and 33rd streets. It continued the tunnel below ground through Manhattan and under the East River to Long Island. This enabled the Long Island Railroad, which the Pennsylvania Railroad had acquired in 1900, to also bring its trains into Manhattan. It also permitted through trains to operate from Boston to Washington, D.C.

Erie Railroad

The Erie initially extended west from Piermont, New York, on the Hudson River (south of Nyack) via the Delaware and Susquehanna River valleys through southern New York State to Dunkirk on Lake Erie, which

Replica of the first train over the Erie Railroad in 1851. Photo courtesy of the Salamanca Rail Museum, Salamanca, New York.

The powerful articulated compounded steam locomotives required massive structures and linkages, as shown by this 2-6-6-4 Mallet. Photo courtesy of the Norfolk and Western Collection at Virginia Polytechnic Institute and State University, Blacksburg, Virginia.

it reached in 1851. Early critics of the Erie referred to it as the railroad "that goes from nowhere to nowhere via nowhere." It was also a railroad that selected a 6-foot gauge while others had begun to standardize on a 4-foot 8.5-inch gauge. This decision cost the Erie hundreds of millions of dollars to correct between 1878 to 1885.

In spite of these deficiencies, the Erie Railroad was an important factor in the development of early American steam railroads. It helped open up the southern regions of Upstate New York by providing settlers in the region with access to the Great Lakes and to New York City. In the late 1800s, the Erie acquired trackage and a terminal opposite Manhattan in Jersey City, New Jersey, extended its trackage to Buffalo and Rochester, New York, and obtained trackage rights west from Salamanca, New York, via Marion, Ohio, to Chicago.

Technological Improvements

Technological improvements continued to play a major role in the expansion of the nation's railroads during the 1800s and early 1900s. Larger and more powerful locomotives

enabled faster train speeds, which in turn forced improvements in track design and construction, and in braking systems. Denser and faster traffic generated more frequent and disastrous wrecks, which fostered the development of automatic signaling systems and safer, all-steel passenger cars.

Steam Locomotive Developments

Improvements in locomotive design and construction became the principal forcing factor in improving railroad productivity until after mid-century. During the early years American railroad entrepreneurs had to rely on British manufacturers for most of their locomotives. Between 1829 and 1840 approximately 100 steam locomotives were purchased from English manufacturers. By 1840, however, American manufacturers had developed the necessary skills and capacity to meet essentially all of the locomotive needs in America.

During the 100 years that steam dominated railroad locomotion, designers focused on three areas of improvement — locomotive power, speed, and efficiency. Improved boiler construction permitted higher steam pressures, which in turn brought about more powerful engines. More powerful engines and improved locomotive suspension systems permitted faster train speeds and greater tractive force (the maximum horizontal pull generated by the locomotive at the rear of the tender). Improved firebox designs produced hotter fires, higher steam pressures, and more efficient fuel consumption.

Improvements in power and speed were dramatic. The earliest American locomotives weighed approximately five tons and produced a tractive force of only 400 pounds. In the peak of steam locomotion during World War II, the Union Pacific Big Boy, the largest type of locomotive ever built, weighed more than 550 tons and produced a tractive force of 135,000 pounds. In terms of relative speeds, the earliest America-built engine, the *Best Friend of Charleston,* was capable of pulling approximately 40 tons

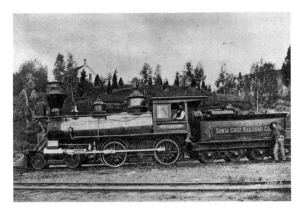

(Left) A 4-4-0 freight locomotive, the Jupiter, *circa 1850. Photo courtesy of the Norfolk and Western Collection at Virginia Polytechnic Institute and State University, Blacksburg, Virginia. (Right) The B&O steam locomotive No. 25,* William Mason *was built in 1856 by Mason Machine Works. The 4-4-0 locomotive was used in general passenger service and is typical of those used prior to the Civil War. Note the large wheel size of the B&O passenger engine. Photo courtesy of the B&O Railroad Museum, Baltimore, Maryland.*

on level ground at a speed of only 12 miles per hour (mph), while the Union Pacific Big Boy could easily pull 4,000-ton trains at speeds approaching 50 mph. The first scheduled run that exceeded 60 mph occurred in 1848 on the Boston and Main between Boston and Lawrence, Massachusetts. A record speed of 112.5 mph was reported to have been achieved briefly by an engine pulling the Empire State Express on the New York Central in 1893.

Through steady improvement in boiler design, steam pressures rose steadily from 50 pounds per square inch (psi) in the earliest engines to 300 psi by World War II in the Union Pacific Big Boy. This yielded a significant improvement since tractive power is directly proportional to steam pressure. To further enhance the efficiency of steam, superheaters were introduced around 1910. Overall, efficiencies of steam locomotion doubled between 1900 and 1930.

Significant improvements to locomotive suspension systems also occurred during the 1800s. The earliest engines were equipped with only four wheels, the axle of one being powered by a single cylinder. The use of dual cylinders mounted externally to the driving wheels on each side of the engine and connected directly to the wheels with driving rods had been adopted by 1840.

When America first started importing locomotives from England, it quickly found that the engines were too heavy and rigid for American roadbeds and frequently jumped the track. While heavy engines were well-suited to English roadbeds, which were built carefully and substantially, they were unsuitable for American roadbeds, which were laid as quickly and as inexpensively as possible. American tracks typically developed undulations that would cause one wheel of a four-wheel rigidly mounted set of drivers to rise above the track. Consequently, the engine frequently left the track when rounding a curve.

Two significant innovations were developed in America during the 1830s to correct this problem. In 1832 John B. Jervis mounted a swiveling four-wheel pilot truck (called a "bogie" in England) under the front of the engine. The pilot truck kept the engine on the track when one of the four drivers left the rail due to a sag in the roadbed. The other significant innovation was the equalizing bar, which was developed in 1838 by Joseph Harrison, Jr. The equalizing bar, or lever, gave stability to the locomotive similar to that provided by a three-legged stool on an uneven surface.

In the late 1800s a two-wheel trailing bogie was added on larger locomotives to support the cab and the increasingly heavy fireboxes. The need for trailing wheels was also brought about by the need to support the heavy mechanical stoker introduced when locomotives converted from wood to coal or oil as fuel.

By the mid-1800s wheel configurations had become quite varied. The industry began to refer to engine types according to the number of leading, driving, and trailing wheels, a scheme that was formalized in 1900 by Frederic M. Whyte of the New York Central. According to this scheme, the first number indicates the number of wheels on the leading truck, the second the number of driving wheels, and the third the number of wheels on the trailing truck under the cab.

The 4-4-0, the so-called American- or Standard-type engine, became the symbol of American expansion and industrial might during the 1830s with its ornate cowcatcher and wide spark-arresting stack. Between 1830 and 1900 approximately 25,000 Standards were built for American and foreign railroads. The more powerful 4-6-0, called a ten-wheeler, became popular in the 1840s and continued to be produced into the 1900s.

By the time of the Civil War, railroads were specifying their own preferred wheel configurations and giving each configuration a name. The Lehigh popularized the 2-8-0, which was given the model name Consolidation, a reference to the origin of the railroad. The 4-4-2 Atlantic, the next generation of the 4-4-0 Standard, was named after the Atlantic City Railroad, which first put it into service in 1895. Similarly, the 4-6-2 Pacific, a popular freight locomotive, was associated with the Missouri Pacific, which started using it in 1902. The huge 2-10-2 Santa Fe was put into service on that railroad in 1903, and the 4-8-4 Northern was introduced by the Northern Pacific in 1927. The widely used 2-8-2 Mikado derived its name because it was first

designed by the Baldwin Locomotive Works to fill an order from Japan in 1897, a time when the Gilbert and Sullivan opera, the *Mikado,* was at its peak of popularity.

While most steam locomotives were capable of being used for both freight and passenger service, many were designed and used for one or the other. Generally, those with larger wheels were built for speed, but at the expense of tractive power, as the latter is inversely proportional to driving-wheel diameter. Thus, the Atlantic, with 80-inch-diameter drivers, and the Pacific, with 73-inch drivers, were frequently used to haul high-speed passenger trains, while the Mikado, with 63-inch drivers, made an excellent freight hauler. The short-distance speed record of 112.5 mph was achieved in 1893 by the New York Central's Model No. 999, a 4-4-0 American with 86-inch driving wheels.

By the turn of the century, engine weights and power had increased to the point that 12, 16, and even 24 driving wheels were needed to support the engine and provide the needed tractive force. These numbers of driving wheels presented problems in negotiating sharp curves on western and mountain railroads where the most powerful engines were needed. As a result locomotive builders adopted the technique of "articulation," which involved the use of two (three in the case of one engine type) sets of driving wheels, each powered by its own set of cylinders, pistons, and driving rods. Articulation was provided by firmly attaching the boiler to the rear set of drivers and then allowing the forward set to move in a slot under the boiler as the locomotive rounded the curves.

Articulated locomotives, which were first built in America around 1904, were referred to as Mallets, after a Frenchman named Anatole Mallet who developed the design in 1885. Mallet also developed the concept of compounding, whereby steam exhausted from the cylinders of one set of drivers was used a second time in the cylinders for the second set, thereby gaining more efficient use of the steam. The wheel designation of an articulated and/or compounded locomotive added a fourth number to the Whyte identifica-

Articulated compounded 2-6-6-4 locomotive pulling a Norfolk and Western freight train. Photo courtesy of the Norfolk and Western Collection at Virginia Polytechnic Institute and State University, Blacksburg, Virginia.

tion scheme. Thus, an articulated-compounded Mallet might be shown as a 2-6-6-4 or a 4-8-8-4. The latter wheel designation identifies the Union Pacific's Big Boy, first built in 1941.

Track Improvements

As has been mentioned earlier, the first rails were constructed merely of wooden logs flattened on top and placed on a stone base. This was sufficient while wheels and carriage frames were also made of wood and loads and speeds were limited to that of a horse or mule. It had been established in the 1600s that a mule could pull at least two and a half times as much weight in a wagon mounted on wooden rails than it could over a typical dirt or cobblestone road.

Early improvements in rail design occurred in England during the 1600s and 1700s. The first improvement involved placing iron strips on top of the wooden rails to reduce wear and friction. As train speed increased the iron strips developed a tendency to snake up through the floor of the carriage, causing injury

and even fatalities. During this period locomotive engineers and firemen often kept a supply of spikes and a spike hammer aboard so that when a loose strip-rail (called a snakehead) was observed, the engineer stopped the train while the fireman spiked it down again.

In 1738 cast-iron rails were developed. This solved the snakehead problem, but the cast-iron rail was brittle and frequently broke. This problem was not solved until 1804, when the malleable-iron rail was developed. An early version of the modern "I"-shaped rail had begun to appear in England by 1820. American railroads adopted its use in the early 1830s. The first steel rails were produced in the United States in 1867 by the Cambria Iron Works in Johnstown, Pennsylvania, and by 1890 practically all malleable-iron rails had been replaced with steel. The welded continuous rail was introduced after World War II to reduce track maintenance. While the early rails weighed only a few pounds per foot, today's high-speed and heavy trains require rails weighing 125 to 150 pounds per foot.

Sketch of a brakeman working in adverse weather conditions, circa 1870. Collection of the author.

During the first half of the 1800s, expansion of America's rail system outstripped the U.S. iron industry's ability to provide the rails to support it. Iron rails were not even produced in America until 1844; as late as 1855 the New York Central still found it necessary to purchase rails in England to meet their requirements. Even decades later, when American mills were producing sufficient steel rails, a number of mountain railroads still preferred to purchase high-strength steel rails for use on curves from German steel mills.

Air Brakes

Air brakes were another important development in the advancement of railroads in America. Until their invention by George Westinghouse in 1869, trains had to be braked by hand. While the engineer shifted the steam-cylinder action into reverse, brakemen ran down the top of the train setting brakes on each individual car by a hand-wheel located on top of the car. In spite of the obvious advantage of the air brake, they were not in general use until Congress made them mandatory in the Railroad Safety Act of 1883. When air brakes were first installed, engineers demanded extra pay to operate them.

Automatic Coupler

The automatic coupler, another safety device made mandatory by the Railroad Safety Act of 1883, had been introduced a decade earlier on the Pennsylvania Railroad. It replaced the old link-and-pin coupler that had maimed so many rail-yard workers. The automatic coupler also brought about a significant decrease in the time it took to couple and uncouple cars in a train.

Automatic Signaling

Signaling systems became necessary as speeds and traffic increased. Before 1847 engineers relied on preprinted schedules and local stationmasters to provide information on the condition of the track ahead. Preprinted schedules were often out of date by the time they reached the train crew, and stationmasters were frequently as ill-informed as the engineer. As a result, collisions were frequent. In 1847 the telegraph was introduced, which helped stationmasters keep more current regarding train movements, but the engineer still retained authority as to whether to proceed or not.

It took another four years before the telegraph was used to control train movements. The first such use is believed to have been by Charles Minot, the superintendent of the Erie Railroad. He had became impatient at a long delay on a siding and telegraphed instructions ahead to hold all on-coming trains at the next station. The engineer of Minot's own train refused to trust the telegraphic instructions so Minot took over the engine and the frightened engineer elected to ride in the last seat of the last car of the train during the successful run.

To further confuse train-dispatching procedures in the early stages of railroading, disagreements arose as to whether the engineer or

Signal structures on three-track main-line of the Norfolk and Western Railroad. Photo from the Norfolk and Western Collection at Virginia Polytechnic Institute and State University, Blacksburg, Virginia.

the conductor was in control of the train. Fist fights between the two were not unheard of when disagreement arose as to whether to proceed to the next station. The railroads finally set firm policies in favor of the conductor, but it took several decades before such policies were universal. This issue was only one of many that focused on the role of the engineer. The practice, for example, of permitting engineers to retain their own personal locomotive, which no other engineer could use, was not completely abolished until late in the 1800s.

Automatic block signaling, an American development, was introduced in 1871. Its use spread slowly at first as evidenced by a report that showed 104 head-on train collisions in 1875 on American railroads. Special automatic signals at drawbridges and where two railroads crossed were the first types of signals to be accepted. Before these automatic signals were accepted, wrecks at cross-over points were common. Also, it was not uncommon for an engineer to run his train off an open swing bridge into a river.

An important ancillary problem faced by railroads in their attempt to schedule and control train movements during the 1800s was the lack of standard times. Until 1883, there were hundreds of local times throughout the nation. Under this chaotic system, noon in Chicago meant 12:31 in Pittsburgh, 11:50 in St. Louis, Missouri, and 11:27 in Omaha, Nebraska. The state of Wisconsin is reported to have had 38 different times. In 1883, out of desperation, the railroads finally adopted for their own use the four standard times we use today. Gradually the rest of the nation accepted these standard time zones, although it took Congress until 1918 to make them the law of the land.

Passenger Car Improvements

When railroads first started carrying passengers in the 1830s, horse-drawn carriages set on four-wheel frames were used as coaches. Most of the early coaches were open, and passengers suffered from smoke inhalation and clothing burns from sparks. Coaches in these early trains were connected by links of chain, and when the train accelerated or decelerated the passengers were jerked backward or forward accordingly. Train crews learned to stiffen the chains with a stick or rod to reduce the jerking. Out of this innovation came the link-and-pin coupler, which was replaced by the automatic coupler in 1883.

Railroading was dangerous for both crews and passengers during the period of its greatest growth, from 1860 to the late 1880s. Accidents were caused by faulty rails and running gear, trestles ravaged by storms, inaccurate information, and human errors of judgment. A major factor in rising fatalities when an accident did occur was the wooden passenger car. The wooden cars easily telescoped in a collision and quickly caught fire when the wood-burning stove used to keep cars warm during the winter overturned. Wooden passenger cars were finally replaced by all-steel ones, starting in 1907.

Other Impediments and Innovations

The proliferation of railroad gauges, that is, the distance between rails, was one of the greatest impediments to railroad efficiency and productivity in America until 1886. Prior to that time, passengers, baggage, and freight had to be transported from one train to another whenever two railroads operating on different gauges interconnected—a common occurrence in the mid-1800s.

One of the most serious problems of gauge became apparent during the Civil War. Southern railroads had been built using a 5-foot gauge and, therefore, could not interconnect with northern railroads when their troops advanced northward. Southern railroads did not shift their 13,000 miles of track over to the standard gauge of 4 feet, 8.5 inches until 1886.

The Civil War has been called the "Railroad War," because the success of so many of its battles and campaigns depended on moving troops and supplies by rail. The North possessed a well-developed railroad network, while the South's was sparse and possessed few alternate routes. The Confederacy had only two east-west rail routes to Chattanooga, Tennessee, and only one from there to the Mississippi River, at Memphis. Further, the Confederacy suffered considerably from shortages of locomotives and rolling stock, while Union forces had more than adequate capacity to move troops and supplies freely.

While the lack of a standard gauge did make travel and transport more difficult than need be, it did not slow down the expansion of railroad mileage. At the end of the Civil War, there were 35,000 miles of track in the United States. By 1880 the nation's railroad track mileage had increased to 93,000 miles and a decade later to 164,000. The peak was reached in 1917 at 234,000 miles. Today, track mileage has shrunk to approximately 150,000 miles.

It took three powerful engines to pull this Denver and Rio Grande passenger train up a steep grade on the main line in Colorado, circa 1920. Photo collection of the author.

Western Railroads

The eastern railroads generally stopped their westward expansion at the Mississippi River. The western railroads generally started west from the Mississippi or Missouri rivers. A few midwestern railroads such as the Rock Island, the Wabash system, and the Burlington provided bridges between the two. Of the western roads, the Northern Pacific, and later James Hill's Great Northern, moved west from the Mississippi River at Minneapolis and St. Paul, Minnesota. The Union Pacific expanded west from the Missouri River at Omaha, Nebraska, while the Santa Fe started from Topeka, Kansas, near the Missouri River. In the south the Southern Pacific expanded east from California and by acquiring the Galveston, Harrisburg & San Antonio Railroad, the Southern Pacific reached the Mississippi at New Orleans.

As the railroads expanded, they frequently fought over access to key points of geography. The Santa Fe, for example, was able to keep the Denver and Rio Grande out of New Mexico and the Southwest, except in a minor way, by being the first to reach Raton Pass in northern New Mexico. On the other hand, the

Denver and Rio Grande was able to keep the Santa Fe out of the Royal Gorge, which blocked the latter's path to the mines at Leadville, Colorado, and to points west in Colorado and Utah.

Another famous contest over a key access point was the Southern Pacific's race with the Texas & Pacific to gain control of the Colorado River crossing and access across the Yuma Indian Reservation in Arizona. After considerable debate in Congress, the Southern Pacific won out. The Southern Pacific also gained control of the other principal access to California over the Donner Summit of the Sierra Nevadas when it leased the lines of its creator, the Central Pacific. As a result it was not until many years later that the Santa Fe and Union Pacific were able to gain entrance into California.

The Union Pacific had been blocked from the Pacific Coast by the Central Pacific at Promontory Point in Utah in 1869. It took until 1884 for the Union Pacific to reach the Pacific Coast at Portland, Oregon, and several more decades for it to reach Southern California. The Union Pacific did not reach San Francisco until it acquired the Western Pacific in the 1980s.

The Chicago, Burlington & Quincy was one of the few east-west railroads to bridge the Mississippi River and, at one time, had an opportunity to reach the Pacific Coast. The Burlington reached the Mississippi River in 1856, but it did not enter Denver until 1883. By then, its possible extension to the West was blocked by the Denver & Rio Grande, to the Southwest by the Santa Fe, and to the Northwest by the Union Pacific. The Burlington did finally make a link to the West Coast via the Denver & Rio Grande and the Western Pacific in 1910.

Jay Gould established another east-west bridge across the Mississippi River when in 1879 he consolidated his holdings in the Missouri Pacific with the Wabash, St. Louis & Pacific. This consolidation provided a direct line from Buffalo, New York, to Kansas City, Kansas, and Omaha, Nebraska, with connections to Chicago. The Wabash system provided considerable competition to the Burlington, since both systems had almost parallel lines with approximately the same termini. While the Wabash system was not able to move west of the Missouri River, it continued to disrupt the equilibrium of western traffic patterns for many years.

Unfortunately, many private investors such as Jay Gould milked and then starved railroads under their control into bankruptcy during this period. Financial speculators such as Cornelius Vanderbilt, Daniel Drew, and James Fisk are only the best-known of those who manipulated railroad stock and bond prices to their own ends.

The Norfolk and Western's Powhatan Arrow *pulled along the New River in Virginia by one of the last of the steam-powered locomotives, a high-wheel 4-8-4. Notice the streamlining that has been applied. Photo courtesy of the Norfolk and Western Collection at Virginia Polytechnic Institute and State University, Blacksburg, Virginia.*

Shift to Diesel Locomotives

The first use of an internal-combustion engine in railroad service occurred in 1906 when General Electric developed a 200-horsepower (hp) gasoline-electric rail car for the Delaware and Hudson Railroad. The first diesel-electric engine used in railroad service was acquired by the Central Railroad of New Jersey in 1926, which assigned it to yard-switching service. During the 1920s diesel locomotives were relatively heavy in relation to their horsepower and were not, therefore, considered suitable for road service except for short runs or where steam power was inappropriate.

The advantages of the diesel engine over steam are that diesel is more efficient, has faster acceleration, is very reliable, and requires less maintenance. The disadvantage of the diesel engine is that its initial cost is higher than a steam engine of equivalent size. However, this is more than offset by its much lower operating cost. Further, in operation diesel has proven to be much more flexible in that the same locomotive can be used effectively in switching, passenger, and long-haul freight service. Also, multiple units can be easily assembled and controlled by a single operator as load conditions require.

In the early 1930s the Electro-Motive Division (EMD) of General Motors pioneered a compact diesel engine using a two-cycle design that substantially lowered the weight-to-horse-power ratio from 80 pounds, typical of the single-cycle diesel engine, to 20 pounds. General Motors then prevailed upon Burlington to install it in a lightweight, integrated three-car train named the *Pioneer Zephyr* that was being built by the Budd Company. In May 1934, the *Pioneer Zephyr*, averaging 77 mph, made a non-stop run from Denver to Chicago, where it became an immediate hit at the Century of Progress Exposition, thereby launching the diesel age of railroading.

EMD went on to design a streamlined, twin-unit passenger locomotive capable of generating 3,600 hp by using two 12-cylinder engines of the type incorporated into the *Pioneer*

Zephyr. Railroads throughout the country showed keen interest and, following their custom when purchasing steam locomotives, immediately started requesting their own individual preferences as to shape, fittings, and style.

At that point EMD made what is now ranked as one of the most successful product-policy decisions of the pre-war period, ranked with Henry Ford's decision to make only black Model Ts. Customers were allowed to buy only standardized models with no deviations except for trim and a few accessories. This policy enabled EMD to keep the price of the locomotive low and substantially accelerated the use of the diesel locomotive in American railroading.

Starting in 1938, EMD, along with several other locomotive manufacturers including American Locomotive Company (Alco), Fairbanks Morse, and Baldwin, began promoting and offering long-haul diesel freight locomotives. These more powerful models typically consisted of three or more individual units, some with cabs and some merely booster units.

As dieselization advanced, the railroads soon realized that the streamlined units with the rounded fronts, while artistically attractive, were awkward to use. Backward visibility for the engineer was severely limited, and unless two units were connected back to back, the engine had to be turned around to travel in the opposite direction. Further, the flush-sided construction made engine maintenance difficult. By the late 1940s, railroads had foregone aesthetics for practicality and settled almost exclusively on the so-called "hood-unit," which eliminated the outer housing, except for the cab.

Transit Systems

The street railway and the railroad were born of the same rail-based parentage, but there the similarities stopped. The streetcar was designed for frequent stops on crowded city streets and essentially limited to carrying masses of people for relatively short distances. Everything about them was on a smaller scale. While the track gauge adopted by street railways was, in the main, the same standard as that used by the long-haul railroads, the rails were lighter and the equipment was of more delicate construction.

The first urban transit system on record was started in New York City in 1827 by Abraham Brower. He used trackless, horse-drawn omnibuses, the first called *Accommodation* and the second, *Sociable*. Each "bus" operated on a set run, could accommodate 10 to 12 passengers, and charged fixed fares per ride. The concept of a public-bus system caught on rapidly, and by 1835 there were hundreds of horse-drawn omnibuses on the streets of New York City.

The first steam-powered urban railway also started in New York City and was called the New York and Harlem Railroad. It started operations with horse-drawn vehicles in 1832 but by 1836 was using steam locomotives. At the time New York City stopped at about 30th Street, and Harlem was a small village to the north. The founder of the New York and Harlem, John Mason, had planned to build a long-haul railroad up the Hudson River to Albany and beyond, but the expansion of the city overwhelmed his resources and the railroad remained essentially an interurban.

In spite of Mason's success, other cities were slow to follow. New Orleans started a horse-drawn rail system in 1835 (known today as the oldest street railway line still in operation),

but little else happened of note until Brooklyn constructed a street rail line in 1853. This was soon followed by street railways in Boston in 1856, and Philadelphia in 1858. Other cities quickly followed.

By 1882 the number of cities and towns with horse-drawn street railways had grown to 415, and the number of streetcars to 18,000. The streetcar made a major contribution to the urbanization and industrialization of America. Along with the bicycle, which came along at about the same time, the streetcar gave the urban population mobility.

Cable-Powered Street Railways

The first step toward mechanically powered streetcars occurred in San Francisco in 1873. Because of its steep hills, the city did not provide an ideal environment for horse-drawn carriages, much less horse-drawn streetcars. An Englishman by the name of Andrew Hallidie obtained permission from the city to construct a cable-powered system from the foot of Clay Street at its junction with Market Street to the top of Nob Hill. It took another seven years before the bugs had been worked out, but the system proved practical.

Chicago was the first city to acquire a license from Hallidie to build its own cable

Cable car turnaround at corner at Seventh Street and Broadway in San Francisco, circa 1880. Sketch collection of the author.

system, which started operating on State Street in 1883. While cable technology was not suitable for most cities, it did catch on rapidly in many. Within a few years, 59 private cable railway systems had sprung up in 27 North American cities. These included all major cities except Boston, Detroit, Atlanta, and New Orleans. At one time San Francisco's system extended for 53 miles; Chicago's, for 41 miles. At their peak in 1893, cable systems powered streetcars on 305 miles of urban streets in North America.

Electric Streetcars

The cable-car craze did not last long, however, as the first electric-powered streetcar was introduced in Richmond, Virginia, in 1888. Boston electrified its rail system in 1889, thereby making its 2,000 horse-drawn streetcars and 8,000 horses obsolete. The shift from horse-power to electric power among American cities occurred quickly. This new technology was clearly right for the times. It was significantly less expensive to install and operate than cable systems, and society welcomed the elimination of horse residue from city streets. By 1902 only a few hundred miles of urban track in the country were still being traveled by horse-powered trams, out of a total mileage of 22,500.

Controversies immediately arose among the cities as to the best form of electric distribution for electric street railway lines. Many people objected to the unsightly overhead lines, so a number of cities built chambers under the tracks to carry the power system and slots to feed electricity to the cars, much like the cable-car slots. Some even tried using rechargeable batteries. The majority, however, accepted the unsightly wires, as they were by far the least expensive and most practical arrangement. The overhead wire brought a new lovable term into our language, the "trolley car," which entered folklore through the popular 1920s and 1930s comic strip, *The Toonerville Trolley*.

Growing competition from trackless buses became evident to street railway officials in the late 1920s. Consequently, the American Electric Railway Association, at its 1929 annual meeting, established a committee to recommend improvements in streetcar performance and construction cost through standardization. The committee, named the Electric Railway President's Conference Committee, was successful in its efforts and produced specifications for a new type of streetcar, which became known as the PCC car. The first PCC prototype was introduced in 1934 and the first order was placed in 1936 by the Brooklyn & Queens Transit Corporation in New York City. Transit systems throughout the country purchased PCC cars, some of which are still in operation today.

The Interurban Railway

Electricity allowed the growth of the interurban railway, which ran to the suburbs, the beach, and to amusement parks. Street railway companies even found it profitable to build and own amusement parks; the Massachusetts Street Railway Company, for example, owned 31. Electric-power companies found it exceedingly profitable to own interurbans and street railway companies, and minor versions of the stock manipulations that brought scandals to the railroad industry occurred in the street railway industry.

Trolley car on Main Street, Salamanca, New York, circa 1910. Photo courtesy of the Salamanca Rail Museum, Salamanca, New York.

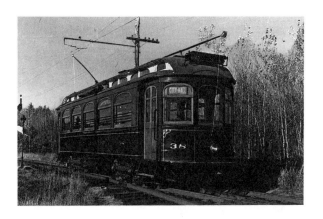

This light interurban car was first used on the lines from Manchester to Nashua and Derry, New Hampshire, and later saw service on the suburban lines of the Manchester Street Railway. Photo courtesy of the Seashore Trolley Museum, Kennebunkport, Maine.

The electric interurban sprang up almost overnight in the 1890s. The first interurban on record is the Newark and Granville Street Railway in Ohio, which started service in 1889. The number of interurbans grew rapidly until 1917, the peak year of their popularity, when there were 18,000 miles of interurban track (compared to a total of 45,000 miles of street railway track). Interurbans were most popular in the Northeast and Midwest. One New England state, Connecticut, contained more than 1,000 miles of interurban track.

During the 1920s a number of long-distance interurbans were constructed. One ran from St. Louis, Missouri, to Springfield, Illinois, a distance of 90 miles. Another, the Chicago, North Shore & Milwaukee, which made an 85-mile run from Chicago, Illinois, to Milwaukee, Wisconsin, operated until 1963. One of the longest interurbans was built in Oregon. It ran from Portland to Eugene, a distance of 143 miles, and took six hours. On some of these longer lines, the interurbans operated dining and parlor cars, much like the long-haul railroads.

The largest interurban rail complex ever created was the Pacific Electric (PE) system, which served the Los Angeles region until the late 1950s. At its peak the PE's big red cars operated over 1,100 miles of track, extending from downtown Los Angeles out to San Fernando to the north, San Bernardino to the east, and Newport Beach to the south. In a series of aggressive takeovers, which they duplicated throughout the country, a combine of General Motors, Standard Oil, and Firestone Tire companies bought up the Pacific Electric from 1938 to 1950. They tore up the track and overhead wiring, sold the rights of way, and replaced the electric trains with diesel buses. The combine was later found guilty by a Chicago jury of criminal conspiracy and illegal monopolistic practices, but the destruction of regional rail-transit systems was permanent.

Buses and Trolley Buses

The heyday of the electric streetcar lasted into the late 1920s. By then subways and elevated rail systems had taken over the major transit task in many of the major cities, and the off-rail transit bus had begun to take over local urban routes. The trolley can still be found in a few cities today, and is experiencing a comeback in the form of the light-rail transit systems.

With the invention of the automobile in the 1890s, the transit omnibus soon began to appear on urban streets. The first motorized buses, powered by a gasoline engine-electric generator system, appeared on Fifth Avenue in New York City in 1905. Fifth Avenue was one of the few streets in New York that had not been disfigured with surface or elevated tracks. By 1912 the company operated more than 80 buses, half of which were double-deckers.

A motor coach service started in downtown Chicago in 1917. Its founder, an Austrian immigrant by the name of John Hertz, had started the Yellow Cab Company two years previously. He soon began manufacturing taxis and buses under the name of the Yellow Coach Company. While all of these ventures were successful, the one that has made his name recognizable throughout the world is his car rental business, which he started in the 1920s. Yellow Coach Company was acquired by General

Motors in 1925, and became one of the two major suppliers of buses in the United States, the other being A.C.F.-Brill.

The electric trolley bus became popular in the 1930s. It provided a quiet and clean type of transit system while avoiding the expensive and disruptive need to install tracks on city streets. The first city to install a trolley-bus system was Philadelphia in 1923, followed by Chicago in 1930. By 1940 there were 2,800 trolley-bus systems, but because of the unsightly overhead wires required, enthusiasm for them waned, and today they can be found in only a few cities, notably San Francisco and Seattle.

The Elevated and Subway

As the gateway for immigrants, New York City became the most densely populated city in the United States around the time of the Civil War. The streets had become clogged with horse-drawn wagons and streetcars at the same time that commuting needs of the city had expanded. The more affluent working population of the city was moving further north on Manhattan Island and east on Long Island. Commuting distances had become too great to be handled by local horse-drawn surface transit systems.

The first elevated railway in America was built in 1871 on the west side of Manhattan. An "el" was added on the east side, on Third Avenue, in 1878. Within a year, four els were operating in New York—on Second, Third, Sixth, and Ninth avenues. By 1880 these els were handling one-half million passengers daily. Within a few years other cities began to construct elevateds. Even relatively small cities such as Sioux City, Iowa, built and operated els for a short time. Many of the early els were steam powered, but converted to electricity in the 1890s.

Chicago built its first system in 1892 and completed the famous downtown "Loop" in 1898. The elevated loop, built by the Union Elevated Railway Company, which operated no trains of its own, provided access to the downtown area for the four separate interurban railroads feeding commuters into Chicago.

When the elevateds were first built in New York City, trains were pulled by steam locomotives. Print from author's collection.

As the major cities began to find the elevated railways inadequate for their need to move people rapidly, subway construction got under way. Boston was the first city to construct a subway-tunnel system, which, like the Loop in Chicago, was designed to bring the three independent surface streetcar lines into the downtown area. The Boston system went into operation in the fall of 1897. Using public funds, New York began to build its first subway in 1900. When it was completed, the city then leased the facilities to private operators. The first New York subway system was completed and opened in October 1904. It extended from City Hall to upper Manhattan, and subsequently to the Bronx.

New York entered into a major subway-building program in 1913, which lasted until 1931, at a cost in excess of $300 million. The construction program became one of the largest in American history at the time, exceeding that of the Erie Canal and rivaling that of the Panama Canal, which had opened in 1914.

Railroad and Transit Museums

Railroads

❖ *MUSEUM OF ALASKA TRANSPORTATION AND INDUSTRY, Milepost 40.2, Glenn Highway, Palmer, Alaska 99501. Tel: 907-745-4493. Open Tuesday to Saturday 10-4. Admission $1.*

Founded in Anchorage as the Air Progress Museum, the museum was renamed to cover all of Alaska's transportation, agricultural, and industrial heritage when it was moved to its present site adjacent to the Alaska State Fairgrounds in 1976. The museum's collection of transportation equipment ranges from a dog sled to fishing boats, and includes cars, trucks, aircraft, and railroad equipment. The railroad exhibits describe the history of the Alaska Railroad and includes rolling stock, railroad artifacts, and the railroad's first diesel engine.

The Alaska Railroad runs between Seward and Fairbanks via Anchorage, with branch lines to Whittier and Palmer. This standard gauge railroad was created by Congress in 1912 out of two existing railroads, one a standard-gauge line and the other a narrow gauge. It operated under the jurisdiction of the U.S. Department of Transportation until 1985, when ownership was transferred to the state of Alaska. The railroad currently operates approximately 60 locomotives, 1,200 freight cars, and 40 passenger cars on 320 miles of track.

❖ *PORTOLA RAILROAD MUSEUM, County Road A-15, Portola, California 96122. Tel: 916-832-4131. Open daily 10-5, June through September; weekends 10-5, October through May. Trains operate weekends; check ahead for schedule. Museum admission free, rides $2, family discount.*

The museum is operated by the Feather River Rail Society and is located on the main line of the former Western Pacific (now part of the Union Pacific) at the summit of its Feather River Canyon entrance to California. The collection of rolling stock includes a wide range of freight cars, plus several passenger cars that were operated by the Western Pacific. The locomotives include 23 diesels, plus one steam and one electric. The

steam locomotive, a 1907 Baldwin 2-6-2, was owned by the Clover Valley Lumber Company of California. This engine is still in operation and is used one weekend each month to pull the excursion train on a one-mile loop track. The loop track was originally built by the railroad for turning helper locomotives around at the top of the grade.

❖ *CALIFORNIA STATE RAILROAD MUSEUM, 125 "I" Street, Sacramento, California 95814. Tel: 916-448-4466 or 916-445-4209. Open daily 10-5; closed major holidays. Admission $3, student discount.*

Opened in 1976 in Old Sacramento State Historic Park, the California State Railroad Museum is considered one of the finest railroad museums in the country. It contains 21 restored locomotives and more than 40 exhibits and dioramas, plus an extensive railroad library. Excursion rides are offered on the restored track of the Sacramento Southern, which served the farm and riverside communities along the

Sacramento River south of Sacramento to the Delta region until the 1970s.

The museum's collection was originally started in 1937 by the Pacific Coast Chapter of the Railway and Locomotive Historical Society, located in the San Francisco Bay area. By 1967, having accumulated 34 pieces of rolling stock and finding it beyond their means to store, rehabilitate, and maintain the collection, the society

The C. P. Huntington *was originally acquired by the Central Pacific Railroad in 1863 and designated as locomotive No. 3. It was transferred to the Southern Pacific Railroad in 1871 where it was assigned No. 1 and used for many years as a corporate symbol. Photo courtesy of the Southern Pacific Railroad, San Francisco, California.*

approached the state of California with the concept of a state-sponsored museum. The state accepted the proposal and began to acquire the collection in 1969. The first phase of the museum facility was opened in 1976. Ground was broken for the main exhibit hall in 1978, and it was opened to the public in 1981.

The most impressive locomotive in the museum collection is a massive Southern Pacific cab-in-front Mallet-type. The 1944 Mallet 4-8-8-4 engine was the last steam locomotive purchased by the Southern Pacific and is the only one remaining of the 256 cab-in-fronts ever built. The Southern Pacific was the only railroad to make use of the cab-in-front design, which it developed to eliminate smoke in the engineer's cab while traversing the snow sheds in the Sierra Nevada.

One of the oldest locomotives in the collection is the Southern Pacific No. 1, the *C. P. Huntington*, which has an unusual 4-2-4T wheel configuration. The four trailing wheels were necessary to carry the weight of the tender, which is an integral part of the locomotive frame (hence the "T" designation).

Another highlight of the museum is the Virginia & Truckee Railroad (V&T) locomotive No. 13, the *Empire*, with its polished brass trim and flared spark arrester. It is set in a mirrored enclosure so that the visitor can view the top of the locomotive. The 2-6-0 *Empire* was built for the V&T as a freight locomotive in 1873. A companion to the *Empire*, the V&T No. 12, called the *Genoa*, is also on exhibit. It is a 4-4-0 passenger locomotive that hauled passengers between Reno, Carson City, and Virginia City from 1873 to 1908.

Among the passenger cars on display is a Canadian National Railways sleeping car, the *St. Hyacinthe*, which is subjected to gentle motion and external flashing lights to simulate high-speed night travel in the 1930s. Alongside the *St. Hyacinthe* is a Rail Post Office (RPO) car in which the visitor is trained to sort mail. The most elegant car in the museum is the private car of well-known railroad buffs and writers, Lucius Beebe and Charles Clegg, called the *Gold Coast*. The two writers purchased a railroad business car of 1890s' vintage in 1948 and had it redecorated to suit their personal tastes.

Denver and Rio Grande 1881 Baldwin 2-8-0 No. 346 pulls a narrow-gauge excursion train at the Colorado Railroad Museum near Golden, Colorado. Photo courtesy of the Colorado Railroad Museum, Golden, Colorado.

❖ *COLORADO RAILROAD MUSEUM, 17155 West 44th Street, Golden, Colorado 80402. Tel: 800-365-6263 or 303-279-4591. Open daily 9-5, except major holidays. Admission $3, student and family discounts.*

Founded by the Colorado Railroad Historical Foundation in 1958, the museum displays locomotives and equipment used on Colorado railroads, mostly narrow gauge. The collection of approximately 60 pieces of rolling stock is one of the largest exhibits of narrow-gauge equipment in the country.

The collection was started in the 1940s by Robert W. Richardson, who owned a motel in Alamosa, Colorado, at a time when many of the narrow-gauge railroad operations were closing down and abandoning their equipment. In 1959 the Richardson collection was moved to Golden and combined with similar collections started by several railroad historical societies.

Historically, Colorado railroads were primarily narrow gauge due to the mountainous terrain and the tendency of mining and logging companies to build railroads as quickly and cheaply as possible. Only after the transcontinental railroads began to cross Colorado did standard-gauge track become common.

Among the museum's collection of standard-gauge equipment is the last remaining standard-gauge steam locomotive used by the Denver and Rio Grande (D&RG) on its line from Denver, Colorado, to Ogden, Utah: a Baldwin 2-8-0 built in 1890. The oldest locomotive in the collection, built in 1881, is a narrow-gauge D&RG Baldwin 2-8-0, No. 346. One of the most modern pieces of standard-gauge equipment on display is the rounded-end last car from the Santa Fe *Super Chief.*

The two-floor indoor museum contains extensive displays on Colorado railroading, including collections of early Colorado railroad records, artifacts, and photographs.

❖ *NATIONAL MUSEUM OF AMERICAN HISTORY, 14th Street and Constitution Avenue, Washington, D.C. 20560. Tel: 202-357-2700. Open daily 10-5:30, except Christmas. Admission free.*

Founded in 1846, the National Museum of American History is one of the largest historical museums in the world. Its exhibits on surface transportation range from early wagons and carriages to modern Japanese motorcycles.

The museum's railroad exhibit features the *John Bull*, the first locomotive run in the United States. The *John Bull* was purchased in England in 1831 by Colonel John Stevens for use on his Camden and Amboy Railroad. It was originally built as an 0-4-0, but was converted to a 4-2-0 in 1833 to reduce its tendency to jump off the hastily-laid American tracks. The *John Bull* is still in operating condition, and is believed to be the oldest self-powered wheeled vehicle in operating condition in the world.

Another piece of equipment from the Camden and Amboy is an eight-wheel passenger car built in 1836, believed to be the oldest such car in existence. Also on display is a Southern Railway 4-6-2 Pacific, built by Alco in 1926, which became famous when it was used to pull Franklin Roosevelt's funeral train from Warm Springs, Georgia, to the nation's capital.

The museum's railroad exhibit features displays on the history of American railroading, including a set of models that depict the evolution of the American locomotive. There are also a full-size model of an early Washington, D.C., streetcar and a diorama of a Brooklyn, New York, elevated station.

❖ *GOLD COAST RAILROAD MUSEUM, 12450 Southwest 152nd Street, Miami, Florida 33177. Tel: 305-253-0063. Open weekdays 10-3, weekends and holidays 10-4; closed major holidays. Admission weekdays $3 and weekends $5, under-12 discount.*

The Gold Coast Railroad was founded in 1957 as the Miami Railroad Historical Society. The organization moved the museum to its present location adjacent to the Miami Metrozoo in 1985.

Currently the museum possesses more than 30 pieces of rolling stock. The most publicized piece is a custom-built Pullman car, the *Ferdinand Magellan*, which was used by four American presidents—Franklin D. Roosevelt, Harry S Truman, Dwight D. Eisenhower, and Ronald Reagan. Another passenger car of interest is the rounded last car of the *California Zephyr*. Built by the Budd Company and named the *Silver Crescent*, it is a unique sleeping, vista dome, bar, and observation car. There are a number of other passenger cars in the collection, including an East Coast Railway chair car and several named Pullman cars.

Among the locomotives in the exhibit are two 4-6-2 Pacifics built by Alco, one in 1913 and the other in 1922. Both engines were operated by the Florida East Coast Railway, owned by Henry M. Flagler, an associate of John D. Rockefeller in Standard Oil. At one time the Florida East Coast served Key West with through Pullman sleepers from New York. Flagler started building a 100-mile viaduct to Key West in 1904 and commenced service in 1912. Service was discontinued in September 1935, when a hurricane washed away 40 miles of the viaduct. The viaduct was ultimately repaired and became the roadbed for U.S. Highway 1.

The Gold Coast Railroad Museum regularly operates an excursion train on 2.5 miles of track within the museum site, using both diesel and steam locomotives.

❖ *ILLINOIS RAILROAD MUSEUM, 7000 Olsen Road, Union (McHenry County), Illinois 60180. Tel: 815-923-2488. Open Monday to Friday 10-4, weekends 10:30-5:30, Memorial Day to Labor Day; weekends 10:30-5, May and September; Sunday 10:30-5, April and October; closed November though March. Admission $4.50, under-12 discount. Rates higher when trains running.*

The Illinois Railroad Museum was organized by a group of local rail fans in 1953. The indoor-outdoor museum possesses approximately 225 pieces of railroad rolling stock. The museum operates a five-mile excursion trip on the former right of way of the Elgin and Belvedere Railroad. The extensive collection of railroad rolling stock is one of the largest in the country.

The collection includes a wide range of locomotives, trolleys, and electric cars. The oldest piece of equipment, a horse-drawn Chicago streetcar, dates from 1859. There is also a railroad business car built in 1889. The museum is most well-known for its five-unit *Nebraska Zephyr*. Built in 1936, this integrated train powered by General Motors diesel engines was owned by the Chicago, Burlington & Quincy. It became part of a family of *Zephyr*s that at one time ran from Chicago to San Francisco.

The locomotives in the collection include 18 steam, 14 diesel, and 6 electric. The diesels include one built in 1937 by the Electro-Motive Company (EMC) and formerly owned by the Missouri Pacific. EMC had been acquired by General Motors in the early 1930s and ultimately became its Electro-Motive Division (EMD). There is also a 1940 E-series EMD diesel, which was the predecessor to the famous wartime F-series.

Also included in the collection are 20 trolley cars and 33 interurbans. These include elevated cars from the North Shore and South Shore interurbans and a Chicago "L" station that has been moved to the museum site and restored. Commuter cars from the Rock Island, the Chicago & North Western, and the Lackawanna are also on view.

❖ *KENTUCKY RAILWAY MUSEUM, New Haven, Kentucky 40051. Tel: 502-549-5470. Open weekends and holidays early May to October; telephone for specific schedule. Admission $3, senior and student discounts.*

The Kentucky Railway Museum was originally founded in Louisville, Kentucky, in 1957. The site was flooded out in 1964, and the museum was moved to a suburb of Louisville in 1977. Lacking sufficient space, the museum was moved again in 1990 to its present location 50 miles south of Louisville.

The museum maintains a collection of approximately 75 locomotives and cars. The oldest locomotive is a 4-6-2 Rogers built in 1905 for the Louisville & Nashville Railroad, and the oldest passenger car dates back to the 1870s.

The museum operates a 22-mile excursion run between New Haven and Boston, Kentucky.

❖ *B&O RAILROAD MUSEUM, 901 West Pratt Street, Baltimore, Maryland 21223. Tel: 410-752-2490. Open Tuesday through Sunday 10-4; closed major holidays. Admission $5, over-59 and student discounts.*

The B&O Railroad Museum was founded in 1953 to preserve the heritage of America's first major railroads. The focal point of the museum, which is located at the starting point of the B&O, is a historical roundhouse built in 1884. Outside the roundhouse are a number of historic steam and diesel engines from

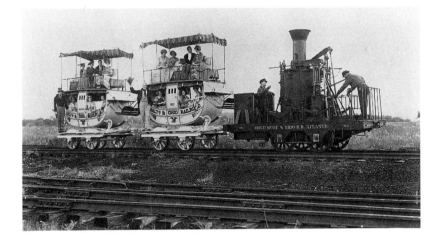

B&O steam locomotive Atlantic with replicas of Imlay coaches Maryland *and* Ohio. *This engine, the* Andrew Jackson, *a grasshopper type, was built by Phineas Davis at Mt. Clare in 1835. Photo courtesy of the B&O Railroad Museum, Baltimore, Maryland.*

This 10-wheel "Camel" passenger locomotive was designed by J. C. Davis and built at the Mt. Clare Shops in 1869. Photo courtesy of the B&O Railroad Museum, Baltimore, Maryland.

the heyday of railroading during the first half of the twentieth century. The historic buildings adjacent to the roundhouse contain a gift shop and several exhibits on the early history of the B&O.

The roundhouse exhibit contains the most extensive collection of antique locomotives in the country. The 22 pieces include restored originals and re-creations of such famous pioneering locomotives of the 1820s as New York-machinist Peter Cooper's *Tom Thumb*, Phineas Davis's *York* and *Atlantic*, and Horatio Allen's *South Carolina*. There are also a variety of steam locomotives built in the second half of the 1800s, such as the 4-4-0 *William Mason* (1856); the 4-6-0 *Thatcher Perkins* (1863); the 2-6-0 *J. C. Davis* (1875); and the powerful 2-8-0 *A. J. Cromwell*, a freight locomotive. (Railroads gave names to their mainline locomotives until around the turn of the century.)

There are several examples on display of non-traditional locomotives, one of which is a 1903 three-truck Shay. Designed by Ephraim Shay for hauling heavy loads in mountainous terrain, primarily in the timber and mining industries, it was capable of climbing grades as steep as 12 percent. The unusually small driving wheels were powered through a set of gears on an externally mounted crank shaft, which was rotated by a set of vertically mounted, steam-driven pistons. Because of this unique drive arrangement, the Shay was also referred to by the name "sidewinder."

Another non-traditional locomotive on display is an 1869 "camelback." Starting in 1848, the B&O was the first to use the powerful 0-8-0 locomotive designed by pioneering railroad-inventor Ross Winans. They were used principally by the B&O (but also by the Pennsylvania and the Erie Railroads, among others) until the early 1870s for the heavy-duty crossing of the Alleghenies. The camelback locomotive derived its name from its camel-like profile caused by placing the engineer's cab astraddle the mid-section of the boiler. This design was necessitated because of a large firebox, which left little room or weight allowance for the engineer's cab in its normal position.

Also in the roundhouse is the first diesel locomotive used in America, a 300-hp Alco-GE-Ingersoll Rand switcher built for the Central Railroad of New Jersey in 1925. Early electric locomotives are represented by a box-shaped 0-4-0 street railway switcher, built by General Electric in 1909, and a 220-volt battery-powered yard switcher, built by General Electric in 1917 for the Chesapeake & Ohio Railroad.

❖ *BALTMORE & OHIO RAILROAD STATION MUSEUM, 2711 Maryland Avenue, Ellicott City, Maryland 21043. Tel: 301-461-1944. Open Wednesday to Monday 11-5, Memorial Day to Labor Day; Friday to Monday 11-5, rest of year. Times may vary without notice; visitors are requested to telephone ahead. Admission $3, senior and under-13 discounts.*

The B&O Railroad Station Museum commemorates the first terminal of the B&O outside of Baltimore. Built of stone in 1831, it is the oldest existing railroad station in America. While it is no longer a functioning station, B&O freight trains continue to pass at regular intervals. The station and an adjoining freight shed, which was built in 1885, provide displays on the creation of the B&O. The museum also shows a film on the beginning of railroading in America titled *The Greatest Railroad Adventure*. A working model of the first 13 miles of the B&O is exhibited in the historic freight shed.

❖ *QUINCY HISTORICAL SOCIETY, 8 Adams Street, Quincy, Massachusetts 02169. Tel: 617-773-1144. Open Monday through Friday 9:30-3:30; Saturday 12:30-3:30. Admission by donation.*

Quincy Historical Society was organized in 1893 to collect and maintain records of the history of the region around Quincy. The society maintains records of the Granite Railway Company, the first railroad company organized to provide transportation facilities to the public.

In addition to the material at the Quincy Historical Society, there is a small privately run museum near the quarry. It is open only sporadically, so visitors should phone ahead to make arrangements (Tel: 617-786-9942). Remnants of the inclined plane used to bring granite out of the quarry can still be observed.

The first commercial railroad car designed by Gridley Bryant. Photo courtesy of the Quincy Historical Society, Quincy, Massachusetts.

❖ *HENRY FORD MUSEUM, 20900 Oakwood Boulevard, Dearborn, Michigan 48121. Tel: 313-271-1620. Open daily 9-5; closed major holidays. Admission $10.50, over-65 and under-13 discounts.*

In 1927 Henry Ford first proposed the idea of an "industrial museum" that would highlight the work ethic of America by displaying the nation's accomplishments in a wide range of industries. The museum opened to the public in 1933 in a 14-acre building with exhibits of products in such diverse fields as agriculture and photography. The transportation portion of the museum includes examples of Ford aircraft built in the 1920s, American locomotives and associated railroad cars, and one of the nation's outstanding collections of automobiles.

The museum's railroad exhibit traces the development of American railroading from the mid-1850s to the 1890s. The earliest locomotive in the collection is a Rogers 4-4-0 American class, built in 1858. The locomotive was originally called the *Satilla* when operated by the Atlantic & Gulf Railroad of Georgia. It was acquired by Henry Ford in 1924. He changed the name to the *President* when President Herbert Hoover dedicated the museum in 1929.

Ford also put together a collection of streetcars. The oldest is a horse-drawn car dating from 1881, which saw duty in Brooklyn, New York, for many years. An electric streetcar that operated in Philadelphia for many years is on exhibit. Built by the J. G. Brill company in 1892, it contains fine mahogany interior trim and features the "dead man" control, a well-publicized safety innovation at the time.

The museum operates an excursion train, called the Greenfield Village Railroad, on a 2.5-mile loop around the Greenfield Village, which is part of the Ford Museum complex.

❖ *LAKE SUPERIOR MUSEUM OF TRANSPORTATION, 506 West Michigan Street, Duluth, Minnesota 55802. Tel: 218-727-8025 or 0687. Open daily 10-5, May to mid-October; Monday to Saturday 10-5 and Sundays 1-5, rest of year. Admission $5, senior, student, and family discounts.*

The Lake Superior Museum of Transportation was founded in 1974 by a group of local rail fans in the Duluth area. It is located on the track-level floor of the historic Duluth railroad station, which now houses the St. Louis County Heritage and Art Center. The station, one of the finest examples of French Norman architecture in the country, was first opened in 1892. During its heyday it handled 50 trains each day from seven railroads. Passenger service to Duluth ceased in 1969.

The collection of locomotives at the museum includes seven steam, nine diesel, and two electrics. The largest is No. 227, a giant 2-8-8-4 Mallet-type Baldwin built in 1941 and one of the most powerful steam locomotives ever developed. It was used for many years by the Duluth, Missabe & Iron Range Railroad to haul iron ore from the mines to the loading docks. The engine is 120 feet long, weighs 566 tons, and was capable of pulling a train of 190 ore cars weighing 18,000 tons at speeds approaching 45 mph.

One of the oldest engines in the collection is the *William Crooks*. Built in 1861, it was operated by the St. Paul & Pacific (Great Northern) until the turn of the century and was the first locomotive operated in Minnesota. This 50-foot-long locomotive, weighing 28 tons, was used in both freight and passenger service. Attached to the *William Crooks* are several wooden passenger cars of the same vintage. Also on display is the Northern Pacific's first engine, the *Minnetonka*. Built in 1870 by Smith and Porter of Pittsburgh, the *Minnetonka* weighed 12 tons and was only 27.5-feet long.

The exhibit also includes a number of freight and passenger cars, plus a variety of service equipment. Among the latter are two snow plows, one of which dates from 1887; several steam wrecking cranes; and a self-propelled log loader that permitted flat cars to be rolled under it for loading.

The museum possesses several old-time trolley cars and provides a short excursion ride on a regular schedule. It also maintains an excellent library of material on regional railroading that is available to researchers by appointment.

❖ *NATIONAL MUSEUM OF TRANSPORT, 3015 Barrett Station Road, St. Louis, Missouri 63122. Tel: 314-965-7998. Open daily 9-5, closed major holidays. Admission $3, senior and under-12 discounts.*

The National Museum of Transport, operated by St. Louis County since 1979, was founded in 1944 for the purpose of preserving a mule-drawn streetcar. It has since grown to become one of the largest and most diverse transportation collections in the country. While the museum continues to be primarily a streetcar and railroad museum, it now also provides a comprehensive collection of carriages, cars, buses, trucks, and aircraft.

There are more than 70 locomotives, approximately half of which are steam, the oldest dating from 1858. One of the more unusual locomotives, a 4-4-0 camelback built in 1905, was displayed at the 1939 New York World's Fair. Also of interest to visitors are the *Burlington Zephyr*, the last of the shovel-nosed integrated trains introduced in the mid-1930s; the Union Pacific *Centennial* diesel No. 6944, the largest diesel ever built; and a Union Pacific Big Boy, the largest steam locomotive ever built.

❖ *NEVADA STATE RAILROAD MUSEUM, 2180 South Carson Street, Carson City, Nevada 89710. Tel: 702-687-6953. Open Wednesday to Sunday 8:30-4:30. Admission free. Check ahead for schedule and fares for train rides.*

The Nevada State Railroad Museum was established by the Nevada legislature when it created the Nevada Department of Museums and History in 1979. Originally called the Virginia & Truckee Railroad Museum, it opened to the public in 1980. Its original objective had been to preserve the heritage of the Virginia & Truckee (V&T), which had served the gold and silver mining community of Virginia City in the Comstock Lode region of Nevada from 1869 until 1939.

Most of the original collection was previously owned by the V&T, although the museum acquired the pieces from Hollywood movie studios that had been using them in Western pictures. Today, about half of the 50 pieces of rolling stock in the collection still have roots in the V&T.

The V&T was originally built as a standard gauge railroad to bring ore from the mines to the smelters along the Carson River near Carson City. Later a connection was made from Carson City to the main line of the Southern Pacific (formally Central Pacific) at Reno. Today all that remains of the V&T is the Nevada State Railroad Museum collection and an excursion railroad that operates on the old roadbed from Virginia City to Gold Hill, a short distance away.

The Nevada State Railroad Museum collection currently consists of four V&T standard-gauge steam locomotives (one of which is on display in Virginia City) and a number of standard-gauge passenger, freight, and service cars. Two of the restored V&T locomotives, both 4-4-0 American-types, were originally built in the 1870s, one in the Sacramento shops of the Central Pacific. There is also a modest collection of equipment that was used on early Nevada narrow-gauge railroads, including three locomotives (one on display in Sparks, Nevada) and several passenger and freight cars.

The museum operates steam excursion trips on the 4,000-foot track within the museum grounds during the summer months. On weekends the museum operates rides on the *Washoe Zephyr*, a self-propelled motorcar built by the Edwards Railway Motor Car Company in 1926.

❖ *NEVADA NORTHERN RAILWAY MUSEUM, 1100 Avenue A, East Ely, Nevada 89315. Tel: 702-289-2085. Open Monday to Saturday 9-5 and Sunday 1-5, mid-May through mid-October; closed major holidays. Admission $2, senior and student discounts. Check ahead for schedule and fare for train rides.*

The Nevada Northern Railway Museum was formed in 1983 by the Ely City Council to preserve the heritage of a historical Nevada railroad that operated for 75 years. The council administers the museum through a city-created non-profit foundation called the White Pine Historical Railroad Foundation, Inc.

The Nevada Northern Railroad was built by the Nevada Consolidated Copper Company (later the Kennecott Corporation) in 1905 to connect the rich copper-mining region around Ely to the main line of the Southern Pacific just east of Wells, Nevada, a distance of 140 miles to the north. The railroad ceased Pullman service in

1920 and all passenger service in 1938. It discontinued ore-hauling operations in 1978, when Kennecott closed the mines, although it continued to provide occasional freight service and excursions until 1983, when the railroad was finally disbanded.

When operations ceased, Kennecott offered the Ely facilities to the newly formed foundation. Along with the 30-building terminal complex, which included the depot, dispatcher's office, roundhouse, shops, and switching yard, Kennecott also donated a number of pieces of rolling stock and 32 miles of trackage. The museum's collection of equipment presently includes three steam, five diesel, and two electric locomotives; five passenger coaches; and more than 70 pieces of freight and maintenance-of-way

equipment. Guided tours of the facilities are offered from May to September.

Several pieces of rolling stock date from the turn of the century, the oldest being several 1886 wooden passenger cars. A 4-6-0 Baldwin, built in 1910, is currently in operation on the excursion railroad, along with several diesels used by Kennecott and built in the early 1950s.

The classic 4-6-0 Baldwin ten-wheeler, designated No. 40, pulls the *Ghost Train of Old Ely* from the depot through downtown Ely and up scenic Robinson Canyon on a 14-mile round-trip journey. A second excursion ride, pulled by an Alco diesel, makes a round trip of 22 miles to the overlook of the historic copper smelter at McGill. The mill was closed in 1978 after 70 years of operation.

❖ *SPENCER SHOPS STATE HISTORIC SITE, 411 South Salisbury Avenue, Spencer, North Carolina 28159. Tel: 704-636-2889. Open Monday though Saturday 9-5 and Sunday 1-5, April through October; Tuesday through Saturday 10-4 and Sunday 1-4, November through March. Trains operate daily from April 1 to early September, then weekends until mid-December. Museum admission free; charge for steam and diesel train tours when operating. Phone ahead for steam and diesel train schedules.*

Historic Spencer Shops were built by the Southern Railway in 1896 to service its fleet of steam locomotives at the midpoint of the railroad's main line between Washington, D.C., and Atlanta, Georgia. The shops continued in operation until 1960, when the facility was permanently shut down after the railroad had completely converted to diesel engines. At one time more than 2,500 people worked at the Spencer Shops.

The facility lay idle until 1979, when the Southern Railway deeded the 57-acre property to the state of North Carolina for a transportation museum. As state employees and volunteers searched for locomotives and rolling stock, others worked to renovate the 37-bay roundhouse, plus several other buildings, for use as a museum. After much effort to restore the facility, the museum was opened to the public in 1983. Plans still exist to renovate the 600-foot open-bay repair shop and several outbuildings on the 55-

acre site, as funds become available.

The Spencer Shop collection of rolling stock now consists of five locomotives, plus a number of passenger, freight, and maintenance-of-way cars. Excursion rides are offered during summer months on a three-mile loop track. The principal steam workhorse for the excursion trips is a Baldwin 2-8-0 (now designated as Southern 604). Built in 1926, it was previously owned by the Buffalo Creek & Gauley Railroad of West Virginia. Several Southern Railway diesels that were left deteriorating in the roundhouse have been restored. An unusual locomotive under restoration is a 1925 Lima three-truck Shay that had served on the Graham County Railroad in the mountains of western North Carolina. It is scheduled to go into operation late in 1992.

While the museum is primarily a railroad museum, it has acquired a modest, but carefully selected automobile collection (see reference in chapter on Automobiles).

Horseshoe Curve west of Altoona, Pennsylvania, enabled the Pennsylvania Railroad to climb over the Allegheny Mountains. Photo courtesy of the Pennsylvania Railroad, Philadelphia, Pennsylvania.

❖ *RAILROADERS MEMORIAL MUSEUM, Station Mall Complex, 1300 Ninth Avenue, Altoona, Pennsylvania 16602. Tel: 814-946-0834. Open Tuesday to Saturday 10-5 and Sunday 12:30-5; closed major holidays. Admission $2.50, over-62 and under-13 discounts.*

Founded in 1980, the Railroaders Memorial Museum contains displays on the development of railroading in Altoona and the region generally. Exhibits include a display about a famous circus-train wreck that occurred nearby in the late 1800s, a working model railroad of the region, and memorabilia from the age of steam.

The outdoor collection of rolling stock includes, among others, an early and rare diesel electric built by the Baldwin Locomotive Works in 1940; a 1942 Pennsylvania Railroad (PRR) streamlined GG-1 electric locomotive, No. 4913; and several Pullman sleepers.

Altoona was founded as a railroad town in 1849 by the PRR when it built its first railroad over the Alleghenies. Located at the eastern base of the mountains, Altoona was the site of the PRR's major shops for fabricating and repairing many of the railroad's locomotives and cars. Under Conrail, Altoona is still a major diesel-overhaul and car-repair center.

Five miles west of Altoona is located the famous Horseshoe Curve that the PRR built to gain elevation on its climb to the summit of the Alleghenies. In this open-loop curve, the track gains 122 feet of the total 1,015-foot climb required in 11 miles to reach the summit. In its time Horseshoe Curve was an engineering marvel, as it required extensive cuts and fills, all done with mules and scrapers. Originally double-tracked, the line west of Altoona through Horseshoe Curve has long since been expanded to four tracks and remains the busiest mountain segment of trackage in the nation.

The federal government has recently designated Horseshoe Curve as a National Historic Site and has funded construction of a visitor center at the base of the curve plus as a viewing platform at track level. The two are connected by an inclined railway, a reminder of the Allegheny Portage Railroad, built 160 years ago. The Horseshoe Curve facility opened in the spring of 1992 and is managed by the Railroaders Memorial Museum.

❖ *STEAMTOWN NATIONAL HISTORIC SITE, 150 South Washington Avenue, Scranton, Pennsylvania 18503. Tel: 717-961-2033. Open daily 9-6, June through October; daily 10-4:30, November through May. Admission free, excursion $7.50, under-13 discount. Check ahead for train schedule and fare changes.*

The collection of rolling stock now at the Steamtown National Historic Site was originally started in Vermont in the 1960s by F. Nelson Blount. In 1984 it was moved to an abandoned Conrail switching yard in Scranton. Before being taken over by Conrail, the site had been a major switching yard of the Delaware, Lackawanna & Western Railroad on its main line from Jersey City, New Jersey, to Buffalo, New York. The site was designated as a National Historic Site by Congress in 1986 and placed under jurisdiction of the National Park Service.

Steamtown's rolling stock consists of 29 steam locomotives and 60 rail cars of various types. The locomotives range in size from an 0-4-0T (includes tender) industrial engine built by H. K. Porter Company for the Bullard Machine Company in 1937, to a 4-8-8-4 Union Pacific Big Boy built by Alco in 1941. The oldest locomotive in the collection is a 2-8-0 built in 1903 by Alco for the Chicago Union Transfer Railway Company.

A visitor center, which will contain exhibits on American railroading, is currently under construction and is expected to open in 1994. Tours of the yard and roundhouse are offered regularly, as are rail excursions of various lengths, one of which is to the nearby historic Scranton Iron Furnaces.

❖ *RAILROAD MUSEUM OF PENNSYLVANIA, East on State Route 741, Strasburg, Pennsylvania 17579. Tel: 717-687-8628. Open daily Monday to Saturday 9-5 and Sunday noon-5, May though October; closed Monday and December 24-25, rest of year. Admission $5, over-64 and student discounts.*

The Railroad Museum of Pennsylvania was authorized by the commonwealth's legislature in 1963. The indoor-outdoor museum opened in 1975 and houses 70 pieces of rolling stock, including 33 locomotives. A display area offers exhibits of railroad memorabilia and descriptions of the state's railroad history. There is a six-minute video on the history of railroading in Pennsylvania and a movie put together by the Pennsylvania Railroad (PRR) in 1946 showing how the railroad operated in the immediate post-war period.

The main part of the collection is located in Rolling Stock Hall, a 150- by 320-foot building, with four tracks down the center containing 24 locomotives and passenger cars. There is a second-floor balcony to permit viewing of the overall collection and a "pit" below one locomotive to allow viewing of its underside. Steinman Station within the hall is a full-size reproduction of an authentic turn-of-the-century station complete with waiting room, ticket office, a working telegraph, and a baggage room that doubles as a mini-theater.

Most of the locomotives and rail cars have been acquired from the PRR, although other Pennsylvania railroads such as the Reading

A GG-1 electric locomotive pulling a Pennsylvania passenger train. Photo courtesy of the Pennsylvania Railroad, Philadelphia, Pennsylvania.

and Lehigh are also represented. The collection of 33 locomotives includes steam, electrics, and diesels, with several steam locomotives built at the Juniata works of the PRR, dating from 1888. The oldest rail car is a wooden combination baggage-passenger car built in 1855 for the Cumberland Valley Railroad.

The GG-1 electric locomotive No. 4935 on exhibit represents one of the 139 GG-1s that were built by Baldwin and in PRR shops from 1934 through 1943. Designed jointly by General Electric, the Baldwin Locomotive Works, and the PRR, it is considered one of the best-designed electric locomotives in the world. Its two trucks, hinged together in an articulated arrangement with three independently suspended axles on each, resulted in one of the smoothest riding locomotives ever built. The GG-1, with its distinctive streamlined look and "pinstriped" decoration created by the industrial designer, Raymond Loewy, was easily recognizable as it flashed by, pulling up to 20 passenger cars at more than 80 mph. Many of the GG-1s remained in service for more than 40 years. No. 4935 was built in 1943 at the PRR shops in Juniata, Pennsylvania.

❖ *THE GEORGE WESTINGHOUSE MUSEUM, Commerce Street, Wilmerding, Pennsylvania. Tel: 412-825-3009. Open Monday to Saturday 10-4; closed Sunday and holidays. Admission free, donations appreciated.*

The museum is located in the original headquarters building of the Westinghouse Air Brake Company, called the Castle, which is now owned and operated by the Education and Research Foundation of the American Production and Inventory Control Society.

The museum contains displays on the many contributions Westinghouse made to railroading, as well as to the industrial development of America in general. Among his contributions to railroading were the air brake, interlocking switches, friction draft gear, and improvements in automatic signaling. His industrial contributions included a system to transmit and use natural gas for lighting and heating, and the distribution and use of alternating-current electricity.

Various displays relate to a number of Westinghouse's 361 patents, including an explanation of how the air brake functions. Other exhibit areas cover his home and family life, his many awards, and examples of the many products he developed.

❖ *TENNESSEE VALLEY RAILROAD MUSEUM, 4119 Cromwell Road, Chattanooga, Tennessee 37421. Tel: 615-894-8028. Open daily May through August and weekends April and September through November; Monday to Saturday 10:30-4:30 and Sunday 12:30-4:30. Admission for train rides varies, so check ahead.*

The Tennessee Valley Railroad Museum was founded in 1961 by a group of Chattanooga rail fans determined to preserve southern railroad traditions. It has grown to become the largest operating historic railroad in the South.

The volunteer members of the museum devoted the first eight years to acquiring equipment for the museum. In 1969 the Southern Railway System donated four acres of land for the museum adjacent to an abandoned stretch of its original main line. After restoring a historic tunnel constructed in 1856, building a bridge across a major thoroughfare, constructing shops and a turntable, and erecting a turnaround wye, the museum railroad made its first run in 1981. The railroad now operates a six-mile round-trip excursion and, on weekends during the summer, a 15-mile round trip to the Chattanooga complex in downtown Chattanooga.

Chattanooga was an important rail center in the South. The first rail service was initiated there in 1849 by the state of Georgia's Western & Atlantic (later becoming part of the Louisville and Nashville and now part of CSX), which provided direct service to Atlanta. Other railroads followed that connected Chattanooga to major cities in Tennessee, Kentucky, Alabama, and Georgia. While passenger service in and out of Chattanooga ceased in 1971, during the heyday of passenger travel in the 1920s, approximately 75 trains stopped at Chattanooga each day.

The museum's collection of locomotives include seven steam, of which two are active, and six diesel, of which four are active. The oldest of these locomotives is No. 349, a 4-4-0 Baldwin built in 1891. The largest locomotive in the collection is ex-Southern Railway No. 4501, a 2-8-2 Baldwin built in 1911. It was purchased by Paul Merriman, one of the founders of the Chattanooga rail fan group, from the Kentucky & Tennessee Railroad in Stearns, Kentucky, for $5,000.

In addition to locomotives the museum possesses 22 freight cars of various kinds, most of which were owned by the Southern Railway, and approximately 60 passenger cars. Most of the passenger cars were built by the Pullman company and include coaches, sleepers, and diners, as well as office, parlor, baggage, and club cars.

❖ *AGE OF STEAM RAILROAD MUSEUM, Texas State Fairgrounds, Dallas, Texas 75226. Tel: 214-421-8754. Open Thursday and Friday 9-1, weekends 11-5, plus daily during state fair in October. Admission $2, student discount.*

The Age of Steam Museum was founded in 1963 by the Southwest Railroad Historical Society. The collection focuses primarily on steam and diesel locomotives and passenger and freight cars of Texas railroads. The oldest locomotive is a 2-10-0 Baldwin built in 1918, followed by a 0-6-0 Baldwin switcher built in 1923 and used by the Union Terminal in Dallas. There is a rare diesel-powered motorcar, called a "doodle bug," built by Brill in 1931 and used for many years by the Santa Fe.

The museum's collection of passenger cars is extensive and varied. It includes a complete train of cars built in the 1920s.

❖ *CENTER FOR TRANSPORTATION AND COMMERCE, 123 Rosenberg Street, Galveston, Texas 77550. Tel: 409-765-1839. Open daily 10-5; closed major holidays. Admission $4, senior and under-13 discounts.*

The Center for Transportation and Commerce was founded in 1982 in the old Galveston Union Station building previously occupied by the Santa Fe Railroad. Displays in the museum focus on the region's railroad history, which includes the five railroads that at one time or another served Galveston—the Santa Fe, Southern Pacific, Missouri Pacific, Burlington Northern, and Missouri Kansas & Texas.

The museum's collection of 46 pieces of rolling stock includes five steam locomotives and two diesels, plus a number of passenger, business, and freight cars. The locomotives include an 1892 Cooke 4-6-0 originally used by the Southern Pacific, a Lima Shay built in 1923, and a 1949 EMD diesel. Among the cars of interest is a self-propelled 1955 Budd diesel car (called an RDC) formally owned by the Southern Pacific; a redecorated superintendent's car owned by the Santa Fe; and a seven-car passenger consist, which includes a Railroad Post Office (RPO), the Budd car, and several Pullman cars. The museum operates a one-mile excursion ride within the museum grounds.

The joining of the Union Pacific and Central Pacific Railroads in 1867 at Promontory Point, Utah. Photo courtesy of Compton's Studio, Brigham City, Utah.

❖ *GOLDEN SPIKE NATIONAL HISTORIC SITE, 32 miles west of Brigham City, Utah 84302. Tel: 801-471-2209. Visitor Center open daily 8-6, late May to early September; daily 8-4:30 rest of year; closed major holidays. Locomotive viewing times variable, but generally 10:30-4. Admission $3 per car, $1 per bus passenger.*

Created in 1965 under the administration of the National Park Service, the historic site at Promontory Point in Utah commemorates the joining of the Central Pacific and Union Pacific railroads on May 10, 1869, to create the first transcontinental railroad. The facility includes a Visitor Center, 1.5 miles of track rebuilt on the original grade, and working replicas of the two vintage locomotives that met at the site—the Union Pacific 4-4-0, No. 119, and the Central Pacific 4-4-0, No. 60, called the *Jupiter.* (The original locomotives were scrapped in 1903 and 1905, respectively.)

Between May and September, the two engines are run out to the "Last Spike Site" each morning and returned in the evening. The original ceremony is reenacted every year on May 10. At the Visitor Center, park rangers, supported by movies and displays, explain the background of the joining of the two railroads and the significance of the completion of the transcontinental railroad.

Construction of the transcontinental railroad by the Central Pacific from Sacramento, California, and the Union Pacific from Omaha, Nebraska, started in 1863. While little track was laid until the end of the Civil War freed the needed labor and supplies, once underway the two railroads vied to see which could lay the most track in one day. The Central Pacific proceeded slowly until it conquered the Sierra Nevadas, but when reaching the plains of Nevada it competed on equal terms, with both railroads laying up to five miles of track per day. By the completion of the 1,776-mile transcontinental railroad, the Central Pacific had laid 690 miles of track, and the Union Pacific, 1,086 miles. Almost overnight, a journey that took six months by ox-drawn wagon was reduced to only six days.

❖ *VIRGINIA MUSEUM OF TRANSPORTATION, 303 Norfolk Avenue, Roanoke, Virginia 24016. Tel: 703-342-5670. Open daily Monday to Saturday 10-5, Sunday noon-5. Admission $3, senior and student discounts.*

The Virginia Museum of Transportation started in 1963 as a joint venture of the city of Roanoke and the Norfolk and Western Railway. In 1983 the Virginia General Assembly designated the museum as the official state transportation museum at which time its current name was adopted. Following a disastrous flood in November 1985, the museum, which contains vintage steam, diesel, and electric locomotives, as well as antique automobiles and carriages, was moved to its present site in the historic Roanoke freight station of the Norfolk and Western.

❖ *NATIONAL RAILWAY MUSEUM, 2285 South Broadway, Green Bay, Wisconsin 54304. Tel: 414-435-7245. Open daily 9-5, May through mid-October. Admission $5.50, senior and under-16 discounts.*

On its 32-acre site, the National Railway Museum contains approximately 20 locomotives and 50 other pieces of rolling stock dating from 1880. Founded in 1958 with only two locomotives, it has become one of the nation's larger railroad museums.

Green Bay's railroad heritage is based on its being located at the junction of three railroads—the Milwaukee Road; the Chicago & North Western; and the Green Bay & Western. The Green Bay & Western was established in 1870 to provide a rail link between the Great Lakes and the Mississippi River without having to pass through Chicago.

Included among the locomotives is a Union Pacific 4-8-8-4 Big Boy, and a recently restored Lima Shay. The oldest locomotive is a 1910 Alco 2-8-0, which was previously owned by the Lake Superior & Ishpeming Railroad on Michigan's Upper Peninsula. Another interesting display is Dwight D. Eisenhower's World War II staff car. The oldest piece of equipment is a Pullman car built by the originally-named Pullman Palace Car Company.

The collection also includes the General Motors-built Aerotrain, an experimental high-speed, lightweight, diesel-powered integrated train consisting of ten cars. General Motors sold the train to the Chicago, Rock Island & Pacific after demonstrating it around the country for two years. Excursion rides are provided on a one-mile track within the museum grounds.

Transit Systems Museums

❖ *ORANGE EMPIRE RAILROAD MUSEUM, 2201 South A Street, Perris, California 92370. Tel: 714-943-3020. Museum open daily 9-5, except major holidays. Rides 9-5 weekends and holidays. Museum admission free; rides $5.*

The Orange Empire Railroad Museum was founded in 1956 by a group of rail fans interested in preserving the electric-trolley era. The museum features more than 150 street railway cars and interurbans, plus several pieces of heavy-rail rolling stock on the 53-acre site. The collection includes a number of Pacific Electric red cars built in the 1920s. There are also other self-propelled cars and locomotives from a number of Los Angeles-area transit and interurban lines.

The museum operates two-mile round trip excursion rides on trains consisting of cars from the Union Pacific and Santa Fe pulled by a 1922 Baldwin Locomotive Company 2-6-2. Rides on interurbans and streetcars are also available. The former Los Angeles streetcars operate on a separate 3.5-foot-gauge loop.

❖ *SAN FRANCISCO CABLE CAR MUSEUM, 1201 Mason Street, San Francisco, California 94105. Tel: 415-474-1887. Open daily 10-6, except major holidays. Admission free, donations accepted.*

The museum houses one of the last operating street cable powerhouses in the world. Visitors can observe the complex machinery used to power the cable and view three vintage cable cars, the oldest of which, built in 1873, is believed to be the world's first.

The museum is operated by the Pacific Coast Chapter of the Railway and Locomotive Historical Society, the same organization that initiated the collection now residing at the California State Railroad Museum.

❖ *WESTERN RAILWAY MUSEUM, 5848 State Route 12, Suisun City, California 94585. Tel: 510-527-9440. Museum open weekends and Monday holidays 11-5. Museum admission $4, student discount.*

The Western Railway Museum was founded in 1960 by the Bay Area Electric Railroad Association. It has become one of the most important collections of electric streetcars in America. There are approximately 80 cars in the collection, including an 1886 New York City "El" car. Although streetcars from England and Australia are also featured, most of the trolleys were once used by Central California transit and interurban companies, including the San Francisco Municipal Railway, the Sacramento Northern, the Petaluma and Santa Rosa, and the Key System.

The collection also contains several heavy-rail locomotives and passenger cars, including Western Pacific diesel engines, Pullman lounge and observation cars, and a 1918 two-truck Shay formally owned by the Robert Dollar Company.

The Bay Area Electric Railroad Association operates various streetcars on a 1.5-mile loop on the 25-acre grounds of the museum. The association is noted for its

These streamlined Key System electric cars operated from San Francisco to the East Bay across the San Francisco Bay Bridge for many years, starting in 1939. The Western Railway Museum maintains three of these trains in running condition. Photo courtesy Western Railway Museum, Suisun City, California.

restoration activities, which can be observed by prior arrangement.

❖ *SHORE LINE TROLLEY MUSEUM, 17 River Street, East Haven, Connecticut 06512. Tel: 203-467-6927. Open daily 11-5, Memorial Day to Labor Day; Saturday and Sunday only in May, September, and October; Sunday only in April and November; closed December through March. Admission $4, senior and under-12 discounts. Admission includes museum and trolley rides.*

The museum was founded in 1945 by the Branford Electric Railway Association. It operates trolleys on the only remaining segment (three miles) of the historic Branford Electric

Railway. The nearly 100 trolleys and interurbans are mainly from extinct Connecticut and New York transit companies.

Among the interurbans and elevateds is the world's oldest surviving steam locomotive used on an elevated. It was built in 1878 and was used on the elevated Third Avenue Railway in New York. The Third Avenue "El" was electrified in 1895 and ceased operation in 1953.

The oldest electric interurban in the collection was built in 1893 and operated on the street railway of Providence, Rhode Island. From 1908 to 1947, when the street railway folded, it was used as a work car. Also of interest is an 1892 cable car used in New York City. It is one of 200 cable cars that were later converted to electric streetcars. Visitors can view the restoration shops and a light-sound show titled, "Birth of the Trolley Era."

❖ *CONNECTICUT TROLLEY MUSEUM, 58 North Road, East Windsor, Connecticut 06088. Tel: 800-252-2372 (USA) or 800-223-6540 (CT). Open daily 10-4, Memorial Day to Labor Day; weekends and holidays 12-5, rest of year; closed major holidays. Admission $4, senior and under-16 discounts.*

The Connecticut Trolley Museum was founded in 1940 by the Connecticut Electric Railway Association. The association considers itself the first incorporated railway museum in North America. Its collection now totals more than 60 trolleys, interurbans, rapid-transit cars, and electric freight equipment, plus several pieces of heavy-rail equipment. Passenger coaches in the collection date back to the late 1800s and include several original wooden coaches from the New Haven Railroad.

Excursion rides are offered on a three-mile segment of the Rockville branch of the Hartford & Springfield Street Railway, built in 1906. The museum expects to open its new indoor museum in late 1992, which will include exhibits on urban railway history, a library, an auditorium, and a gift shop.

❖ *SEASHORE TROLLEY MUSEUM, Log Cabin Road, Kennebunkport, Maine 04046. Tel: 207-967-2712. Open daily 10-5:30, May through mid-October; open early spring and late fall at reduced hours; telephone ahead for schedule. Admission $5.50, senior and student discounts.*

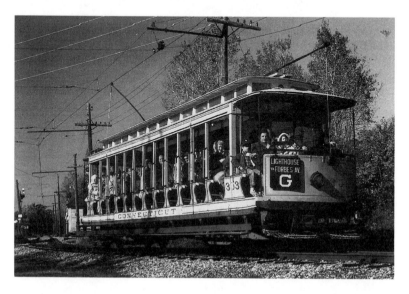

Connecticut Company Car 303 was built in 1901 by the J. G. Brill Company of Philadelphia and served the New Haven, Connecticut, area until 1947. Photo courtesy of the Seashore Trolley Museum, Kennebunkport, Maine.

The genesis of the Seashore Trolley Museum dates back to the mid-1930s. At that time a group of rail enthusiasts in New England, observing street railway and interurban systems being abandoned in increasing numbers, began to collect cars headed for the scrap heap. They found a piece of land near Kennebunkport on which they built a short stretch of track to enable them to operate their collection and named their newly born operation the Seashore Electric Railway.

By 1941 their efforts had developed sufficient permanence that they incorporated in Maine as the New England Electric Railway Historical Society, retaining the name Seashore Electric Railway for the operating property. Following World War II members of the society began acquiring dismantled railway equipment such as tracks, poles, overhead wires, and other paraphernalia from which they assembled an operating replica of a combined interurban and street-railway system.

Today, the museum complex has a collection that approaches 200 interurbans, streetcars, and maintenance-of-way equipment and has become one of the largest in the world, providing examples from throughout the United States and Canada, as well as Europe, Japan, and Australia. Equipment ranges from horse cars built in the 1880s to diesel buses and electric trackless trolleys from the 1950s. Among the cars of special interest are several trolley parlor cars, open-sided horse cars and trolleys, freight trollies, subway cars, snow-removal trolleys, and nearly one dozen PCC streamlined streetcars.

The society operates a number of its trolleys and interurban cars on a three-mile excursion ride along the main line of the former Atlantic Shore Line interurban. By special arrangement, visitors can view the extensive car-restoration work being performed continually by society members.

❖ *NEW YORK CITY TRANSIT MUSEUM, Boerum Place and Schermerhorn Street, Brooklyn, New York 11201. Tel: 718-330-3060. Open Monday to Friday 10-4 and Saturday 11-4; closed major holidays. Admission $1, student discount.*

Founded in 1976 by the New York Transit Authority, the museum contains 18 restored subway and elevated cars dating back to 1903. The collection was originally assembled as a temporary exhibit in celebration of the nation's bicentennial anniversary, but it proved to be sufficiently popular that the transit authority has retained it as a permanent showcase for the city's transit system. The story is told that when transit authorities went looking for antique cars for the exhibit, they found that obsolete cars had been hidden away by subway personnel in abandoned tunnels of the 714-mile system for just such an occasion.

Exhibits also include antique turnstiles, fare boxes, a working signal tower, a display showing the evolution of subway maps, and models of early New York streetcars. On the mezzanine floor is a display on the first contract issued by the city in 1904 that started construction of the complex system.

The New York Transit Museum is located on two levels of the former Court Street subway station in Brooklyn Heights. Built in 1936, the station of the Independent City Owned Rapid Transit Railroad (known as the IND) was one end of a short shuttle line between Hoyt and Schermerhorn streets that operated from 1936 to 1946.

FIRST AUTO RACE by Roger White, oil, 29 x 42 inches, courtesy of the Smithsonian Institution.

Automobiles

The automobile is such an integral part of our daily lives that it is hard to believe that well within the twentieth century the nation was still relying on the horse and buggy for transportation. Even as late as World War I, which has been called "the last of the horse wars," a major portion of the American population still relied on the horse to meet its transportation needs. By then steam-powered boats had been plying the rivers, lakes, and coastal shores for almost a century, and steam locomotives were already busily puffing along 255,000 miles of railroad track.

The automobile, like the railroad, was of European origin. Unlike the railroad, however, automobile development had its genesis in Germany and France rather than England. In fact, Great Britain had laws against the use of the automobile until 1896, several years after France had developed a viable auto industry.

Two Germans, Gottlieb Daimler (1844-1929) and Karl Benz (1834-1900), were the leaders in the development of the automobile gasoline engine. In 1886 each of these inventors independently built a successful gasoline-engine-driven car. Each founded successful automobile manufacturing companies. Ironically, these two pioneers apparently never met, although their two companies ultimately merged in 1926, long after Karl Benz had died, but within the lifetime of Gottlieb Daimler.

In spite of the innovations made in Germany, France is often referred to as the mother of the automobile industry. Germany, unlike France, lacked a viable road network in those pioneering days. Consequently, most of the autos produced by Daimler and Benz were exported to France. By 1895 there were 350 autos in France while only 75 were in Germany.

In Europe point-to-point automobile races became very popular in the 1890s as manufacturers vied with each other to excel in speed and endurance. The first recognized point-to-point race took place between Paris and Rouen, France, in July 1894. It was followed by a Paris-Bordeaux-Paris race the next year. The Auto Club of France sponsored 34 intercity races over the next eight years, culminating with a Paris to Madrid race in 1903.

By then, races on public roads had become very dangerous as speeds had increased dramatically. Hundreds of cars entered these popular races, and spectators along the roadways numbered in the millions. The Paris-Madrid race was cancelled after the first leg to Bordeaux, because of the number of accidents and fatalities among both racers and spectators. From then on speed races were run on closed-off streets or private tracks.

The first closed-street speed race involving a trophy occurred in Paris in 1900. It was sponsored by Gordon Bennett, owner of the *New York Herald Tribune*. The Paris race was replaced in 1906 by the Grand Prix de France at Le Mans. Intercity road races were replaced by rallies, beginning with the 1907 rally from Peking to Paris via Siberia, which took two months to complete.

American Racing

Starting at the turn of the century, speed racing in America developed at Ormand Beach and Daytona Beach in Florida. Ormand Beach, adjacent to and north of Daytona Beach, is considered the birthplace of American auto racing. It was here that such car-making pioneers as Alexander Winton, R.E. Olds, and the Duryea brothers competed with foreign car makers to establish the first American land-speed records. Barney Oldfield, a leading bicycle racer before turning to racing cars, broke several speed records at Ormand Beach. Daytona Beach soon became the most popular straightaway race track in the country, however, and continues to be the scene of major auto races.

The Indianapolis Motor Speedway in Indianapolis, Indiana, was constructed in 1908 in the form of a two-and-one-half-mile oval. The "Indy 500" quickly became known throughout the world as the most important race of the year. It was first held in 1911 and has been run every year since except for two years during the First World War and from 1941 to 1945 during the Second World War. It has become the oldest continuous auto speed contest in the world. The Indianapolis and Daytona Speedways have been major proving grounds for automobile advancements in speed and durability during essentially all of the life of the American car industry.

Steam-Powered Vehicles

In the early years of automobile development, speed was mainly a function of engine power, which, in turn, was limited by engine technology. In the late 1800s and early 1900s, steam technology was the most advanced and, therefore, was the first to be installed in an automobile.

The first successful steam-driven vehicle was a three-wheeler built by a Frenchman, Nicolas Joseph Cugnot, in 1765. It weighed 4 tons and could attain a speed of 6 miles per hour (mph). The vehicle proved impractical, however, because the boiler-engine combination rested on the single front wheel, making it very difficult to steer. In 1802 an Englishman, Richard Trevithick, built a successful steam-operated passenger vehicle capable of speeds up to 9 mph. Both Cugnot and Trevithick were also pioneers in developing steam-powered railroad locomotives in Europe.

The first recorded attempt in the United States to develop a steam-driven vehicle was undertaken by Oliver Evans, who also pioneered steam railroad locomotion in the United States around 1800. In 1787 he was awarded the first patent on a steam-driven vehicle. But by 1804 he had only succeeded in mounting a steam-powered barge on a wagon and connecting the drive shaft of the barge to the wheel shaft of a wagon. This strange vehicle caused considerable consternation when Evans drove it through the streets of Philadelphia.

The Cugnot steam tractor was one of the first mechanized vehicles. It was the French forerunner of the horseless carriage. Photo courtesy of the Smithsonian Institution, Washington, D.C.

By 1821 the steam engine was well-developed, and in 1825 an Englishman named Sir Goldsworthy Gurney initiated the first regular steam-carriage service. The service ran between London and Bath, a distance of 171 miles. The carriage was capable of carrying 18 passengers (6 inside and 12 outside) at an average speed of about 8 mph. Thus a trip that today takes approximately three hours on the motorway, then took two or perhaps three days in Mr. Gurney's carriage.

During the next 50 years, a number of steam-carriage services were initiated in both England and France. By 1873 speeds of 22 mph were being attained regularly, and by the early 1880s steam-carriage speeds were approaching 40 mph. Steam-vehicle technology reached its peak in 1894, when a French vehicle built by De Dion-Bouton won the Paris-Rouen city-to-city race (mentioned earlier). While steam power was reliable, the engine was excessively heavy and required frequent stops for refueling.

The first successful American steam-driven car was introduced by Sylvester Roper of Roxbury, Massachusetts, in 1863, the year that Henry Ford was born. Roper made only ten of his vehicles during the 1870s and 1880s. They were viewed as curiosities and were mainly

F. E. and F. O. Stanley, the Stanley twins, in their first Stanley steam-engine car, designed about 1897. Photo courtesy of the Smithsonian Institution, Washington, D.C.

exhibited at county fairs. Roper also attempted to produce a steam-driven motorcycle but was unsuccessful.

The first popular American steam-powered car was introduced in 1897 by two brothers, Francis E. and Freelan O. Stanley of Newton, Massachusetts. By 1906 a Stanley steamer had set a world speed record of 127.66 mph at Ormand Beach, Florida. The following year the same race driver, Fred Marriott, reached a speed of 197 mph but lost control of the car and was critically injured in the resulting crash. The attending press made much of the fact that the Stanley racing car's boiler, which was operating at a pressure of 1,300 pounds per square inch (psi), did not explode. The Stanleys gave up racing following the accident but continued making steamers until 1929.

The Stanleys' chief competitor during the first decade of the 1900s was the White Sewing Machine Company of Cleveland, which began producing a steam-powered car in 1900. White's principal advertising theme was that its car could "steam up" faster than a Stanley. "Gives steam in five minutes," was the company's motto. White shifted over to making internal-combustion-driven automobiles in 1910. Another competitor appeared in 1912, when Abner Doble introduced a large automobile capable of vibrationless riding up to 85 mph. Doble continued making steamers until 1930.

Electric-Powered Vehicles

Development of electricity as the most popular source of automotive power took the lead for a brief time around the turn of the century. The electric motor made a simple engine, the electric battery had been developed, and it was a clean source of power. Other advantages of the electric auto included efficiency, speed, quietness, lack of vibration, and ease of maintenance. Its disadvantages, however, were its limited range and the weight of the necessary batteries. During the three decades starting in the 1880s, inventors worked feverishly to make longer-lasting and lighter batteries, but without success. The advantages and disadvantages of electric-powered vehicles and the need for lighter-weight batteries are as applicable today as they were in the late 1800s.

The first successful electric power-driven auto was built in France in 1893. It produced 3.5 horsepower (hp) at 1,300 revolutions per minute (rpm), using two batteries weighing a total of 925 pounds, and was able to maintain a speed of approximately 12 mph. By 1897 speeds had reached 45 mph, and by 1899 speeds of 65 mph were being attained.

During the heyday of the battery-powered car, the range between battery charges continued to be less than 60 miles. While this limitation made long-distance travel impractical, it was sufficient to permit use of the electric car in major cities. In 1897 the city of New York purchased and operated a number of electric taxis made by the Electric Carriage and Wagon Company of Philadelphia.

Thomas Edison getting into his Model 43 Detroit Electric car. Photo courtesy of the Smithsonian Institution, Washington, D.C.

and several of the original experiments used gunpowder as the spark to ignite a mixture of marsh gas and air inside the engine cylinder—hence the term "internal combustion." In 1777 an Italian named Alessandro Volta replaced gunpowder with an electric spark. Michael Faraday extracted benzene from coal in 1825, thereby producing the first liquid fuel. Other developments came slowly until the development of the four-stroke engine by Frenchman Alphonse Beau de Rochas in 1862. In 1876 Nikolaus Otto, using the de Rochas principle, introduced a commercially successful stationary engine that produced 8 hp.

It took another nine years, however, before Benz and Daimler in Germany were able to commercialize a vehicle powered by an engine using the Otto principle. Benz's engine produced 0.9 hp at 400 rpm while Daimler's produced 1.5 hp at 700 rpm. The Daimler engine was produced for a number of years in the United States by Steinway & Sons, the American piano manufacturer.

In the same year that Otto introduced his engine in Europe, an American inventor,

One-third of the new car models introduced in 1900 were electrics. The leading producer was Columbia Electric, founded by bicycle-maker Albert A. Pope. Electrics remained popular, particularly with women, even after the self-starter was introduced on gasoline-powered cars in 1912. The Anderson Electric Car Company of Detroit continued to make their famous "Detroit Electrics" until 1942. Because of gas rationing during World War II, tiller-steered electrics dating from the first decade of the 1900s could be found on America's city streets.

A few years after the turn of the century, Studebaker started producing electric vehicles, but it shifted to the internal-combustion engine around 1910. By 1912 there were 20,000 electric vehicles operating in the United States—more than the rest of the world combined. However, interest in electrical automotive power waned soon thereafter when the internal-combustion engine took over as the most popular form of vehicle power.

The Internal-Combustion Engine

The internal-combustion engine is based on the principle of the power of an explosion,

An authentic replica of the world's first successful operable automobile, an 1885 Benz. Photo courtesy of the Owls Head Transportation Museum, Rockland, Maine.

The 1895 Duryea automobile which J. Frank Duryea drove to victory in the Chicago Thanksgiving race. Frank Duryea's brother, Charles, is shown here driving the car. Photo courtesy of the Smithsonian Institution, Washington, D.C.

George Brayton, developed an engine based on the de Rochas principle. The following year, 1877, George Baldwin Seldon took out a patent on a vehicle using the Brayton engine. While Seldon never actually produced a commercial vehicle, he forced other manufacturers to pay him royalties on his patent for a number of years. Henry Ford contested the patent in 1902, but it wasn't until 1911 that the courts finally declared Seldon's claim invalid and the American automobile industry was free to proceed on its own.

The first successful automobile powered by an internal-combustion engine in the United States is credited to two bicycle makers in Springfield, Massachusetts, Charles and Frank Duryea, who demonstrated their vehicle in 1893. The following year, Elwood P. Haynes, a metallurgist in Kokomo, Indiana, became the second. Ransom Eli Olds, who formed the Olds Motor Vehicle Company in Detroit in 1892, built his first experimental model in 1895, and offered his first vehicle for sale in 1897. Henry Ford test drove his first vehicle, which he called a quadricycle, in 1896. By then, the Duryea brothers were already offering internal-combustion-powered automobiles for sale. By 1900 Olds was selling his cars at a rate of 1,400 per year.

Another pioneer was Henry Leland, founder of the Cadillac Automobile Company, who brought out his first Cadillac in late 1902. Ford produced his first Model A in 1903, and David Buick, who like R. E. Olds had been a builder of marine engines, produced his first car in 1904.

Of this group of pioneers, Henry Leland is perhaps the least known. Leland learned precision manufacturing at a U.S. Army arsenal before joining Henry Ford at his first enterprise, the Henry Ford Company. When Henry Ford left to start the Ford Motor Company in 1902, Leland took over the company and renamed it the Cadillac Automobile Company. In 1909 Leland sold Cadillac to General Motors and then created the Lincoln Motor Company, which he sold to Ford in 1922. Leland-built cars were always superbly made and his peers referred to him as "The Master of Precision." Unfortunately for him, he proved to be a better car builder than businessman.

Automobile Matches America's Needs

While Europeans had immediately fallen in love with the automobile mainly for their love of racing, Americans took it seriously from the beginning as a means of transportation. Americans, who had greater distances to travel than Europeans, needed faster means of travel than that provided by the horse and buggy. At the turn of the century, the railroads of the country were well-developed, but the nation was demanding better off-rail transportation than could be provided by horse-drawn wagons and carriages. The rural population was becoming isolated from the increasingly urbanized commercial centers of the country.

A 1904 Cadillac touring car with rear entrance. This model, with its 10-hp, single-cylinder engine, continued to be built by Henry Leland until 1909, when he sold the company to William Durant. Leland established Cadillac's reputation for precision-built cars. Photo courtesy of Car & Carriage Caravan, Luray Caverns, Virginia.

Europe maintained the lead in racing-car technology during the first two decades of the twentieth century, but Americans immediately recognized the importance of reliability. Early cars were constantly breaking down. Among car manufacturers, Alexander Winton of Cleveland was one of the first to recognize the need to build reliable cars. He had been a bicycle manufacturer until he shifted to making automobiles in 1897. Two years later, to advertise the reliable performance of his cars, he drove from Cleveland to New York in 47 hours, and received accolades from cheering throngs as he drove down Broadway.

The first motor vehicle to be driven from coast-to-coast was a 20-hp, 2-cylinder Winton. In 1903 a young Vermont doctor by the name of Nelson Jackson, accompanied by a mechanic, undertook the trip from San Francisco to New York on a bet that he could do it in less that 90 days. Although forced to follow a circuitous route into the Northwest, frequently negotiating deep ruts on old wagon roads, and periodically suffering mechanical breakdowns, Jackson and his mechanic completed the trip in only 63 days.

Commercial Vehicle Development

Commercial use of the motorized vehicle expanded rapidly. In 1901 the world's first trucking service was initiated in New York, and an American residing in Connecticut by the name of John Collins had developed the world's first mechanical street sweeper. Motorized sightseeing buses were on the streets of New York City by 1904. Bus service appeared on Fifth Avenue in 1905. Power steering was introduced on trucks and buses soon thereafter.

In 1903 the newly formed Automobile Club of America sponsored the world's first truck-performance contest. Competition was in two classes, delivery wagons and heavy trucks; the latter competition was won by a steam-powered truck. Two years later, the first American motor truck show was held in Chicago, Illinois, which received considerable interest by Europeans as well as Americans.

Articulated trucks (now called semis), built by Knox in Springfield, Massachusetts, came into use in 1909. Many of the gasoline-powered trucks made use of a cab-over-engine design; the tilt-cab feature was developed by a Hartford, Connecticut, manufacturer in 1912. By 1914 Ford had built the first true truck-assembly line in Dearborn, Michigan.

Automobile Mass Production

Soon after the turn of the century, automobile production grew rapidly. In 1899 there were 30 manufacturers in America and they produced a total of 2,500 cars. By 1905 there were a total of 77,000 cars in the United States, and by 1910 the number had grown to 181,000. During the first decade of the century, 485 manufacturers entered the market, many of which dropped out or were acquired within a year or so. Annual automobile production climbed to 187,000 in 1910 and to 485,000 in 1913. By then, America dominated the world market, as the rest of the world produced only 121,000 cars in 1913.

The development of mass-production techniques was started by R.E. Olds in 1902, and accelerated by Ford later in the decade. Olds's factory-style production concept outmoded the costly custom-shop approach developed in Europe and followed in America at the time. It enabled Olds to build 2,500 cars in 1902 and increase production to 6,500 in 1905. Using these techniques, Ford produced 25,000 Model Ns in 1907, while Daimler in Germany, still using hand-crafted techniques, was able to produce only 1,000 Mercedes.

The use of continuous production gave America dominance in the industry, but it also made the industry more capital-intensive, thereby raising the price of entry into the industry. The number of American producers dropped from a high of 253 in 1908 to 44 in 1929. The subsequent Depression reduced the total even further during the 1930s. Besides Ford, General Motors, and Chrysler, only Nash, Hudson, Studebaker, and Packard, among the more well-known manufacturers, were able to hang on through the Depression. They,

too, faltered during the early post-World War II period.

As automobile production expanded, progress was being made in automobile technology. During the 1920s the drive shaft replaced the chain drive; pneumatic tires replaced solid ones; and open touring cars were being replaced by closed sedans. The 1920s brought the self-starter, all-steel bodies, the high-compression engine, and hydraulic brakes, and the synchro-mesh transmission was introduced. The automatic transmission came into being in the 1930s.

While over 2,000 automobile manufacturers came into existence at one time or another in the United States, by the 1960s the American automobile industry had essentially boiled down to the Big Three—Ford, General Motors, and Chrysler—plus several specialized car-makers.

Henry Ford

Henry Ford was born of Irish parents in 1863 on a farm near Dearborn, Michigan. By the time he entered his teens, Ford had already committed his life to things mechanical. He left

A 1926 Model T Ford Runabout. Photo courtesy of the Smithsonian Institution, Washington, D.C.

157

the farm at the age of fifteen and went to work as a machinist in Detroit. In 1887, at the age of twenty-five, he became chief engineer for the Detroit Edison Illuminating Company.

Through articles in technical magazines, Ford became fascinated with Nikolaus Otto's gasoline engine. In his spare time Ford built a shop at the back of his Detroit home where he started to experiment with his own gasoline-engine design. By 1893 he had perfected an engine based on the Otto principle, and by 1896 had installed it in his first car, which Ford called a Quadricycle. Soon thereafter, Ford left Detroit Edison to devote full time to the development of the automobile.

Henry Ford founded the Ford Motor Company in 1903 and produced his first car, the Model A, that same year. When he started the company, Ford's total assets consisted of his home, a large number of patents, and $28,000 of capital that had been contributed by 12 friends and business acquaintances. The Model A was powered by a two-cylinder, 8-hp engine connected to the rear wheels through a two-speed gearbox and a chain drive. Within a little more than one year his company built 1,700 Model As. The Model A was followed in quick succession by seven other alphabetic series models—B, C, F, K, N, R, and S—before the introduction of the Model T in 1908.

Ford started his famous mass production line with the Model T in 1908. The Model T was introduced as a simple, reliable car at a price of $850. All during its 19-year life, Henry Ford worked to reduce the cost of production. He was so successful that by 1925, he had been able to reduce the price of the least-expensive model to only $260. In 1909 Ford produced 12,000 Model Ts, in 1913 he produced 183,000, and by 1923 production had grown to two million Model Ts annually. When the last Model T rolled off the assembly line in May, 1927, Ford had built 15,007,033.

In 1925 Ford had gained 55 percent of the total U.S. automobile market. Within two years, however, American car buyers wanted more than a black Model T and his share of the market dropped substantially. The Chevrolet Division of General Motors surpassed Ford in sales for the first time in 1927 and did so again in 1928. Ford started production of the second Model A late in 1927 and within the next four years regained part of its lost market share. By the time the Model A was phased out in 1931, Ford had produced five million of them. Not to be caught short again, Ford brought out the V-8 engine in 1932, long before General Motors (1954) and other competitors shifted over to the V-8 design.

Ford started making trucks and tractors in 1917, and acquired the Lincoln Motor Company in 1922. In 1926 the company diversified into aircraft production, building the famous Ford Trimotor, which became known as the Tin Goose. While Ford withdrew from the aircraft industry in 1933, during World War II Ford produced 8,600 B-24s and 57,000 aircraft engines.

In addition to pioneering the automobile assembly-line, Ford also pioneered the concept of the multinational company. He formed a British subsidiary to produce Model Ts in England as early as 1911 and created a German subsidiary in 1926. Other automobile manufacturers in Europe, slow to adopt Ford's innovative production concepts, did not do so until the late 1920s. By then, Ford had become well-established in Europe.

Starting in the late 1930s and continuing after World War II, Ford introduced a number of automobile innovations. The company introduced the Mercury line of mid-range family cars in 1939, and in 1940 introduced the elegant Lincoln Continental convertible. In 1954 Ford offered its first sports car, the 193-hp Thunderbird, followed a decade later by the very popular Mustang. Ford's most successful car, the Fairlane 500, was introduced in 1958, and its popular compact, the Falcon, came out in 1960. The Pinto sub-compact was first produced in 1970.

A 1914 Chevrolet convertible coupé with gas tank on rear luggage rack. Photo courtesy of the Smithsonian Institution, Washington, D.C.

General Motors

William C. Durant, a major carriage builder, acquired the Olds Motor Vehicle Company in 1903. Five years later Durant created General Motors when he acquired the Cadillac Automobile Company and the Oakland Motor Company (which later became the Pontiac Division of General Motors). Durant was forced out of General Motors in 1910 and joined the Chevrolet Motor Company, which had just been started by Louis Chevrolet, a Swiss-born racing driver.

At about this same time, General Motors founded the General Motors Truck Company through a merger of Reliance Motor Company and the Rapid Motor Vehicle Company. Rapid Motor is considered America's first truck manufacturer. In 1925, the General Motors Truck company acquired the Yellow Cab Manufacturing Company.

Durant again took over leadership of General Motors through a stock manipulation when it acquired Chevrolet in 1915. He was ousted a second time, however, when the company ran into financial problems in 1920. At that point Durant was replaced by Alfred P.

Sloan Jr., whom Durant had brought in to General Motors to form an accessories subsidiary. Sloan served as president of General Motors from 1923 to 1936, its period of greatest development. During Sloan's tenure General Motors acquired the Fisher Enclosed Body Company, which had been providing car bodies since its creation by coach-builder, Lawrence P. Fisher.

In the late 1920s Sloan developed the policy of planned obsolescence by introducing new models each year. Also, while Ford was ending production of the Model T and shifting to the Model A, Sloan was dropping the practice of manufacturing a single model with variations. He started the practice of producing multiple models in different price ranges. By the late 1930s, General Motors had acquired 50 percent of the American automobile market. During this period each of the individual divisions of the company operated independently within its own market.

While General Motors was built on its prowess in manufacturing and marketing, it does have a number of technical accomplishments to its credit. It developed the synchronized gearbox in 1928, independent wheel suspension in 1933, a two-stroke diesel engine for trucks, buses, and railroad engines in 1934, and the automatic gearshift in 1939. The automatic gearshift developed into the Hydromatic, Dynaflow, and Powerglide transmission systems of the 1950s. During World War II the company produced everything from airplanes (13,000) to machine guns (1.9 million) to trucks (854,000). Its conversion to war work was total, and following the war, the company was slow in returning to automobile manufacturing.

In 1951 General Motors built an experimental XP Sabre racing vehicle with a completely new engine and suspension system. This development subsequently became the very popular Corvette sports car which was introduced by Chevrolet in 1953. The Corvette was the first car in America to have a fiberglass body. In the 1970s Chevrolet introduced the Impala line, which became one of its most popular cars.

All four General Motors divisions continued to innovate with new styles and features during the 1960s and 1970s. By the 1980s, however, the energy crisis and Japanese competition had begun to affect General Motors' ability to retain its position in the market. Nevertheless, all four divisions remain to this day as viable automobile manufacturers, much as they were when established by Alfred P. Sloan Jr., in the 1920s.

American Motors

American Motors was started by Thomas B. Jeffrey, previously a manufacturer of bicycles, as the Thomas B. Jeffrey Company in 1902. Until 1914 he sold his cars under the Rambler marque, at which time he switched to the Jeffrey marque. Jeffrey specialized in four-wheel-drive vehicles and attained fame with his reliable army trucks during World War I. Charles W. Nash, a former executive of General Motors, bought the Jeffrey company in 1916 and changed its name to the Nash Motor Company.

In 1937 Nash again changed the name of the company to the Corporation of American Motors when he bought the Kelvinator Company. In 1954, when Nash bought the Hudson Motor Company that had been founded 1909, he changed the name of his company a third time, this time to American Motors Corporation. The company resurrected the Rambler marque in 1950 when it introduced America's first convertible compact.

Keeping with the company's tradition as specialists in four-wheel drive, in 1970 Nash purchased Wyllis-Overland, developers of the famed World War II four-wheel-drive Jeep. In 1979 Renault of France acquired a 46.6 percent interest in American Motors Corporation and the company now builds both French- and American-designed cars in its American factories.

Chrysler

Chrysler was formed in 1925 when Walter P. Chrysler took over the Maxwell Motor Company and renamed it the Chrysler Corporation. Walter Chrysler started out with Buick in 1911 and rose to become a vice president of General Motors until his departure in 1920 to become head of Wyllis-Overland. After saving Wyllis-Overland from bankruptcy, he moved over to Maxwell to accomplish the same feat. In 1928 he brought out the Plymouth and De Soto lines of cars and acquired the Dodge brothers' company.

Chrysler's most distinctive cars were the Airflows which incorporated a streamlined design of the hood. They appeared in both the Chrysler and De Soto lines during the 1930s. The Airflow was the first car to incorporate an automatic overdrive, now standard in many modern cars in this age of gas-mileage improvement. It also introduced such innovations as rubber mountings for the engine to give a smoother ride and the concept of streamlining. For all of its advantages, the Airflow did not become popular. The public considered it ugly, a fatal flaw in an era of cars with classic beauty.

The De Soto line was dropped after World War II, but in the post-war period Chrysler continued to introduce innovative models in its other three lines.

The Studebaker Story

The Studebaker Corporation was started as a blacksmith shop in South Bend, Indiana, by Henry and Clem Studebaker in 1852. Joined by three other brothers, they built the company into the largest wagon manufacturer in the world. They developed one of the first American international companies and sold wagons in almost every country in the world.

In spite of its heavy commitment to wagon production, Studebaker was one of the first wagon makers to shift over to making automobiles. At the suggestion of Thomas Edison, the company produced its first car, an electric, in 1902. Recognizing the future was in gasoline-engine-powered automobiles, Studebaker shifted over two years later. By 1913 Studebaker was the third largest automobile manufacturer in America, behind Ford and General Motors.

As a result of the Great Depression, the company went into receivership in 1933, but it was one of the few companies to work its way back to health. Harold Vance and Paul Hoffman took over leadership of the company in 1935 and brought in the famous industrial designer, Raymond Loewy, to design the company's cars. This started a 20-year relationship that resulted in some of the automotive industry's most imaginative and style-setting designs.

In 1946 Studebaker became the first American car maker to come out with a post-World War II design, thanks to Raymond Loewy and Studebaker engineers. The bullet-nosed styling of the 1950-51 models brought temporary renewed success to the company, but it began to encounter severe price competition from the Big Three auto-makers.

A merger with the Packard Motor Car Company was arranged in 1954, but it failed to help the situation. In 1955 a new management team was brought in, and they decided not to renew Loewy's contract. As a result the company lost its styling edge and conditions worsened. Loewy was brought back in 1961 with the hope he could design a new winner for the company. Unfortunately it was too late, even though he did help bring an outstanding car onto the market, the Avanti. The end of Studebaker in South Bend came in December 1963, when the company suddenly announced that it was shutting its doors. Studebaker Canada continued to produce cars until March 1966.

The 1963 Avanti designed by Raymond Loewy, shown on the left, with Sherwood Egbert, president of the Studebaker Corporation. Photo courtesy of the Studebaker National Museum Archives, South Bend, Indiana.

Automobile Museums

❖ *MUSEUM OF AUTOMOBILES, Petit Jean Mountain, Morrilton, Arkansas 72110. Tel: 501-727-5427. Open daily 10-5, closed Christmas. Admission $4, student discount.*

The museum was built by Winthrop Rockefeller in 1964, before he became governor, to house his personal collection of antique and classic automobiles. Following his death in 1975, most of the collection was sold to Harrahs Automobile Museum in Reno, Nevada. In 1976 a group of Arkansas automobile collectors and enthusiasts formed a non-profit tax-exempt foundation to reopen the museum with cars on loan from collectors around the country. The museum currently displays approximately 50 cars at any one time.

Rockefeller's personal 1951 and 1967 Fleetwood Cadillacs are part of the museum's permanent collection. Also retained from the original collection is a unique 1914 Cretor popcorn wagon. Cretor, located in Chicago, has for many years built mobile popcorn machines that are mounted on various vehicle bodies, including pushcarts.

Another unique car in the collection is a 1923 Arkansas-built, 6-cylinder Climber. Climber was a Little Rock, Arkansas, automaker from 1919 to 1923 that built cars specifically for the southern market. They were designed to withstand the rigors encountered on poorly constructed southern roads and had an unusually high wheel base. Climber built a total of 275 automobiles.

The oldest car on display is a 1904 Olds with a rare so-called French Front. This design gives the car the look of a standard car rather than the carriage look of the more common Curved-Dash model built by Olds at that time. The collection also includes a 1913 Metz, a 1915 Model T Ford Doctor's Coupe, and a rare 1930 Model A Ford Town Car. Henry Ford built only a few of these Model A limousines, which featured open-air chauffeur's compartments, in his unsuccessful attempt to enter the luxury car market.

❖ *THE BEHRING MUSEUM, Blackhawk Road and Camino Tassajara, Danville, California 94526. Tel: 415-736-2277. Open Tuesday through Sunday 11-5, except major holidays. Admission $6, student and senior discounts. Guided tours available by appointment.*

The Behring collection has been assembled since 1982 by Kenneth Behring and Donald Williams. It emphasizes both European and American cars of the fine coach-building era from the mid-1920s to World War II. The museum has a large collection of Mercedes, Rolls-Royces, Packards, and Cadillacs. An exquisite 1935 yellow supercharged Duesenberg owned by Clark Gable is frequently on display. The museum claims it has one of the best automotive libraries in the country.

❖ *TOWE FORD MUSEUM OF CALIFORNIA, 2200 Front Street, Sacramento, California 95818. Tel: 916-442-6802. Open daily 10-6, except major holidays. Admission $5.00, senior and student discounts.*

The Towe Ford Museum of California was created in 1986 by the California Vehicle Foundation when it acquired a large portion of the 250 Ford cars owned by the Towe Antique Ford Foundation collection in Deer Lodge, Montana. The California foundation had been created in 1983 by a group of Sacramento car enthusiasts. It then entered and won a competitive bidding contest for the Towe collection against a number of other cities throughout the country. (See separate listing for the original Towe Museum in Deer Lodge, Montana.)

A 1931 Ford Model-A convertible with covered rumble seat. Note extended carryall over the rear bumper and the runningboard luggage holder. Photo courtesy of the Smithsonian Institution, Washington, D.C.

The Sacramento museum contains approximately 180 automobiles, 80 percent of which are Ford products (including Lincolns and Mercurys). The oldest car in the collection is from the first production model produced by the Ford Motor Company, a 1903 Model A Runabout. Each of the eight alphabetic series models (A, B, C, F, K, N, R, and S) that preceded the introduction of the Model T in 1908 are represented. There is another 1903 Model A, but with a Cadillac marque. It was designed in part by Henry Ford and became the first model produced by the then-new Cadillac Motor Car Company headed by Henry Leland.

The 1908 Model T on display is a rare example from the initial run of 800 cars. One of the two 1913 Model Ts on display was called an Express Wagon. It could hold nine passengers or, by unbolting the seats, serve as a delivery truck. This model ultimately proved to be the forerunner of the Ford Station Wagon and Panel Truck. The 1919 sedan on display was a unique design in that it was equipped with center doors. It also possesses an electric starter motor, the first year Ford offered this option.

The Towe Museum has 32 different styles of the second Model A on exhibit and 38 pre-World War II V-8s. The V-8 stayed in production until Ford shifted over to making Jeeps, trucks, and tanks for the military in early 1942.

The museum's collection contains cars from most of the post-war years through 1971. Among these are two Edsel sedans, a station wagon, and two 1964/1965 V-8 Mustang convertibles. The Mustang was one of Ford's most popular cars, with 500,000 being sold between mid-1964 and the end of 1965.

❖ *SAN DIEGO AUTOMOTIVE MUSEUM, 2080 Pan America Plaza, Balboa Park, San Diego, California 92101. Tel: 619-231-2886. Open daily 10-4:30, summer 10-5. Admission $4, senior, student, and military discounts.*

The San Diego Automotive Museum, founded by a group of local car enthusiasts, opened its doors in December 1988 in a building owned by the city of San Diego, which dates from the 1935 San Diego World's Fair. Among the 69 vehicles currently on display are a 1904 Model B Ford; a clay prototype model of a Mark X Lincoln; the presidential limousine used by Richard Nixon, Gerald Ford, Jimmy Carter, and Ronald Reagan; a Model J Duesenberg; the seventeenth Tucker (1948) ever built; and an Allard racing car once owned by Steve McQueen. Among the classic cars on display are a 1933 Pierce Arrow Silver Cloud (one of five known to be in existence), a restored red 1936 Auburn 852 Bobtail Speedster, and a 1932 Cadillac V-12 Convertible Coupe.

Also on exhibit is a factory replica of Karl Benz's first car which he built in 1886, and a special display of 15 motorcycles. In addition to the rotating exhibit, the museum offers special shows that focus on specific aspects of automotive history, such as historic race cars, town cars, the development of the BMW over time, and historic trends in styling.

❖ *MERLE NORMAN CLASSIC BEAUTY COLLECTION, 15180 Bledsoe Street, Sylmar, California 91342. Tel: 818-367-1085. Admission free, no children under 13 admitted. Reservations required.*

The Merle Norman collection was assembled by J.B. Nethercutt, chairman and co-founder of the Merle Norman Cosmetics Company, and his wife Dorothy. The collection is exhibited in a luxuriant showroom with marble floor and pillars, which is, beyond a doubt, one of the most ornate classic automobile facilities in the United States.

The collection emphasizes automobiles at the peak of their elegance. They date mainly from the 1930s and include classic pre-World War II Cadillacs, Packards, and Rolls-Royces. The Rolls-Royce Room contains 11 Rolls-Royces, among which are a 1913 Silver Ghost, a 1958 Silver Wraith limousine, a 1963 Silver Cloud, and a 1968 Silver Shadow. Also included are several Duesenbergs. The most spectacular example is a one-of-a-kind light-blue 1933 Duesenberg built for display at the Chicago World's Fair. A red 1932 Packard 12-cylinder convertible coupe on display is of no less grandeur.

In addition to the fine automobile collection, the Nethercutts have also accumulated outstanding examples of musical instruments and devices.

❖ *FORNEY TRANSPORTATION MUSEUM, 1416 Platte Street, Denver, Colorado 80202. Tel: 303-433-3643. Open summer Monday through Saturday 9-5, Sunday 11-5:30; rest of year Monday through Saturday 10-5, Sunday 11-5; closed Christmas. Admission $3, student and over-62 discounts.*

Mr. Forney, an inventor who specialized in arc welding equipment for the farm market, started collecting cars in the 1950s when he bought a 1919 Kissel. When his company's sales force found out about his interest in old cars, they started ferreting them out of their customer's barns in exchange for welding equipment. The museum originally opened in 1961 in Fort Collins, where Mr. Forney's business was located, but in 1968 he moved it to Denver.

Currently there are 150 cars in the collection, 40 of which are owned by the Forney family. Of particular interest in the collection is a 1923 six-wheeled Hispano-Suiza convertible touring car originally owned by the famous American film director D.W. Griffith (*Birth of a Nation*). Cars owned by famous personalities also include a Kissel Gold Bug owned by Amelia

Earhart and a Rolls-Royce owned by Ali Kahn. Of historical interest are several motorized wagons from the late 1800s, which were essentially buckboards equipped with 1-cylinder engines. Also on display is a curved-dash 1903 Olds, which was part of the styling transition from carriage designs to modern automobile styling, and a 1905 Ford two-seater with a modern engine-under-hood design.

In addition to its car collection, the Forney Museum contains exhibits of railroad locomotives and rolling stock, 25 antique bicycles, and several horse-drawn carriages. In total the museum has on display approximately 300 pieces of transportation equipment.

❖ *COLLIER AUTOMOTIVE MUSEUM, 2500 South Horseshoe Drive, Naples, Florida 33942. Tel: 813-643-5252. Open Tuesday through Saturday 10-5, Sunday 1-5, May through November; daily 10-5, December through April. Admission $6, under-13 discount.*

The Collier Museum was opened in 1988 by Miles C. Collier as a non-profit corporation dedicated to the preservation and display of one of the world's most significant collections of classic racing and sports automobiles. Miles C. Collier named the museum in honor of his father, C. Miles, and two uncles, Sam and Barron Jr., all of whom were active racing enthusiasts in the 1930s. They also were the first MG agents in the United States and founded the Automobile Racing Club of America in the 1930s, which is the predecessor to today's Sports Car Club of America.

In December 1986, Miles C. Collier acquired the 50 antique-automobile collection of his close associate, racing driver Briggs Cunningham, when the latter closed his own museum in Southern California. Among the many important racing cars Collier acquired are two that Cunningham entered in the 1952 race at Le Mans in France, which were the first American-built cars in this classic race. There is also a Ford GT-40 that won at Le Mans and a Jorgensen-Eagle that Bobby Unser drove to victory in the 1975 Indianapolis 500.

Containing more than 80 automobiles, the museum is divided into five themes: sports and sports racing cars; American racing cars; cars of "conspicuous consumption"; Grand Prix racing cars; and Porsche racing cars. The collection of approximately 25 Porsches is one of the largest and most important in the world outside of the Stuttgart, Germany, headquarters of Porsche. One of the prize sports cars in the permanent collection is a 1912 Hispano-Suiza T-15 Alfonso XIII, which is one of the oldest cars in the display. Another is a 1912 Mercer Raceabout, which is as austere as the Hispano-Suiza is luxurious.

There are a number of elegant automobiles with unique pedigrees, including Gary Cooper's supercharged 1935 Duesenberg SSJ. It is one of only two of its kind; the other was ordered by Clark Gable after seeing Cooper's. Only 480 Duesenbergs were ever built by the time E.L. Cord closed down his Auburn-Cord-Duesenberg empire in 1937.

All of the cars in the Collier collection are kept in excellent running condition by Collier Historic Motorcars, a separate for-profit automobile restoration business located within the museum complex. "These fine cars can only be fully appreciated when they are seen on the road in their element," commented Frank Gardner, the museum's director.

❖ *DON GARLITS MUSEUM OF DRAG RACING, 13700 Southwest 16th Avenue (off I-75 at Exit 67), Ocala, Florida 32676. Tel: 904-245-8661. Open 9-5, closed Christmas. Admission $6, student discounts.*

The Don Garlits museum, which opened in 1984, provides an exhibit on the 30-year history of drag racing. This collection of cars, engines, and photographs, was put together by Garlits, a pioneer drag racer. Garlits, more frequently referred to as "Big Daddy," introduced the rear-engined racer, the bicycle-wheel front end, use of spoilers, and the enclosed cockpit. He started racing in 1950 and won his first major race in 1955. His best speed is 287.81 mph, which he achieved in 1989. While Garlits has retired from full-time drag racing, he continues to be active in the field.

In 1976 Garlits created a nonprofit corporation for the purpose of building a museum to house his collection of 100 drag racers and antique cars. The museum contains most of Don Garlits series of "Swamp Rats," which he built and raced in the 1960s and 1970s. Dragsters raced by most of the famous drivers in the sport are on display, including the first "rail" dragster. Named the "Bug," it was built in 1941 by Dick Kraft, who raced it for a number of years at America's first drag strip in Santa Ana, California. The introduction of the rail dragster marks the departure of drag racing from "stock car" racing.

A historically interesting drag racer on display is a yellow pre-rail dragster called the Bean Bandit Special, built in 1952-3 by Joaquin Arnett in San Diego. Coming out of the hot rod craze in San Diego, it was the first car built solely for drag racing.

In an exhibit area adjacent to the display of drag racers is the Garlits collection of antique and classic cars. The oldest car in the exhibit, a 1913 Metz roadster with a split windshield, was the first Metz model equipped with doors. Next

This jaunty 1912 Metz Roadster was equipped with a four-cylinder, water-cooled, 22-hp gasoline engine. Notice the brass bulb-operated air horn and water-carbide tank for headlights. The car's friction-type drive was introduced by Charles Metz in his 1909 model. Photo courtesy of the Car & Carriage Caravan, Luray Caverns, Virginia.

to it sits a 1914 Metz speedster, believed by Garlits to be the only one now in existence. It has been restored to its original glory with leather bucket seats, brass trim, and ornate brass lanterns on the side of the hood. As was the custom in those days, the car was not equipped with a windshield. Charles Metz was a pioneering car maker in Waltham, Massachusetts, who specialized in sports cars during the period 1908 to 1920. He was the first to offer a do-it-yourself kit to home car-builders.

Also on display is a beautiful 1915 Lozier Roadster, one of America's lesser-known production cars, but appreciated for its performance and durability, which experts consider comparable to that of the best European cars of its time. Another interesting classic car is a 1932 Ford Delux coupé. Painted black, this enclosed stately car is one of only 800 built by Ford. Of the post-World War II cars, two 1968 Dodge Coronet R/Ts are unusual because they were built for racing and contain 225 hp engines. Only 200 of these "family hot rods" were ever built.

❖ *BELLM CARS AND MUSIC OF YESTERDAY, 5500 North Tamiami Trail, Sarasota, Florida 33580. Tel: 813-355-6228. Open Monday through Saturday 8:30-6, Sundays 9:30-6. Admission $6.50, early-school discount.*

The Bellm collection of automobiles is a diversified grouping of American cars from throughout the industry's development. It includes a 1901 Oldsmobile, a rare 1918 Willys Knight touring car, a 1933 boat tail Auburn, and a 1937 Lincoln Zephyr, among others. The collection also contains several trucks, including an International Harvester built in 1911, a Lincoln pickup truck built in 1921, and a Ford Model T truck built in 1924. Post-World War II attempts to create new car companies are represented by a 1948 Tucker, two Kaisers built in the early 1950s, and a 1981 DeLorean.

In addition to the automobile collection, the museum has a collection of 2,000 mechanical musical instruments and 150 working examples of game machines popular during the 1930s.

❖ *VINTAGE WHEEL MUSEUM, 218 Cedar Street, Sand Point, Idaho 83864. Tel: 208-263-7173. Open daily 9:30-5:30, except major holidays. Admission $2.50, senior and ages 14 to 18 discounts.*

The Vintage Wheel Museum contains 16 antique cars, ranging in age from a 1907 International high-wheel "horseless carriage" to a 1955 Cadillac Coupe de Ville. An early Cadillac of 1913 vintage is also on display. It is uniquely equipped with an electric starter and dual spark plugs to enable starting by either crank or battery. The 1919 Buick on display represents the first year that Buick offered electric headlamps and starter as standard equipment. The 1923 Stanley steamer on display exemplifies the approaching demise of the steamer. By then the self-starter had become standard on many gasoline-powered cars, which helped make the steamer, with its 10- to 20-minute warm-up time, obsolete.

In addition to its automobile collection, the Vintage Wheel Museum displays several historic carriages, including a Queen Anne carriage, a U.S. Mail RFD coach, and a sporty self-driven Trap with a rumble seat.

❖ *AUBURN-CORD-DUESENBERG MUSEUM, 1600 South Wayne Street, Auburn, Indiana. Tel: 219-925-1444. Open daily 9-6, except for major holidays. Adult admission $6, school-age, over-65, and family discounts.*

Established in 1973 as a non-profit corporation, this specialized museum focuses on cars produced in and around Auburn, Indiana, particularly those manufactured by the Auburn Automobile Company between 1900 and 1937. Also included in this collection of approximately 150 automobiles, however, are cars from other American manufacturers, plus several European makes. The museum is housed in the art deco-style building erected in 1930 as the Auburn Company's factory showroom.

Of special note in the collection is a 1932 Duesenberg Model J, originally purchased by Cliff Durant, the son of the founder of the General Motors Corporation; a 1932 Auburn V-12 sedan; a one-of-a-kind Cord built to the specifications of the president of the Champion Spark Plug Company; and a rare 1898 Winton.

Auburn-Cord-Duesenberg was put together by an automobile super-salesman and entrepreneur with the improbable name of Errett Lobban Cord. The Auburn Company had been founded in 1900 by two brothers named Eckhart in Auburn, Indiana. By 1924 the company was badly ailing and had an inventory of 700 unsold cars. A group of the company's investors asked Cord to take it over. Cord added more dramatic paint and shiny metal to the existing cars and quickly sold them to dealers. He then added a more powerful engine to the new cars and by 1929 had raised the sales of Auburns tenfold.

In 1926 Cord worked out a partnership arrangement with the Duesenberg brothers. Out of this arrangement came the Duesenberg J and the super-charged SJ series. Only 480 super-charged SJs were ever built, but the series made American automotive history. These Duesenbergs became the only American cars ever to rival the quality and elegance of the British-made Rolls-Royce. In 1929 Cord started making cars under the Cord marque, such as the L-29 and the coffin-nosed 810 series. Cord's insistence on having adequate power in his cars caused him to eventually acquire his engine supplier, the Lycoming Engine Company. Unfortunately, the bad economic times of the 1930s caught up with E.L Cord, and his empire, which by then included the Stinson Aircraft Company, fell apart.

❖ *INDIANAPOLIS MOTOR SPEEDWAY HALL OF FAME, Indianapolis Motor Speedway, 4790 West 16th Street, Indianapolis, Indiana 46222. Tel: 317-241-2500. Open daily, except Christmas. Admission $1, under-16 free.*

The Indianapolis Speedway's Hall of Fame was created in 1956 as a means of honoring and perpetuating the contributions of outstanding personalities in racing and the automotive industry. The original Hall of Fame Museum was housed just inside the main gate of the speedway. This facility proved inadequate, and in 1976 a larger building, which also housed the speedway's administrative offices, was constructed on the infield of the track.

Eddie Rickenbacker in a 1915 Maxwell at the Indianapolis Speedway. Photo courtesy of the Smithsonian Institution, Washington, D.C.

The Hall of Fame Museum contains over 75 racing cars along with racing memorabilia and car accessories. It includes exhibits of memorabilia from the three periods of track ownership: Carl Fisher (1908-1925), the original organizer of the speedway; Eddie Rickenbacker (1926-1945); and Tony Hulman (1946 to present). Mr. Hulman moved his personal antique automobile collection to the Hall of Fame Museum from his Early Wheels Museum in Terre Haute, Indiana.

The Speedway's Hall of Fame Museum captures the heritage of the Indy 500 over the years by exhibiting more than 30 of the winning cars. The Marmon Wasp, driven by Ray Harroun, that won the first race in 1911 is prominently featured. Four two-time winners are on display, including the Boyle Maserati driven by Wilbur Shaw in 1939 and 1940 and the car driven by Mauri Rose in 1947 and 1948. All four of A.J. Foyt Jr.'s winning race cars are featured. The Lola-Chevrolet that won the 1990 Indianapolis 500 is the latest winner to join the collection of racing cars.

The collection also contains approximately 60 examples of vintage cars from the early 1900s, many produced in Indiana. These include automobiles manufactured by such pioneers as Duesenberg, Stutz, and Marmon, all three of which raced cars at the speedway.

The 1950 Studebaker coupé with wraparound rear window and bullet nose front grill, its two most distinctive features. Photo courtesy of the Studebaker National Museum Archives, South Bend, Indiana.

❖ *STUDEBAKER NATIONAL MUSEUM, 525 South Main Street, South Bend, Indiana 46601. Tel: 219-284-9714. Open Monday through Friday 10-4:30, Saturday 10-4, Sunday noon-4. Admission $3.50, senior and student discounts.*

The Studebaker National Museum is located in a building erected in 1919 by the Studebaker Company to house the company's largest dealership. The Studebaker vehicle collection was started by the company around 1900 and was donated to the city of South Bend in 1966 when the company ceased operations. The collection contains more than 100 carriages, wagons, cars, and trucks. It spans 130 years of transportation history, starting with the Studebaker family's Conestoga wagon and ending with the company's last car off of the production line in 1963, a Daytona hardtop.

The more interesting and significant cars on display include:

■ a 1920 Light Six, the first car Studebaker made in South Bend;

■ a 1928 Commander Roadster, tested for 25,000 miles in 23,000 minutes;

■ a 1939 Champion, Loewy's first design for Studebaker;

■ a 1950 Champion, Loewy's bullet-nosed design that became the company's best seller;

■ a 1953 Commander Hardtop, another famous Loewy design; and

■ a 1963 Avanti, Loewy's last great car design for Studebaker.

An important feature of the museum is the collection of Studebaker horse-drawn wagons used by the U.S. Army in the Civil War and in World War I. Another significant feature of the museum is the company archives, which are the most definitive collection of company records in existence (accessible by appointment).

❖ *VAN HORN'S ANTIQUE TRUCK COLLECTION, Mason City, Iowa 50401. Tel: 515-423-0655. Open Monday through Saturday 10:30-4, Sunday 11-6. Admission $3, early school age discount.*

The Van Horn collection of pre-1925 trucks is the largest such exhibit in the United States. Its more than 70 restored antique trucks have been assembled by Lloyd and Margaret Van Horn, who started collecting in 1972. Van Horn, who has operated the same auto salvage yard in Mason City for 39 years, started collecting trucks rather than automobiles because, he

169

says, "I figured that everyone had seen all the antique cars." Van Horn has a workshop devoted to truck restoration and is proud that almost all of his trucks are operable. A number of the trucks in the collection are placed in period settings such as a gas station or in front of a general store.

One of his prize trucks is a 1912 Reo farm truck with a 2-cylinder engine and chain drive. Another is a 1914 Bessemer that he had to rebuild starting with only the frame and running gear. Van Horn also has an unusual steam-driven Rapid truck built in 1908 that doubled as a steam-operated carpet cleaner. The engine had

been modified so that the owner of the cleaning business could use the steam from the engine to clean carpets at the customer's residence or place of business.

As part of his collection, Mr. Van Horn has several circus trucks that he has restored with loving care and in full color. One is built on a 1920 General Motors truck chassis and is complete with a calliope. The circus exhibit also includes a miniature circus covering an area 12 feet by 30 feet. The circus is complete with three tents, including action scenes in the big tent, plus 43 wagons and a 64-foot circus train. The creator of the model took 34 years to build it.

❖ *OWLS HEAD TRANSPORTATION MUSEUM, State Route 73, Rockland, Maine 04854. Tel: 207-594-4418. Open daily 10-5 from May to October, weekdays 10-5 rest of year. Admission $4, over-65 and student discounts.*

The Owls Head museum was established as a non-profit foundation in 1974 under the leadership of James S. Rockefeller Jr. and Stephan Lang. Rockefeller, a member of the famous Rockefeller family, is a boat builder and

A 1925 Ford Station Wagon. In New England these wooden-bodied vehicles were called "Beach Wagons" since they were used to transport passengers to and from the beach. They were later called station wagons because they carried commuters to and from railroad stations. Photo courtesy of the Owls Head Transportation Museum, Rockland, Maine.

has lived in the Owls Head area for many years.

The museum's collection includes approximately 60 antique cars, 15 horseless carriages, 20 bicycles dating from 1885, 25 pioneer aircraft dating from World War I, and a number of stationary and aircraft engines. The museum also maintains a library containing 5,000 volumes and thousands of periodicals, photos, and videos on transportation vehicles.

Among the automobiles displayed are a 1903 Curved-Dash Olds Runabout, a 1903 Model A Ford, and several early Model Ts. The Curved-Dash Olds was the first mass-produced car in America; 427 were produced in 1901, which expanded to 4,000 in 1903. An equally important car on display from a historical standpoint is a 1903 Mercedes Simplex. The Simplex is considered the first "real" automobile ever made since it was the first to be equipped with a steering wheel and a hooded engine in the front.

The museum exhibits several early steam cars of significance, one of which is a 1903 Prescott. A Prescott steamer won the New York to Boston reliability race in 1902 and the Mt. Washington Hill Climb in 1904. The J.L. Prescott Company was a manufacturer of stoves that built steam cars as a sideline between 1900 and 1905. The other steamer is a 1903 Stanley Runabout. The Stanley brothers built their first steamer in 1897 in Newton, Massachusetts, and sold more than 200 the first year.

A 1907 Cadillac Model K Runabout provides one of the early examples of inter-changeability of parts in the American automobile industry. Cadillac became the first manufacturer to adopt the policy of absolute inter-changeability when, in 1904, Henry M. Leland joined the company as chief engineer.

An interesting car on display from the 1920s is a Ford Beach Wagon with a wooden body. This predecessor to the station wagon was basically a modified Model T. Another modified Model T on display is a 1928 Model A Racer, which consists of a Model T body and a Model A drive train, plus other modifications. This racer was capable of 125 mph.

❖ *WELLS AUTO MUSEUM, Route 1, Wells, Maine 04090. Tel: 207-646-9064. Open daily 10-5, mid-June through September; Saturday and Sunday 10-5, from Memorial Day to Columbus Day. Admission $3, student discount.*

The basic collection contained in the Wells Auto Museum was put together by Glen C. Gould Jr., the original owner of the museum. Gould's most active period of collecting was from 1946 to 1973. He first opened his museum in Massachusetts in 1950, but has been located in Wells since 1975.

The museum contains approximately 130 antique cars, of which 80 are on display at any one time. Kenneth Creed, museum director, says that the collection focuses on cars from the early 1900s to 1920—what he calls the "brass era."

The earliest cars in the collection are a 1902 Thomas, a 1908 Baker electric, and three steamers: a 1907 Stanley Gentleman's Speedy Roadster, Model H-5; a 1907 White Model HH with a 20-hp engine; and a rare 1905 Grout touring car (the last year Grout remained in business). Another interesting antique car is a 1912 Pathfinder Roadster. The Pathfinder company produced cars in Indianapolis from 1911 to 1918.

Restored Stutz Bearcats are always welcome sights in any museum and the yellow 1918 model with a 4-cylinder, 90-hp engine on display here is no exception. Harry Stutz started his own company in 1911 and produced a long line of award-winning cars, particularly sports cars, until he went out of business in 1933.

Among the classic American cars pro-

A 1918 Stutz Bearcat with 4-cylinder motor rated at 90 hp. It was manufactured in Indianapolis, Indiana, and cost $2,850. Photo courtesy of Wells Auto Museum, Wells, Maine.

duced following World War I is a restored red four-passenger 1918 Pierce-Arrow Model 48 Roadster. Three of the most interesting "modern" classic cars in the museum are a 1941 Packard Model 160 Convertible Coupe; a 1955 Chrysler Model C-300A Coupe; and a 1963 Studebaker Avanti. The Packard is one of the last of the classic large cars that made Packard so famous in the 1920s and 1930s.

A young Henry Ford in his 1896 Quadricycle. Photo courtesy of the Smithsonian Institution, Washington, D.C.

❖ *HENRY FORD MUSEUM, 20900 Oakwood Boulevard, Dearborn, Michigan 48121. Tel: 313-271-1620. Open daily 9-5 except on major holidays. Admission $9.50, school-age and over-62 discounts.*

In 1927 Henry Ford first proposed the idea of an "industrial museum" that would highlight the work ethic of America by displaying the nation's accomplishments in a wide range of industries. The transportation portion of the museum contains one of the nation's outstanding collections of vehicles.

The automobile collection contains over 200 cars (although they are not all on display at any one time) and includes more than 60 Fords and Lincolns, plus cars made by both American and European manufacturers. The exhibit features an 1863 Roper steam carriage, which is the oldest car known to exist; the only known Duryea automobile in existence, circa 1896; Henry Ford's Quadricycle (1896); and the Ford 999 racer in which Henry Ford established a speed record of 92 mph in 1904.

The collection of early cars also includes White and Stanley steamers from 1902-3; a 1903 Ford Model A; a convertible-top Model T built in 1908; and a 1958 four-door hardtop Edsel. In addition to a number of Ford and Lincoln models from the 1920s and 1930s, there are similar models of other American car manufacturers such as Packard, Chrysler, and Chevrolet.

❖ *ALFRED P. SLOAN JR. MUSEUM, 1221 East Kearsley Street, Flint, Michigan 48503. Tel: 313-760-1169. Open Tuesday to Friday 9-5 and Saturday-Sunday noon-5. Admission $3, senior and early-school discounts.*

The Sloan Museum in Flint, which opened in 1966, focuses on cars produced by local manufacturers, particularly Buick and Chevrolet. It was founded by a publicly sponsored non-profit foundation that built a cultural complex called Flint Cultural Center. The museum's initial collection was put together by local automobile collectors. From this base, the collection has grown to more than 80 cars, principally Buicks and Chevrolets, plus examples of carriages built in Flint during the late 1800s.

Flint's history as a vehicle-making center goes back to the mid-1800s, when its wagon makers gained international recognition. By the turn of the century, Flint had become the largest carriage-making center in the world. The first automobile maker in Flint, the Flint Automobile Company, was founded in 1901. In 1903 Flint Wagon Works bought out the Buick Motor Company in Detroit and moved its operations to

Flint. Buick was soon taken over by William Durant, who founded General Motors in 1908, using Buick as a base. Louis Chevrolet, who worked for Durant as a racing team driver, started his own company in 1911. By 1920 Flint-based companies were rivaling Detroit as the largest automobile producing center in America.

The earliest Buick in the collection is a Model C 2-cylinder touring car built in 1905. The collection also includes a 1910 Buick Bug, a torped- shaped, 4-cylinder racer in which Louis Chevrolet raced at the Indianapolis Motor Speedway. On display is one of the earliest cars built by Chevrolet, and the only one of its vintage in existence—a model 1912 touring car called the "Classic Six." In addition, the collection includes a Little Roadster, which was built by Louis Chevrolet in 1911, before he started his own company.

The collection also features a number of Cadillacs, the earliest being a 1912 Cadillac touring car. A special feature of the museum is a collection of General Motors prototype models from the immediate post-World War II period.

❖ *GILMORE-CCCA MUSEUM, 6865 Hickory Road, Hickory Corners, Michigan 49060. Tel: 616-671-5089. Open daily mid-May through mid-October 9-5; Saturday and Sunday September-October and mid-May through June. Admission $6.*

The Gilmore Museum opened in 1966 and displays a diverse collection of mainly American cars with emphasis on Packards and Cadillacs. The collection was initiated by Donald Gilmore, a past chairman of the Upjohn Pharmaceutical Company. It was supplemented in 1982 by the collection of the Classic Car Club of America (CCCA) Museum. The exhibition is housed in five wooden barns, several of which were dismantled from neighboring farms and reconstructed on property acquired by Gilmore in the early 1960s.

The exhibit features an elegant 1937 dark-green four-door Cadillac convertible produced by the Fleetwood Body Company, a subsidiary of General Motors. General Motors bought Fleetwood in 1925 to provide custom bodies for its top-of-the-line Cadillacs. The Gilmore-CCCA collection contains a number of Rolls-Royces dating from 1910, including a 1929 Rolls-Royce phaeton manufactured in Rolls's United States plant in

A 1938 Packard-Dietrich convertible, Model 1607, with a V-12 engine. Photo courtesy of the Gilmore Car Museum, Hickory Corners, Michigan.

Springfield, Massachusetts. Rolls opened this factory in 1920 and continued production of Rolls-Royces there for the America market until 1932.

The museum houses Duesenberg, Cord, Auburn, and Tucker cars, plus the 1930 Rolls-Royce and movie set from Walt Disney's movie *The Gnomemobile.*

❖ *R.E. OLDS TRANSPORTATION MUSEUM, 240 Museum Drive, Lansing, Michigan 48933. Tel: 517-372-0422. Open Monday through Saturday 10-5, closed major holidays. Admission $3, senior and student discounts.*

The R. E. Olds museum, which was founded in 1977 as a community effort among local collectors, is a modest but interesting exhibit of approximately 30 antique cars and trucks produced in Lansing by such companies as Oldsmobile, Reo, Star, Durant, and Bates. The collection includes an Olds Motor Wagon built in 1897, Curved-Dash Oldsmobiles built in 1901 and 1904, and a 1906 Reo. The Reo Automobile Company was started by R. E. Olds in 1904 after he sold his Oldsmobile Company to William C. Durant.

❖ *AUTOMOTIVE HALL OF FAME, 3225 Cook Road, Midland, Michigan 48641. Tel: 517-631-5760. Open Monday through Friday 9-4:30. Admission free.*

The Automobile Old Timers (AOT) organization, now called the Automotive Hall of Fame, was founded in 1939 in New York City by a group of automobile executives. Its stated purpose was to honor the key leaders and contributors to the evolution of the American automobile industry. The founding committee included, among others, Eddie Rickenbacker, the World War I flying ace, builder of Rickenbacker motor cars from 1921 to 1927, and the owner of the Indianapolis Motor Speedway from 1926 to 1945. The first board of directors included Henry Ford, Ransom E. Olds, and William K. Vanderbilt (sponsor of the Vanderbilt Cup car racing trophy from 1904 to 1916).

In the Hall of Fame, there are individual presentations on the lives and careers of each of the 106 inductees. The Hall of Fame organization has also developed one of the largest libraries and archives in the world of pictures, publications, and private correspondence concerning the companies and individuals that represent the heritage of the American automotive industry.

❖ *TOWE FORD MUSEUM, 1106 Main Street, Deer Lodge, Montana 59722. Tel: 406-846-3111. Open daily 8 a.m.- 9 p.m., June through August; Wednesday to Friday 9-4; Saturday and Sunday 10:30-5, rest of year. Admission $7, student, senior, and family discounts.*

Edward Towe, born in Iowa in 1914, is a retired farmer and businessman who started tinkering with old Fords at an early age. He bought his first true antique Ford, a 1923 Model T, in the early 1950s for $75. That purchase started him on his quest for at least one example of every model year Henry Ford ever produced. Although not fully realizing his objective, he did succeed in assembling the most extensive collection in the world of Fords built from 1903 to 1952, plus an assortment of additional models through the 1980s.

Mr. Towe opened his museum in 1952 and built the collection up to 250 Fords. By 1986 the collection had grown beyond the capacity of the museum and he sold a major portion of it to the Towe Ford Museum of California in Sacramento. The remaining 100 Fords and Lincolns at the Deer Lodge museum still represent one of the largest Ford collections in the world. On exhibit are a Fordson tractor and Henry Ford's personal Lincoln camper. The museum's library maintains an extensive collection of books on the Ford company and manuals pertaining to Ford cars.

❖ *CHEVYLAND U.S.A., Exit 257 from I-80, Elm Creek, Nebraska 68836. Tel: 308-856-4208. Open daily May 1 to Labor Day 8-5, other times by appointment. Admission $4, student discounts.*

The Chevyland collection is owned by La Monte (Monte) Clark who founded the museum in 1976. Clark, a farmer by profession and life-style, decided to start collecting Chevrolets in 1970 after reading a book by George Dennis entitled *Sixty Years of Chevys*. While he is still missing a few years around 1920, Clark essentially succeeded in acquiring 60 years of Chevys and now owns 110 Chevrolets dating from 1914 to 1975. He and his son Allan have restored 42 of the cars; an additional 24 were found to need little or no restoration when acquired. The remainder are still in need of overhaul, or at least a new coat of paint.

The collection includes mainly roadsters, two-door hardtops, and coupes. Clark considers a 1932 Sports Roadster, a 1947 Country Custom Club Sedan with wood-panel siding, a fuel-injection 1957 convertible, and the continuous line of 20 years of two-door Chevrolets, as the most prized features of his collection. Among the non-Chevrolet-produced cars, he is especially fond of a rare 1930 Whippet, a car made by the Whippet Company of Kansas City, Missouri, from 1926 to 1931.

❖ *HAROLD WARP PIONEER VILLAGE, Junction US 6/34 and SR 10, Minden, Nebraska 68959. Tel: 308-832-1181 (out-of-state 1-800-445-4447). Open daily 8-dark. Admission $5, student discount.*

The Pioneer Village Foundation was founded by Harold Warp in 1952. Warp, the inventor of Flex-O-Glass, founded a company in Chicago by that name to produce plastic bags in the mid-1920s. Warp set out to collect at least one of everything that he believes has "made America great," and boasts that he has "collected something of everything from 1830 to present." Warp's collections are now housed in a complex of 26 historical and museum buildings. These collections include steam locomotives; early outboard boat motors; airplanes, including the first plane flown by Warp in 1927; motorcycles; cars; tractors; and decorative arts.

Harold Warp started collecting antique cars in 1948, and today his collection contains 350 antique automobiles. The oldest cars in the collection are a 1897 Milwaukee steam car, a 1898 Duryea Buggy, a 1902 Cadillac designed by Henry Ford, and a 1905 Buick, the oldest known

A 1907 Stanley Steamer, Model H5. The auto was capable of speeds of 70 mph. Photo courtesy of the Wells Auto Museum, Wells, Maine.

Buick in existence. The 26 Buicks in the collection date from 1905 to 1965. There are also 29 Chevrolets and 51 Fords dating from the early days of those companies.

175

❖ *IMPERIAL PALACE AUTO COLLECTION, 3535 Vegas Boulevard, Las Vegas, Nevada 89109. Tel: 702-731-3311. Open daily 9:30 a.m-11:30 p.m. Admission $6.95, early-school-age and over-65 discounts.*

The Imperial Palace collection is owned by Ralph Engelstad, owner of the hotel/casino complex. The exhibit opened in 1981 and focuses on a wide variety of American cars dating back to the 1890s, including Cadillacs, Pierce-Arrows, Duesenbergs, and Packards. There are also a number of excellent examples of European-built cars, such as Alfa Romeo and Rolls-Royce. Approximately 200 cars are displayed, although the total collection consists of 700 vehicles. The cars are regularly rotated into the exhibit space and onto nationwide tours.

Excellent examples of pre-World War I cars include an attractive cream-colored, battery-powered convertible coupe built by Detroit Electric in 1914, and an early commercial steam-powered vehicle, a 1900 Mobile.

The exhibit contains a number of cars previously owned by famous and infamous personalities, including Al Capone's 1930 Cadillac, with a 16-cylinder engine, bulletproof glass, armor plating, and gun ports; and Howard Hughes' 1954 Chrysler. There is also a bulletproofed and armor-plated 1939 Mercedes-Benz that was custom-built for Adolf Hitler.

Englestad's collection contains approximately 25 Model J Duesenbergs, the largest such collection in the world. The museum recently completed a $50-million extension that includes a special Duesenberg Room to house them. On display are Duesenbergs owned by such well-known celebrities as actor James Cagney, chewing-gum manufacturer Phillip K. Wrigley, razor mogul Colonel Jacob Schick, showman Billy Rose, heavyweight boxing champion Max Baer, Father Divine, and an Indian prince.

Rounding out the museum's exhibits is a collection of commercial vehicles, including trucks, taxis, and buses. The oldest example is a seven-passenger, 1904 omnibus, called the Great Arrow, and manufactured by Pierce-Arrow. There is also a 12-passenger Stanley Steamer, which was built in 1913 and used as a touring bus by the Stanley Hotel in Estes Park, Colorado. A number of Ford trucks built in the 1910s and 1920s are on display, including a picturesque 1914 Model T pie wagon. The taxis on display include a 1924 Ford Model T depot hack and a 1923 Yellow Cab built by the Yellow Cab Company of Chicago.

A 1918 Pierce Arrow, Model 48. This four-passenger roadster with standard 3-speed transmission and aluminum body cost $6,400. Photo courtesy of Wells Auto Museum, Wells, Maine.

❖ *NATIONAL AUTOMOBILE MUSEUM, 10 Lake Street South, Reno, Nevada 89504. Tel: 702-355-3500. Open daily 9:30-5:30 except major holidays. Admission $7.50, student and over-62 discounts. Annual passes are available for adults at $15, $5 for students, and $35 for families.*

The National Automobile Museum is the successor to the Harrah's Automobile Museum and is operated by the William F. Harrah Foundation. At one time William Harrah's automobile collection consisted of 1,500 cars and was one of the world's largest. He started collecting antique cars a few years after he built his first casino in Reno, Nevada, in 1946. When he opened the collection to the public in Sparks, Nevada, in 1962, it consisted of approximately 600 cars.

Following Harrah's death in 1978, his hotel and casino holdings, including the automobile collection, were acquired by Holiday Inn. The Holiday Inn Corporation auctioned off more than 700 of the cars and helped establish the William F. Harrah Automobile Foundation to perpetuate the remaining collection of approximately 175 cars. Subsequent acquisitions have brought the exhibit to approximately 200 automobiles.

The current museum in downtown Reno opened in late 1989. It was designed to present the cars in the context of the period in which they existed. There are, for example, four authentic street scenes, representing the four quarters of the twentieth century. There are multi-media theater presentations on various aspects of automotive history, and a personal audio guide is also available for touring the exhibit.

The exhibit includes a number of cars owned by Hollywood stars, such as James Dean, John Wayne, and Al Jolson. Other featured cars in the museum include a 1933 black-and-white supercharged Duesenberg speedster and a 1907 Thomas Flyer that won the New York-to-Paris automobile race in 1908.

Harrah's staff is known for its expertise in car restoration, and these facilities are open to public view.

❖ *SPENCER SHOPS STATE HISTORIC SITE, 411 South Salisbury Avenue, Spencer, North Carolina 28159. Tel: 704-636-2889. Open Monday though Saturday 9-5, Sunday 1-5, April through October; Tuesday through Saturday 10-4, Sunday 1-4, November through March. Museum admission free; charge for steam- and diesel-train tours when operating.*

While Historic Spencer Shops is primarily a state-owned railroad museum, it does have a select collection of approximately 30 antique automobiles. These cars are housed in the old steam-locomotive Flue Shop. Although Ed Robinette, the exhibit supervisor, displays only half of the cars at any one time, the entire collection can be viewed if advance arrangements are made.

The oldest car in the collection is a 1904 Curved-Dash Oldsmobile, which inspired the song, "In My Merry Oldsmobile." Another of the early cars in the collection is a strikingly restored 1912 Huppmobile touring car. It is painted red with yellow outlining, brass trim, and black fenders. The Hupp Motor Car Company produced 12,000 cars in 1913 and reached a peak of 38,000 cars in 1928. Hupp, like so many other automobile manufacturers, floundered in the 1930s, and the company finally went out of business in 1940.

Of particular interest in the collection is an elegant 1921 Lincoln convertible touring car designed and built by Henry Leland, the founder of the Lincoln Motor Company as well as Cadillac. The car was capable of reaching 70 mph and became a favorite of both gangsters and police.

The earliest Ford in the collection is a 1913 Ford Model T Depot Hack or Canopy Delivery Vehicle. An interesting car among the Fords on display is a 1935 gray Ford Roadster with a souped-up, 90-hp V-8 engine and capable of achieving 80 mph. It was one of 28 cars first

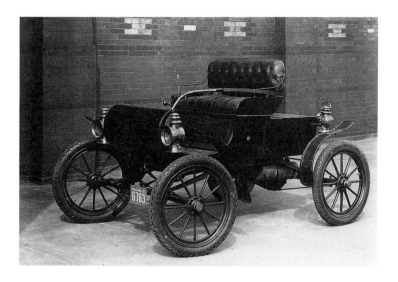

This 1903 Curved-Dash Oldsmobile was the first mass-produced car in the world. Ransom Olds started custom-building cars in 1897 and created the first production line in 1902. Four thousand cars were built in 1903, representing one-third of total U.S. production. Photo courtesy of the Smithsonian Institution, Washington, D.C.

purchased by the North Carolina Highway Patrol in 1935 and ultimately became very popular with police throughout the country.

Another historically significant car of the period immediately following World War I is a 1919 Dodge Roadster Four. The Dodge brothers were noted for building rugged cars from the company's inception in 1919, and the Roadster Four became a standard U.S. Army vehicle in the 1920s. Several were used by General John Pershing during his pursuit of Pancho Villa into Mexico.

Among the more modern cars in the collection, one of the most exotic is a 1963 Studebaker Avanti designed by Raymond Loewy. An even more recent unique car in the collection is a 1970 Plymouth Road Runner Super Bird. The Super Birds were only built in 1970 for the sole purpose of qualifying the car on the NASCAR stock car racing circuit. Only 1,920 cars were built, approximately one for every two dealers. Famous racing driver Richard Petty drove the 425-hp Super Bird to four victories on the racing circuit in 1970.

❖ *FREDERICK C. CRAWFORD AUTO-AVIATION MUSEUM, 10825 East Boulevard, Cleveland, Ohio 44106. Tel :216-721-5722. Open Tuesday through Saturday 10-5; Sunday noon-5. Admission $4, school-age and over-60 discounts.*

The Crawford Museum features approximately 120 cars, several of which date from the 1890s. The majority of the collection was put together by Frederick C. Crawford, past chairman of the board of TRW Inc. TRW's Thompson Division has been a major supplier of automotive parts since the beginning of the twentieth century. The collection emphasizes cars built by Cleveland manufacturers. Cleveland was a major automotive center until the early 1930s, spawning such pioneering automobile

creators as Peerless, White, and Winton.

The exhibit includes a number of electric cars built by Cleveland companies such as Baker and Rauch, and Lang Electrics. On display are also several steamers built by White Sewing Machine prior to World War I. The collection also includes cars from dozens of other American manufacturers such as Ford, Cadillac, Packard, and Dodge. Foreign car makers such as Mercedes-Benz, Ferrari, Jaguar, and Rolls-Royce, are also well-represented.

❖   THE SWIGART MUSEUM, Route 22 East, Huntingdon, Pennsylvania 16652. Tel: 814-643-3000. Open daily 9-5 July through Labor Day; Saturday and Sunday 9-5 June, September, and October; closed November through May. Admission $5, over-65 and under 13 discounts.

The Swigart collection was started by William Swigart in the mid-1920s and it continued to grow into the 1940s. It has been available for public viewing since 1927. Swigart specializes in collecting cars from the pioneering period prior to World War I. His collection is considered the best exhibit of one- and two-cylinder cars in America. It includes examples of cars built by such early pioneering companies as Reo, Franklin, Mitchel, Black, and Oldsmobile.

The collection features a number of examples of cars built by the largest carriage maker in America, Studebaker, and the largest bicycle manufacturer, Pope Manufacturing Company of Hartford, Connecticut. Also shown is a Locomobile Steamer and a Sears Car. In 1902 the Locomobile Steamer was the number-one selling car in America. The Sears Car was manufactured on contract for Sears and sold through their catalog in the early 1900s. Of more recent vintage on display is one of the first post-World War II cars, the Tucker.

❖   GAST CLASSIC MOTORCARS, SR 896, 421 Hartman Bridge Road, Strasburg, Pennsylvania 17579. Tel: 717-687-9500. Open daily 9 a.m.-9 p.m., May to October; rest-of-year Friday and Saturday 9 a.m.-9 p.m., Sunday through Thursday 9-5; closed December 24-25. Admission $6, under-13 discount.

Sam Gast had a long-standing hobby of collecting and trading antique and classic cars, a hobby in which his wife Joan and his elder son Jeff became involved. In 1976 Sam and his family decided to turn the hobby into a business and opened a shop in a local warehouse with a 13-car collection. Finding that most people came to reminisce, not to buy, the Gasts built and opened an attractive museum in 1985 as a commercial enterprise. The business is now run by Jeffrey Gast, whose mother manages the gift shop. His father has retired.

The exhibit consists of approximately 50 cars, which are changed periodically. While there are several antique cars from the pioneering years of the automobile industry, the Gasts have emphasized exceptional automobiles from the decades of the '40s, '50s, and '60s.

The oldest vehicle in the collection is an 1875 Studebaker Conestoga wagon, while the

This Sears 1911 Runabout was used as a commercial vehicle by an exterminating company. Photo courtesy of the Smithsonian Institution, Washington, D.C.

oldest automobile is a 1910 Ford Model T. One of the most popular automobiles in the collection is a 1948 waltz-blue Tucker Torpedo, one of only 51 ever made. The Tucker was acquired from Tom Monahan, president of Domino's Pizza, for $275,000 in 1989. Two of the most interesting features of the Tucker are its third headlight in the center that turned with the wheels and the interchangeable front and back seats, which was designed to reduce wear and tear.

Also on exhibit are the first and last MGs to be imported into the United States. These were originally acquired by Edsel Ford and Henry Ford II, respectively, and placed in the Henry Ford Museum. The Gasts acquired the two MGs from the Ford Museum in 1983.

Also of interest among the Ford cars in the exhibit are a 1958 Edsel and a 1959 retractable hardtop convertible. Ford made the hardtop convertible model, called a Skyliner, for three years, starting in 1957. The most unusual car in the collection is a 1967 Amphicar, the only car ever built to travel in the water as well as on land.

❖ *CLASSIC CARS INTERNATIONAL AUTO MUSEUM OF THE WEST, 355 West 7th Street South, Salt Lake City, Utah 84101. Tel: 801-582-6883. Open daily 9:30-4. Admission $3, children and senior discounts.*

The Classic Cars Museum was founded in 1983 by Dick Williams who started collecting antique and classic cars in the 1960s and now possesses more than 200 automobiles. Mr. Williams' collection emphasizes automobiles from the 1920s and 1930s, the heyday of classic cars. Of particular interest are a 1929 dual-cowl Model J Duesenberg, a 1931 dual-cowl phaeton Pierce-Arrow, Secretary of the Treasury Henry Morgenthau's dual-windshield V-12 Lincoln phaeton, and Al Capone's 1925 four-door Packard convertible with a dual windshield.

The earliest cars in the collection include a 1903 Stevens-Duryea, a 1906 two-passenger Cadillac Tulip roadster with a 1-cylinder engine, and a 1907 four-passenger International High Wheeler. The Stevens-Duryea employed a tiller steering mechanism and had a fabric-covered passenger seat in front of the driver.

One of the most impressive machines in the collection is a 1930 Cadillac phaeton convertible with a V-16 engine, 1930 being the first year Cadillac built this engine. Almost as impressive is a 1936 Packard two-door convertible Victoria with a Dietrich-designed body.

❖ *CAR & CARRIAGE CARAVAN OF LURAY CAVERNS, Luray, Virginia 22835. Tel: 703-745-6551. Open daily 10-7:30 from mid-March to mid-November, 10-5:30 mid-November to mid-March. Admission $10, senior and school discounts. Admission includes tour of the caverns.*

The Car and Carriage Caravan is part of the Luray Caverns complex owned by Ted Graves. The caverns were discovered in 1878 and acquired by Graves's grandfather, Colonel T.C. Northcott, around 1900. Colonel Northcott formed the Luray Caverns Corporation, which has remained in the family ever since.

Ted Graves took over the operation in the early 1950s. For a number of years, Graves had been restoring antique cars as a hobby, so in the late 1950s he built a museum to display his collection of cars. The museum opened in 1957 and now contains approximately 80 antique cars

and wagons, plus other items relating to the history of vehicle transportation. All of the vehicles are fully restored to running condition.

The oldest automobile in the exhibit is a 1892 Benz. It was one of the first cars in the world to be produced in any quantity. The oldest American-built car is a 1900 Curved-Dash, tiller-steered Oldsmobile with a 1-cylinder, 4.5-hp engine. Two unusual early cars on display were manufactured in Massachusetts. One is a Waltham Manufacturing Company (of watch-making fame) 1903 Buckboard, whose frame was made almost entirely of wood. The other is a

A 1907 International Autowagon. When the automobile became popular the International Harvester Company, which had produced farm machinery for a number of years, added a gasoline engine to its best spring wagon and called it the Autowagon. Photo courtesy of the Car & Carriage Caravan, Luray Caverns, Virginia.

1903 seven-passenger touring car made by the Knox Automobile Company of Springfield, Massachusetts.

Evidence of customer-oriented styling features in the early 1900s is provided by two four-passenger touring cars, one a 1904 Cadillac and the other a 1903 Winton. Both cars feature rear entrance access to the rear seat and quick conversion to a two-passenger roadster through the removal of four bolts. Another sign of elegance in this period is provided by a 1906 Cadillac Double Tulip Touring car. This early vintage Cadillac shows the elegance of finishing that has continued to characterize Cadillacs to this day.

The collection contains a number of excellent examples of cars produced prior to World War I. Of particular interest are three pre-World War I Roadsters, a 1910 Maxwell, a 1911 Huppmobile, and a 1912 Metz. The 1910 Maxwell contained a 2-cylinder engine, while the other two manufacturers had advanced to 4-cylinder engines. The Metz came with a mother-in-law seat in the back, a forerunner to the rumble seat. The Metz Company was another Waltham, Massachusetts, car builder. More recent cars of special interest in the collection are a 1930 Packard Touring car, a 1930 front-wheel drive Cord L-29 phaeton, and a 1931 Pierce-Arrow.

❖ *FOUR WHEEL DRIVE MUSEUM, Foot of East 11th Street, Clintonville, Wisconsin 54929. Tel: 715-823-2141. Open Memorial Day to Labor Day Saturday and Sunday 1-4, weekdays by appointment. Admission free.*

The FWD Company, originally called the Four Wheel Drive Company, was founded in 1909 by two inventors who built America's first four-wheel drive automobile, a high-wheel steamer. They nicknamed the car the "Battleship," because it could go almost anywhere, including through four to five-foot snow drifts. Today the FWD Company concentrates on heavy-duty special-purpose vehicles such as

cranes, telephone- and power-company vehicles, snow plows, cement trucks, and fire engines.

The FWD Company opened the museum in 1948 to display its heritage of various types of civilian and military four-wheel-drive vehicles. Among the cars on display are an FWD race car that ran in the Indianapolis 500, one of the few four-wheel-drive steamers (1908) ever produced, a number of four-wheel vehicles designed and manufactured for the U.S. Army in World War I, and several Seagrave fire engines. Seagrave is a manufacturer of fire engines that was purchased by the FWD Company in 1971. The military vehicles include a FWD army truck called the John Payne, an FWD army scout car named the Nancy Hanks, and a three-ton FWD ammunition carrier.

The Battleship on display at the museum is one of only ten such cars the company ever produced (1909-1911). It contained a number of automobile innovations, including a free-working differential, which was equipped with a differential lock to keep the four powered-wheels from spinning on muddy or icy roads. The car also pioneered the four-wheel dual braking system. The company shifted from steam to internal-combustion engines after completion of the first ten Battleships.

The FWD ammunition carrier became famous during World War I. More than 20,000 were built and used at the European front. After the war they were sold to various state highway departments and became the start of the nation's fleet of highway maintenance trucks.

A 1907 Cadillac Model K Runabout. This car is one of the first in a series of Cadillacs with interchangeable parts, which became the standard of the industry. Photo courtesy of the Owls Head Transportation Museum, Rockland, Maine.

❖ *HARTFORD HERITAGE AUTOMOBILE MUSEUM, 147 North Rural Street, Hartford, Wisconsin 53027. Tel: 414-673-7999. Open Monday through Saturday 10-5, Sunday noon-5. Admission $4, senior and student discounts.*

The Hartford Museum is operated by a non-profit organization founded in 1982 by a group of local citizens. One of the principal missions of the museum is to perpetuate the heritage of the Kissel Motor Company, which built cars in Hartford from 1906 to 1931.

Kissel built a total of 35,000 cars, trucks, and fire engines during its 25 years of existence. The museum collection includes 13 Kissel car models and 2 Kissel fire engines. One of its most popular Kissel cars was the Gold Bug speedster, one of which is on display at the museum.

Among famous American personalities who owned Gold Bugs were Amelia Earhart, Al Jolson, Fatty Arbuckle, and Jack Dempsey.

The museum has a total collection of 85 cars and trucks. Among these are three Kaisers; a fiber glass Darin, of which only 400 were made; a 1982 DeLorean; and Henry Ford's personal 1925 Lincoln Continental. The oldest automobile in the collection is a 1902 Rambler, which was built by the Thomas B. Jeffrey Company, which subsequently evolved into American Motors. The museum also possesses several Hudsons, another ancestor of American Motors. One of these Hudsons is an unusual 1931 boat tail coupe and the other is a 1937 four-door Terraplane.

Other makes of cars in the collection include Auburns, Pierce-Arrows, Locomobiles, and a Stutz.

❖ *BROOKS STEVENS AUTOMOTIVE MUSEUM, 10325 North Port Washington Road, Mequon, Wisconsin 53092. Tel: 414-241-4185. Open daily 10-5, May 1 though September 30, rest of year open five days a week 10-5, closed Tuesday and Thursday and major holidays. Admission $5, over-65 and student discounts.*

Brooks Stevens grew up in the automotive business. His father, William Clifford Stevens, invented the pre-selective gear shift in 1915. Brooks Stevens created his own design consulting firm and worked closely with such companies as Willys, Kaiser, Studebaker, and American Motors. Brooks Stevens Design Associates has designed over 40 vehicles during the past 55 years, many of which have received awards at prestigious car shows.

Stevens started his collection of antique and classic cars in the 1930s and opened the museum in 1958. He has stated that his objective in collecting cars is to acquire those that have significant technical or design innovations.

The oldest car in the exhibit is a 1905 one-cylinder Cadillac roadster. Another pioneer-

ing car in the collection is a rare 1914 Marmon race-about. This car was equipped with the same engine as the Marmon racer that won the first Indianapolis 500 in 1911. Another innovative automobile in the collection is a 1919 Paige Daytona Roadster, which created a world speed record of 117 mph at Daytona Beach, Florida. The collection includes several experimental cars, such as an all-aluminum car designed for the Olin Aluminum Company in 1959, and several prototypes of the famous Excalibur design.

The Brooks Stevens Museum also has on display a collection of motorboats (Evinrude) and snowmobiles. One of the snowmobiles, made by Johnson Pegasus, established the world speed record of 141 mph.

A 1929 Packard Phaeton. The distinctive well-balanced styling made Packard one of the most popular prestige cars at the time. Photo courtesy of the Owls Head Transportation Museum, Rockland, Maine.

AIR MAIL PIONEER by R. E. Pierce, acrylic, 13 x 24 inches, courtesy of the United States Air Force Art Collection.

Aviation and Space

The Wright brothers were the first to make a sustained controlled flight under power. The two Ohio bicycle makers made their first flights at Kitty Hawk on the Atlantic shore of North Carolina in December of 1903. They had selected this sight several years previously when they began experimenting with glider techniques in preparation for achieving powered flight.

Orville and Wilbur Wright had built and tested their first glider in 1901, based on then-current aeronautical data. These first tests proved disappointing, but rather than question their own capabilities, they began to check the validity of the data they had used. This approach was considered heresy among aviation scientists of the time since the data had been developed over many years by the father of glider design, the German aeronautical engineer Otto Lilienthal.

After testing Lilienthal's theory of aerodynamics in a crudely made wind tunnel, the Wright brothers satisfied themselves that the German scientist had overestimated the amount of lift obtained from a given wing area. Based on their own experimental data, the two brothers rebuilt their glider and confirmed their own theories at Kill Devil in 1902.

With hundreds of glider flights at Kill Devil behind them, the Wrights returned to Dayton and began to assemble the parts of a powered airplane. They first searched for a lightweight engine that produced the 12 horsepower (hp) they calculated was needed. Finding that engine builders were all preoccupied with developing automobile engines, the Wrights turned to the gifted mechanic in their bicycle shop, Charles Taylor. Although Taylor had never built an engine, he was able to assemble a 4-cylinder engine weighing only 180 pounds, using standard bicycle-shop tools, an aluminum engine block, cast-iron pistons and rings, and a steel crankshaft.

During the remainder of the winter of 1902 and into the summer of 1903, Orville and Wilbur Wright wrestled with design problems such as steering controls, propeller design, and power transmission. Their wind-tunnel experiments concerning wing design helped them immeasurably in shaping the propellers. They concluded that two propellers rotating at a slower speed were more effective than a single higher-speed propeller. The brothers also concluded that two counter-rotating propellers would avoid a torque effect, a phenomena that troubled many of the early single-propeller aircraft pioneers.

By September of 1903 the brothers were moving their newly built plane from Dayton to Kill Devil. The first flight was taken by Wilbur on December 17, 1903. While the flight ended in a minor crash, it proved that powered, controlled flight was practical. Three days later, Orville made the first successful powered flight that landed at a spot no lower than the point of takeoff.

While others went on to make outstanding contributions to aircraft performance, the wide range of sound innovative accomplishments achieved by Orville and Wilbur Wright in the short period of two years was remarkable. They were the first to use a wind tunnel to analyze air foil and propeller aerodynamics successfully. They were the first to build an engine designed specifically for flight, and they were the first to create a regime for controlling flight in three dimensions. While Wilbur Wright died in 1912, Orville Wright went on to make a number of additional contributions to aviation before his death in 1948. Among these was the automatic stabilizer, which proved so useful in improving bomber accuracy during World War II.

Professor Samuel Langley

One of the earliest American pioneers in powered flight was Professor Samuel Langley (1834-1906), a distinguished astronomer who served as the third secretary of the Smithsonian Institution. Langley started research into powered flight in 1887. After experimenting with a

Langley's Aerodrome No.5. Photo courtesy of the Smithsonian Institution, Washington, D.C.

variety of propulsion systems, he finally succeeded in making the first successful flights of an engine-driven aircraft on May 6, 1896, using a single-cylinder steam engine. The unmanned, tandem-winged aircraft, designated Langley Aerodrome *No. 5*, was 13 feet long, 4 feet high, and had a wingspan of almost 14 feet. Two flights were made that day from a spring-loaded catapult on the shore of the Potomac River. One flight lasted for 2,300 feet and the other for 3,300 feet before the plane dived into the river. (Landing gear had been eliminated to save weight.)

Based on his initial success, the War Department awarded Langley the then-unheard-of sum of $50,000 to create a man-carrying version of the Aerodrome. After carefully constructing a larger version of the unmanned aircraft, he launched it from a houseboat on the Potomac on October 7, 1903. The plane was damaged in takeoff. Another flight was attempted two months later on December 8, nine days before the Wright brothers made their successful powered flights at Kitty Hawk on December 17. This flight also ended in failure, and Langley gave up his efforts in disgrace. He died three years later, a very disappointed and discredited scientist.

Glenn Curtiss

The success of the Wrights' early experiments spurred the creative efforts of a well-established bicycle and motorcycle racer and engine builder, Glenn Curtiss of Hammondsport, New York. In 1904, Curtiss had established a land speed record of 67 miles per hour (mph) on one of his own motorcycles, almost twice the speed the Wright brothers' plane had achieved in the air the year before. With his pre-occupation with speed, Curtiss soon developed an intense interest in flying and, in 1906, held a number of extensive conversations with the Wright brothers.

By 1908 Curtiss had produced his own biplane, the *June Bug*, with which he won a trophy (established by *Scientific American* magazine) for making the first straight-line flight of one kilometer (3,281 feet). In 1909 Curtiss won an important speed trophy in France, which impressed the U.S. Navy. The following year, with the Navy's assistance, one of Curtiss's planes was the first to take off from the deck of a ship, and in 1911 a Curtiss aircraft made the first shipboard landing. The concept of the arresting cable still in use on aircraft carriers was developed for that test. In 1911 Curtiss also made the first successful takeoff and landing on water, thereby developing the concept of the seaplane.

In 1909, the Wright brothers formed a company to produce their planes and also to defend their patent position. They sued Glenn Curtiss for patent infringement, claiming he obtained their patent-protected technology through the extensive conversations he had with them in 1906 and had incorporated the concepts into his own planes for purposes of making a profit. After protracted litigation, the Wright brothers essentially won their case.

In 1912, ten years after Langley's unsuccessful attempts to fly the Aerodrome, Glenn Curtiss modified Langley's plane and tried to fly it at his Hammondsport facility, but also without success. His purpose in attempting to prove the Aerodrome could fly was to discredit Orville and Wilbur Wright's patents by proving that Langley had been the first to develop a flyable engine-powered aircraft.

The Wright Aeronautical Company and the Curtiss Airplane Company were the most significant aircraft manufacturers in the United States until the late 1920s. By then both companies had been taken over by New York financiers. It is one of the ironies of American industry that, in 1930, the two firms were merged into a single company named the Curtiss-Wright Corporation.

At about this same time other famous U.S. aircraft pioneering companies began to appear on the scene, including Martin, Boeing, Lockheed, Douglas, and Ryan. The Curtiss-Wright Corporation continued to make contributions to American aviation through World War II, producing such outstanding planes as the P-36 and the P-40 Warhawk. Unfortunately, the decline of business during the early postwar years was more than the company could weather, and it ceased making aircraft in 1948.

Blériot in the plane he used to cross the English Channel. Photo courtesy of the Smithsonian Institution, Washington, D.C.

Early European Developments

During the period following the Wright brothers' accomplishments and leading up to World War I, Europeans took the leadership in aircraft design and development. The French were particularly motivated to experiment with powered flight after witnessing flying demonstrations by the Wrights in Paris in 1908.

Louis Blériot of France was one of the early European pioneers of aviation. He was the first to fly across the English Channel (1909), and he built a number of planes flown by other pioneering French flyers. Blériot produced 500 of the Blériot XI in 1911 and an additional 800 during World War I.

Blériot was the first to see the speed advantages that could be obtained from eliminating one wing of the biplane. He began to experiment with the monoplane, which, with the limited knowledge available on aerodynamic stresses at the time, proved to be a dangerous aircraft to fly. Excessive speeds resulted in collapsed wings and dead pilots. For a time several countries grounded monoplanes because of the high rate of pilot attrition. In spite of these setbacks, progress continued as military planners began to see the value of high-speed aircraft.

Another French pioneer, Armond Deperdussin, formed a company called SPAD (*Société pour les Appareils Deperdussin*) in 1910. His engineer, Louis Béchereau, created the Deperdussin racer, which was one of the first aircraft to exceed 100 mph, achieving 106 mph in 1912. Béchereau's design included a powerful

140-hp rotary engine. In his design he gave detailed attention to the reduction of drag through streamlining, including the use of an unusually large streamlined propeller hub.

The rotary engine, a radial engine with a fixed crankshaft, was a French development. The propeller was fixed to the engine so that both the engine and the propeller rotated around the fixed crankshaft. The advantage of this engine was light weight per horsepower since the rotating cylinders made cooling more efficient. Its disadvantage was that the torque forces generated by the rotating engine required the pilot to compensate differently when turning left or right. Still, the engine was effective until horsepower approached 200 hp and torque forces became extremely difficult to manage. Aircraft designers then returned to the in-line, water-cooled, automobile-type engine until the offspring of the rotating engine, the radial engine, was developed in America in the late 1920s.

The Germans also became active around 1910. Anthony Fokker, a Dutchman who started an aircraft manufacturing company in Germany after his offer to assist the Allies was refused, was one of the leaders. Hugo Junkers was another German aircraft producer who contributed to German aviation before and during World War I. Both Fokker and Junkers developed the use of steel in aircraft body construction—Junkers being the first to design an all-steel aircraft. The Fokker D VII is considered by many experts to have been the finest fighter plane in the First World War.

While the French, Germans, and English were the pioneers in pre-World War I aviation, Nicolas, Czar of Russia, was the first European

Sikorsky and his plane in Russia, 1913. Photo courtesy of the Smithsonian Institution, Washington, D.C.

monarch to sense the potential of aviation. He formed the Imperial Russian Flying Corps in 1910 and held a design competition, which was won by a Russian, Igor Sikorsky. Sikorsky designed a number of fighter and observation planes for the Russian Flying Corps. Just prior to immigrating to America in 1919, he successfully demonstrated the value of multi-engine aircraft able to carry passengers and heavy loads. After coming to America, Sikorsky continued to build large, multi-engine aircraft and began to develop the concept of the helicopter; his efforts finally reached fruition in 1939.

During the pre-World War I period, except for a very few pioneers in the U.S. military, Americans were content to exhibit their new-found toy at fairs and other gatherings around the country. One of the most dramatic achievements in the United States during this period was the 49-day transcontinental junket flown by Calbraith Perry Rodgers in 1911 in a Wright EX biplane, nicknamed the *Vin Fiz.*

Rodgers had attempted to win a $50,000 prize offered by William Randolph Hearst to the first pilot who could cross the country in 30 days or less. While Rodgers lost the prize, having only reached Illinois after 30 days, he picked up financing for the remainder of the journey from the Armour Meat Packing Company. Armour was marketing a new grape drink called *Vin Fiz*, which Rodgers agreed to paint on the underside of the lower wing of his biplane. During the many-stop voyage, Rodgers crashed 19 times, 5 of which were serious, and by the time he reached Pasadena, California, his plane had few of the original parts. While in flight his average speed had been 60 mph.

World War I

When World War I started in 1914, most of the aircraft then flying were mono-planes. By the end of the war, practically all sides had shifted back to biplanes (and even several versions of the triplane). The reason for this regression was structural reliability. The trade-offs between wing area, wing loading, and structural strength were not well-understood at the time and as the demand for performance increased, it was safer to revert back to the multiple-wing plane.

The French were the first of the allies to go into mass-production of aircraft. They designed and manufactured the famous SPAD (*Société pour Aviation et ses Dérivés*) single-engine fighter. The SPAD was produced by Blériot, who had taken over Deperdussin's company. While changing the company name, he kept the acronym made famous by Deperdussin. He also retained the creative Louis Béchereau as his chief engineer.

The British were also able to gear up quickly. T. O. M. Sopwith, who had formed the Sopwith Aviation Company in 1912, was able to quickly expand its production of the Sopwith Pup, Camel, and Triplane. In 1913 Sopwith had only seven employees, but by the end of WW I he was employing 3,500 people and had produced 16,000 aircraft. Another famous British World War I aircraft, the S.E. 5a, was produced

A replica of the 1917 SPAD XIII. The SPAD XIII was one of the great fighter planes of World War I. Eddie Rickenbacker flew this type of plane when he led the 94th Hat-in-the-Ring Aero Squadron. Photo courtesy of the Owls Head Transportation Museum, Rockland, Maine.

by the British Royal Aircraft Factory.

While a number of American pilots flew in combat during the First World War, they mainly flew in French SPADs and Nieuport 17s, and, to a lesser extent, British S.E. 5s. American aircraft, principally the Curtiss JN-4 "Jenny" biplane, found their way to the front in the waning phases of the war, and only a few actually flew in combat. Most Jennys were used as trainers. They were reliable aircraft, and most importantly, they were kind to inexperienced pilots. There had been so many Jennys produced during World War I that in the 1920s they became popular with barnstorming pilots who acquired them as war surplus for less than $100.

At the start of World War I, the U.S. Army Air Service had a complement of 1,100 men, of which 35 were pilots, and several hundred planes—none fit for combat. The United States was fourteenth in rank among the world's air forces. By the end of the war, the Air Service had expanded to 195,000 men and 750 planes and had moved up to third in rank. While it was in combat for only seven months before the German surrender, the Air Service did manage to perform well under the leadership of Brigadier

General Billy Mitchell. American pilots shot down 781 German planes and 73 surveillance balloons. Eddie Rickenbacker was the outstanding ace with 26 enemy aircraft to his credit.

Immediate Post-World War I

Following the war, the race was on to establish long-distance flying milestones. One such milestone was the first flight across the Atlantic. In May of 1919 a U.S. Navy Curtiss flying boat, NC-4, made the first flight across the Atlantic, but it required 28 days to complete. The flight from Long Island, New York, to Plymouth, England, was routed via the Azores and Lisbon, Portugal. The NC-4 was initially accompanied by the NC-1 and NC-3, but the two other aircraft ran out of fuel and were damaged when forced to land at sea. In June of the same year, two British pilots in a two-engine Vickers bomber made the first non-stop flight, flying from Ireland to Newfoundland.

The 1920s

The 1920s became a race for speed. Prior to World War I, the Deperdussin racer had set a record of 124.5 mph, but most military aircraft at the start of the war only had top speeds in the 80-90 mph range and engine sizes of 90 hp. By the end of the war, engine sizes had more than doubled but speeds had only increased by 50 percent. The SPAD XIII, for example, was capable of a top speed of 138 mph, using a 235 hp Hispano-Suiza water-cooled V-8 engine.

During the 1920s a succession of faster and faster racing planes was built. In 1922 a low-wing monoplane designed by Alfred Victor Verville and built by Lawrance Sperry in Dayton, Ohio, achieved a speed of 223 mph. The plane, which was equipped with a Curtiss D-12 water-cooled engine, was one of the first to have retractable landing gear. Lieutenant James Harold "Jimmy" Doolittle flew a U.S. Army Curtiss R3C-2 seaplane at 233 mph in the 1925 Schneider Cup race.

The Schneider Cup races were an important stimulus to attempts to increase speed—somewhat similar to the "Indy 500" in advancing automobile technology during approximately the same period. The Schneider Cup had been held annually from 1913 to 1927 (except during WW I) and biannually until 1931, when it was terminated. The cup was first won in 1913 by a French Deperdussin aircraft at a speed of 45 mph. By 1921 the winning speed, achieved by an Italian aircraft, had slightly more than doubled to 110 mph.

The British gained dominance in the Schneider Cup races during the 1927-1931 period with their series of Supermarine seaplanes designed by R. J. Mitchell. In 1927 a Supermarine S.5 established a speed record of 282 mph, and in 1931 a Supermarine S.6B equipped with a 2,350 hp Rolls-Royce engine established a Schneider Cup record of 340 mph. A few weeks later, another S.6B became the first aircraft to exceed 400 mph. The Supermarine series evolved into the Supermarine Spitfire that was instrumental in winning the Battle of Britain.

American Air Developments

Unlike military leaders in Europe, who had realized the potential of aviation in World War I, U.S. Congressional leaders and army generals remained unconvinced all during the 1920s of the benefit of aviation. While both the army and the navy continued to conduct experiments and demonstrations, Brigadier General William "Billy" Mitchell was almost alone in the crusade to develop American air power. In his controversial bombing of an obsolete German naval ship in 1921, Mitchell was forced to use German Fokker high-wing transports. During the 1920s the U.S. Post Office was the most progressive federal agency in developing the use of aviation. It had started the U.S. Air Mail Service in 1918, using war-surplus British de Havillands.

Naval aviation was born in 1910 when a civilian pilot, Eugene Ely, took off in a Curtiss pusher biplane from the cruiser USS *Birmingham*, in Hampton Roads, Virginia, and landed on the beach. Two months later, he took off from shore and landed on a platform on the cruiser USS *Pennsylvania* in San Francisco Bay. Distrusting the reliability of deck landings, the navy pursued the development of seaplanes. While the use of aircraft to extend fleet surveillance had proved valuable, it was not until the 1930s that aviation became an integral part of navy operations.

The Army Air Service continued its attempts to convince army leadership to intensify the development of military aviation. In 1923, after several aborted attempts the previous year, two Army Air Service pilots, Lieutenants John A. Macready and Oakley Kelly, made the first non-stop transcontinental flight. The 27-hour flight from Long Island to San Diego, which yielded an average air speed of 92 mph, was made in a Fokker high-wing transport modified with a Packard Liberty engine. Also in 1923 the Army Air Service began to experiment with in-flight refueling since typical aircraft range at the time was less than 600 miles (approximately four hours) under normal flight conditions. In 1929, using in-flight refueling techniques, an Army Air Service Fokker set a record of 150 hours of continuous flight.

In furtherance of its promotion of aviation, the Army Air Service achieved the world's first around-the-world flight in 1924. The effort initially involved four modified two-wing Douglas World Cruisers with Liberty engines, although only two of the aircraft completed the 175-day voyage. The flight, which started in Santa Monica, California, on March 17, 1924, involved 363 hours of actual flying time for an average air speed of 72 mph. The Army planes made 57 stops and the average leg was approximately 460 miles.

Charles A. Lindbergh's flight from Long Island to Paris on May 20, 1927, in the *Spirit of St. Louis* probably did more than any other demonstration to make the general public aware of the potential of aircraft. His transatlantic flight in a Ryan single-wing aircraft equipped

Lindbergh taking off in the Spirit of St. Louis. *Photo courtesy of the Smithsonian Institution, Washington, D.C.*

with a Wright air-cooled Whirlwind engine, was not the only one during the 1920s, nor the most significant, technically. It was, however, the first solo non-stop flight across the Atlantic, and it captured the imagination of the public. Lindbergh said later that his biggest problem on the 33.5-hour flight was his battle with fatigue.

Excluding Lindbergh's flight, there were 60 attempts at transatlantic crossings between New York and Paris during the period from 1926 to 1932. Less than 20 were successful and more than 20 crashed or vanished.

American Aircraft Engine Development

Lindbergh's flight further substantiated the reliability of the Wright Aeronautical Company's radial air-cooled engine, the Whirlwind. The Wright Whirlwind engine and its successor, the Cyclone, along with Pratt & Whitney's air-cooled Wasp engine, were the standards for reliable engine performance for more than 20 years.

Both the Wright and Pratt & Whitney families of radial air-cooled engines were basically created by the same pioneering engine designer, Charles J. Lawrance. He designed his first radial engine in 1922. It so impressed the U.S. Navy, which preferred air-cooled engines for shipboard

Wiley Post in front of his plane, the Winnie Mae. *Photo courtesy of the Smithsonian Institution, Washington, D.C.*

use due to ease of maintenance, that it pressured the Wright Aeronautical Company to acquire Lawrance's small development company. Lawrance designed the Whirlwind J-1 for Wright. He then moved over to Pratt & Whitney when Wright executive Frederick B. Rentschler took over that ailing company in 1925. At Pratt & Whitney he designed the famous Wasp line of engines.

Transpacific Crossing

With the conquering of the Atlantic crossing in 1919, interest turned to achieving the much more difficult Pacific crossing. The U.S. Army succeeded in flying to Hawaii from the mainland on June 28, 1927, in an American-built Fokker trimotor. The first complete transpacific flight occurred the following year when two Australian pilots, Charles Kingsford-Smith and Charles Ulm, flew from Oakland, California, to Brisbane, Australia, with stops in Hawaii and Fiji, in a Fokker trimotor named the *Southern Cross.* The flight made one of the first uses of radio navigation on the initial leg to Hawaii.

The first successful non-stop transpacific flight did not occur until 1931, after a number of failed and even tragic attempts. Two American flyers, Clyde Pangborn and Hugh Herndon Jr., completed a 4,883-mile flight from Tokyo to Wenatchee, Washington, in 41 hours in a Bellanca named *Miss Veedol.*

The first transpolar flights were made in

1928 by two American pilots, Hubert Wilkins and Carl Eielson, who successfully flew a Lockheed single-engine Vega from Point Barrow, Alaska, over the North Pole to the Norwegian possession of Spitsbergen. Later in the same year, the two pilots accomplished the same feat over the South Pole.

In 1931 Wiley Post, accompanied by an Australian navigator named Harold Gatty, set an around-the-world record of 8 days and 15 hours in a Lockheed Vega called the *Winnie Mae.* Post's flight demonstrated the value of the Sperry autopilot and an advanced radio direction finder.

American Commercial Aircraft Development

Prior to World War I in the United States, passenger-carrying flights were limited to thrill-seeking rides at fairs. In the summer of 1914, however, the first commercial passenger service was operated in Florida between St. Petersburg and Tampa using a flying boat capable of carrying one passenger. In 1919, a Curtiss flying boat was used in a passenger service between San Pedro harbor and Catalina Island, in California. Commercial aviation was slow to develop during the 1920s in America.

First produced in 1926, the high-winged Ford Trimotor was one of the first aircraft built for commercial use. In 1927, Boeing produced the 40-B2 biplane, which was used by United Airlines in the first transcontinental air service. The high-winged, single-engine Lockheed Vega was also introduced in 1927. It became a popular passenger aircraft for its time, as well as being popular with adventuring pilots.

The Boeing 247, first introduced in 1933, was the first of the modern multi-engine, low-wing commercial transports to go into service. It was a joint effort by Boeing, United Airlines, Pratt & Whitney (engine), and Hamilton-Standard (propellers). United and this group of manufacturers tried to establish a monopoly on commercial transports, so a number of other airlines, notably Continental, Transworld Airlines (TWA), and Western, prevailed upon Donald Douglas to develop a competing transport. The DC-1, -2, and -3 came out of this decision by Douglas to enter the commercial aircraft field. The first DC-1s were delivered to TWA in 1933 and the DC-3 first went into service in 1936. As a result of subsequent competition between these two pioneering commercial aircraft, Boeing produced only 61 of the 247s, while Douglas turned out 13,000 DC-3s (including the military transport version, the C-47).

Passengers boarding a United Airlines Boeing 247. Photo courtesy of the Smithsonian Institution, Washington, D.C.

Pan American Initiates Transpacific Service

A major milestone in commercial aviation came in 1935, when Pan American Airways (Pan Am) initiated commercial flights from San Francisco, California, to Manila, Philippines, via Hawaii, Midway, Wake, and Guam. The inaugural passenger flight in 1936 to Manila took 60 hours, with the first leg to Hawaii taking 18 hours. Passengers disembarked at each fueling stop and spent the night in a hotel. In 1937 Pan Am extended service to China and New Zealand.

Pan Am initially used four-engine flying boats from Sikorsky and Martin Aviation, which they advertised as Pan American "Clippers." Later, Pan Am added Boeing 314 flying boats. The commercial flying boats contained passenger comforts that have never been matched, such as a dining salon and private suites with a dressing room and toilet facilities. Many provided Pullman-type sleeping accommodations and some even came equipped with a honeymoon suite. When transoceanic flights exceeded 12 hours, extra passenger comforts were almost necessary, but as commercial aircraft speeds improved and need for bigger payloads increased, these amenities were eliminated.

Pan Am became the first airline to initiate commercial flights to South America in 1935 using a Sikorsky S-42 flying boat. Non-stop service across the Atlantic, however, was not instituted until 1939. For the Atlantic service, Pan Am used the same Boeing B-314 flying boats that were in regular service in the Pacific.

In 1937 Russia attempted to initiate commercial over-the-pole flights to the United States, but after several crashes, the attempt was aborted. Also in 1937 Amelia Earhart was lost over the Pacific Ocean in a twin-engine Lockheed Electra while trying to become the first female pilot to circle the globe.

In 1938 Howard Hughes demonstrated how far aircraft reliability and technology had come by flying a Lockheed twin-engine L14 around the world in less than four days, cutting Wiley Post's 1931 record by more than half.

Sikorsky flying boat over San Francisco Bay. Photo courtesy of the Smithsonian Institution, Washington, D.C.

By the 1930s engine power had reached 2,500 hp, a long way up the scale from the 12-hp engine built by the Wright brothers in 1902, and even the 200- to 400-hp engines used in World War I aircraft. The increased flying speeds attainable with these powerful engines had also increased landing speeds so that braking was needed. This introduced the use of wing flaps and wheel brakes. The electric engine starter was also introduced in the early 1930s.

Faster flying speeds also created icing problems and much experimentation occurred during the 1930s to alleviate this problem. Thermal and vibration techniques were employed to remove excessive ice from wings and propellers. A mechanism to spray alcohol on the rotating propeller was even used for a short period.

Hughes made extensive use of weather forecasts and radio navigation techniques. Upon arriving back in New York City, Hughes commented that the industry had developed to the point that any airline pilot could have achieved what he had just done. It was not until 1949 that the first non-stop round-the-world flight was accomplished by a U.S. Air Force B-50A, using four in-flight refuelings. The flight covered the 23,500-mile trip in 94 hours.

Aircraft Technology in the 1930s

Starting in the late 1920s and continuing throughout the 1930s, many of the aeronautical innovations introduced in the early 1920s came into common use. These included retractable landing gear; variable-pitch propellers; and flush-rivet, all-metal fuselage construction.

One of the most striking improvements of the early 1930s was the development of a cowling for the radial engine by the National Advisory Committee for Aeronautics (NACA). This innovation, developed after extensive analysis and wind-tunnel testing, reduced drag sufficiently to enable improvements in speed of 20 percent in most aircraft.

World War II Buildup

When World War II began, the United States military was still behind the times. It had only a few hundred planes and ranked sixth among world air forces. As it had at the beginning of World War I, the American aircraft industry overcame this poor starting position. Five years later, by the end of the war, the U.S. Air Force had nearly 80,000 planes and was the largest air force in the world. The performance of the U.S. Air Force and that of its allies proved conclusively that air power had become an integral part of modern warfare.

Military aircraft developments during World War II achieved the peak of propeller-driven performance. Improvements to commercial propeller-driven aircraft continued during the 1940s and 1950s through adoption of these wartime developments. Pratt & Whitney produced the last piston-engine, a 28-cylinder radial engine capable of producing 3,500 hp. Military aircraft designers had begun to develop jet-engine technology by the end of the war.

194

Jet Aircraft

Design of the first jet engine was attempted by a British designer named Frank Whittle, who took out the first patent and finally succeeded in building a workable engine in 1938. An experimental aircraft based on the Whittle's concepts made its first flight in May 1941.

Work on a jet engine also started in Germany during the mid-1930s, led by Hans von Ohain working under aircraft designer Ernst Heinkel. They flew their first experimental jet in 1939, two years before the British test flight. Germany went into production of a jet engine, designated the Junkers Jumo 004, during World War II and installed it in a Messerschmitt called the Me 262. This jet fighter became the first operational jet fighter aircraft in the world and flew in combat late in the war. While the Me 262 had no effect on the outcome of the war, it made a revolutionary contribution to aviation and established the superior performance of jet aircraft.

By the end of World War II, jet engines had already gone through one generation of development and were on a par with the best of the piston-driven aircraft engines, even in the United States. Further improvements in reliability and efficiency were achieved during the years immediately following the war. The first American jet aircraft to become operational, the Lockheed F-80 Shooting Star, provided the backbone of U.S. Air Force fighter capability in the Korean War.

The successor to the F-80, the F-86, was the first American swept-wing aircraft. The Germans were the first to discover the advantages of the swept wing for supersonic flight. They had originally used a slightly modified swept wing on the Me 262 in order to achieve a proper center of gravity due to the weight of the engines. When the Germans entered into the age of supersonic aircraft, they found that the swept-wing design helped alleviate some of the vibration encountered when approaching the sound barrier. At the end of the war, when the Allies found the German data on the swept wing and talked to German aircraft designers, they quickly converted their own high-performance jet aircraft to swept-wing designs. The first American fighter designed to operate at supersonic speeds was North American Aviation's F-100 Super Sabre.

In the early 1950s Richard T. Whitcomb, a scientist at NACA's Langley facility, made one of the most exciting technical discoveries in jet aircraft design. He determined that the performance of a supersonic aircraft could be substantially improved if the cross-sectional area of the fuselage was reduced in the vicinity of the wings. This came to be known as the "area rule" and was first applied to Convair's delta-wing fighter, the F-102.

Post-War Commercial Aircraft Development

Until 1946 commercial airlines relied principally on propeller-driven flying boats. The concept of modern airports with concrete runways had not taken hold in most parts of the world and water was the most effective landing and takeoff medium. As late as 1945 most airports in Europe were still covered with grass. By 1946, however, modern airport facilities were becoming available, and land-based commercial transport began to replace the seaplane.

A significant footnote to history is that Henry Ford was one of the pioneers in the construction of long concrete runways. He first applied them at the Dearborn, Michigan, airport, which opened in 1926, and they became the model for airports throughout the United States. By the late 1930s hundreds of American cities had built concrete runways at their local airports.

Following World War II aircraft manufacturers introduced large four-engine propeller-driven transports. Boeing introduced the Model 377 Stratocruiser with its eye-catching double-bubble fuselage, and Lockheed offered the L.049 Constellation, affectionately known as the "Connie." Douglas's DC-4, -5, -6, and -7s appeared in rapid succession. The final versions of these dynasty-ending families of piston-engine transports were all built for ranges exceeding 3,000 miles in order to be able to fly non-stop across continents and oceans. Speed did not become a primary factor until the late 1950s.

By 1958, when Boeing delivered the first American-built commercial jets to Pan Am, commercial air travel had finally come of age. Passenger miles flown by American carriers had grown from 8.8 billion in 1949 to more than 30 billion by 1958 and were continuing to grow. Business travelers and vacationers alike had begun demanding faster and more-frequent service.

Propeller-driven transports were not able to meet the public's demand for faster aircraft and shorter flying times. For example, while the DC-7 had a cruising speed of 360 mph, the Boeing 707 could cruise at 570 mph. Douglas introduced its first commercial jet airliner, the DC-8, in 1959, and it also had a cruising speed of 570 mph. Thus within two years, the flight time from Los Angeles to New York was reduced from 7 hours and 40 minutes to only 4 hours and 40 minutes.

The next generation of American commercial jets was led by the Boeing 727 and the Douglas DC-9. The Boeing 727, with the distinctive three-engine configuration mounted at the rear of the fuselage, quickly became the favorite of the airlines. Because of the location of the engines, the passenger cabin was much quieter, and it proved to be a much more efficient aircraft than the previous-generation 707. By the time Boeing phased the 727 out of production in 1984, it had built 1,830 in various configurations. The engine-in-rear arrangement was not new to American travelers who were familiar with the French Sud Caravelle, which first started flying in Europe in 1959 and had been flown by United Airlines in the United States starting in 1961.

The next major step in the evolution of air travel was the introduction of the wide-bodied jumbo jet in the form of the Boeing 747, which first appeared in 1970. Developing the 747 was a major challenge for Boeing and might not have been undertaken except for the loss of a substantial air force contract and a pre-design commitment of orders by Juan Trippe, then head of Pan Am. In the mid-1960s Boeing had lost the

bidding on the Air Force C-5A transport to Lockheed and was looking for a way to salvage the effort they had put into the competition.

Boeing was not alone in the wide-bodied jet field. Lockheed introduced the L-1011, although it stopped production in 1984 after having produced only 250 aircraft. Douglas, who by then had merged with McDonnell Aircraft to become the McDonnell-Douglas Corporation, brought out the DC-10, followed by its successor, the MD-11. Another important competitor in the market for wide-bodied jets was the European-built Airbus. Currently, the Boeing 747, the McDonnell Douglas MD-11, and the Airbus, in its various configurations, are still in production.

Supersonic Commercial Aircraft

Supersonic flight was first achieved on October 14, 1947, when Captain Chuck Yeager flew the X-1 at Mach 1.06. In 1953 a Douglas D-558 Skyrocket achieved twice the speed of sound. That same year the first fighter designed to operate at sustained supersonic speeds, the North American F-100 Super Sabre, was introduced.

While the military has continued to develop supersonic aircraft, airlines and aircraft manufacturers have come to realize that commercial supersonic travel is not economically sound—at least in the foreseeable future. Recognition of this economic limitation came slowly.

In the early 1960s the British and the French were attempting to leapfrog U.S. domination of commercial aircraft manufacture by developing a supersonic transport (SST). They quickly realized that the development effort would be too expensive for either country to finance alone. So in 1962 the two countries formed a jointly owned company called Aérospatiale-British Aerospace Corporation for the purpose of building the supersonic Concorde. During this period, the Soviet Union had also initiated a commercial SST program.

In 1963 President John F. Kennedy, fearing the United States would lose its preeminence in commercial aviation, initiated a competition between Boeing and Lockheed for the design of an American SST with federal funding. It was clear that the cost of developing the SST would be prohibitive for private industry. The original design specifications called for the SST to fly at Mach 3 and to have a seating capacity of 290 passengers. The competitive bidding took four years to complete, and in 1966 a contract was awarded to Boeing. The program proved to be overly ambitious, and after spending hundreds of millions of dollars with little to show for it, Congress finally cut off funding in 1971, and the SST project died. The Soviets also terminated their commercial supersonic jet aircraft program at about the same time.

In the meantime the French-British consortium had built the Concorde, and by March 1969 it was in the air. Regular service was initiated by Air France and British Airways in 1976, each airline having acquired seven of the 14 total Concordes built. As it finally evolved, the Concorde is capable of flying at a supersonic speed of Mach 2.2 and has a seating capacity of 125 passengers. Currently both of the sponsoring governments continue to subsidize the Concorde's operation.

Aviation Developments Approach Space

The vision of aviation scientists has long been to develop a space plane capable of taking off from an ordinary airfield, accelerating into outer space, performing assigned functions in space, returning to earth's atmosphere, landing in a normal fashion, and then repeating the process many times. To escape the earth's atmosphere, this aerospace plane would need to reach orbital speed and withstand the intense heat associated with hypersonic (over Mach 5) and reentry speeds.

The first hypersonic flight, which occurred on October 3, 1967, was achieved by the North American X-15. Built of titanium and high-alloy steel able to withstand temperatures approaching 1,200 degrees Fahrenheit, the X-15 reached Mach 6.72 and an altitude of almost 60

miles, close to that of space. The X-15 proved to be a useful test vehicle for the Space Shuttle. The original concept of the Space Shuttle had been an aerospace vehicle capable of operating as an aircraft when in the earth's atmosphere and as a spacecraft when in space. Based in part on the X-15 program, government scientists concluded that with existing technology such a vehicle would be prohibitively expensive. A joint effort between NASA and the Department of Defense, called the National Aero-Space Plane Project, is currently underway, however, with the long-term objective of developing a true aerospace craft.

The U.S. Space Program

While the aerospace craft has been a dream of aerodynamicists since before World War II, the development of space flight has actually been rooted in an entirely different scientific community. Propulsion and reaction-type guidance technologies were the technical challenges of space, not aerodynamics. With its preoccupation with atmospheric flight advancements, the United States all but ignored its space program until the Russians launched Sputnik I on October 4, 1957. Then, as the United States was just beginning to get its space program underway, the Russians announced the successful launching of a manned space flight involving Yuri Gagarin on April 12, 1961.

Ironically, the United States pioneered modern rocketry in the 1920s under the leadership of physicist Robert Hutchings Goddard. Goddard made his first contribution to rocketry during World War I, when he developed a prototype bazooka weapon—although it did not come into combat use until World War II. His most famous contributions to rocketry started in 1926, when, as a professor of physics at Clark University in Worcester, Massachusetts, he launched the world's first liquid-fueled rocket. In 1935 one of his rockets became the first vehicle to break the sound barrier. During World War II Goddard supervised the U.S. Navy's jet propulsion program, much of which was devoted to developing JATO (jet-assisted

Dr. Robert H. Goddard standing beside the first successfully-launched liquid-propelled rocket, launched at Auburn, Massachusetts, March 16, 1926. This flight demonstrated the possibility of using liquid propellants in actual flight. Photo courtesy of the National Aeronautics and Space Administration, Washington, D.C.

takeoff) engines for use on heavily loaded navy seaplanes. Goddard, along with Dr. James A. Van Allen at the Applied Physics Laboratory at Johns Hopkins University, provided the genesis of the navy's post-war missile program, which led to the navy's Viking family of rockets.

The United States chose not to pursue the lead in rocketry provided by Goddard's efforts during the 1920s and 1930s, but the importance of the results of his research was not lost on the German military scientists. The German Wehrmacht initiated its rocket development program in 1932 under the command of Artillery Captain Walter Dornberger who, two years later, hired a young college graduate physicist named Wernher von Braun.

By 1942 the German rocket scientists had test-flown the 46-foot-long V-2 missile capable of a 190-mile range with a one-ton explosive warhead. It was committed to the field in September 1944. By March of the following year, 3,000 V-2s had been launched against Allied targets on the continent and in England before allied bombers were able to eliminate the launching facilities. German scientists also developed the winged V-1 rocket-powered "Buzz-Bomb," which could be fired from mobile launchers. It was 25 feet long, had a range of 150 miles, and could carry a payload of almost one ton. The V-1 became operational in 1944 and rained terror on London, England, and Antwerp, Belgium, until May of the following year.

Following the war the U.S. Army brought 80 V-2s to White Sands Proving Ground in New Mexico, where they became the starting point for the army's missile program. The Army Ballistic Missile program was headed by the Redstone Arsenal in Alabama, which developed the Jupiter family of missiles. The Jupiter-C provided the launch vehicle for the United States' first satellite launch on January 31, 1958. That same year, the army's Redstone missile, equipped with the Jupiter launcher, was declared operational.

While the army and navy pursued their ground-based rocket development programs, the air force worked toward the development of smaller aircraft-based missiles, particularly air-to-air tactical weapons. It was not until the mid-1950s that the air force concluded that it needed a large, ground-based ballistic missile capability to carry strategic nuclear warheads. This led to the Titan liquid-fuel and Atlas solid-fuel rocket programs and the creation of the U.S Air Force Ballistic Missile Division in 1957. The Atlas and Titan were declared operational in the early 1960s.

While the air force and army were busily competing for jurisdiction over the use of missiles for strategic defense, Congress became embroiled in a debate over the roles and missions of the various military and civilian agencies with respect

Launch of a French communications satellite on December 6, 1965, by a NASA-developed Scout rocket. Photo courtesy of the National Aeronautics and Space Administration, Washington, D.C.

to the nation's space activities. This debate had been triggered by Russia's launching of Sputnik in October 1957. By then the military services had taken over the nation's leadership in space research. The only civilian agency involved, the National Advisory Committee for Aeronautics (NACA), which had been founded in 1915 to further the nation's aviation technology, was deemed too committed to research into atmospheric flight to be up to the task of developing a space program.

Consequently, a new agency was formed on October 1, 1958, the National Aeronautics and Space Administration (NASA). It combined the NACA research activities along with the army's rocket development program headed by Wernher von Braun at Huntsville, Alabama, and several Defense Department-managed programs. As part of this Congressional action, the air force was given jurisdiction over land-based intercontinental and intermediate-range ballistic missile weapons. Congress also authorized the air force to proceed with the development of the Minuteman solid-fuel missile.

NASA immediately attempted to bring under its wing all of the satellite and propulsion capabilities needed to accelerate the nation's space travel and exploration program. By the end of 1958, the Russians had launched several more Sputniks, and there was a strong national sense of urgency to catch up in the space race.

During the first decade of its existence, NASA lacked rockets capable of lifting satellites and spacecraft into space and was forced to call upon the military services for its launchers. The only notable exception was the Scout rocket that was developed at Langley Research Center. A small satellite launch vehicle first flown in 1960, the Scout was capable of putting a 130-pound satellite into a 300-mile orbit. Later versions increased the payload to 425 pounds.

For larger payloads NASA relied on such military launchers as the army's Jupiter rocket, which launched the three Explorer satellites, the first of which was launched on January 31, 1958. NASA used the air force's Thor launchers for a number of unmanned satellites and spacecraft, including the Pioneer lunar probe in 1958. The Navy's Viking rocket was used to launch three Vanguard satellites, the last being launched on September 18, 1959. A number of NASA's unmanned satellites and space probes were launched by an Agena B upper-stage booster. The development of this rocket, which had sophisticated control features, was started by the air force in 1959 but was taken over by NASA in 1961.

For the nation's first manned space flight, the suborbital flight made by Alan Bartlett Shepard Jr. in the Mercury program's Freedom 7 on May 5, 1961, NASA chose an army Redstone launcher. For the first manned orbital flight

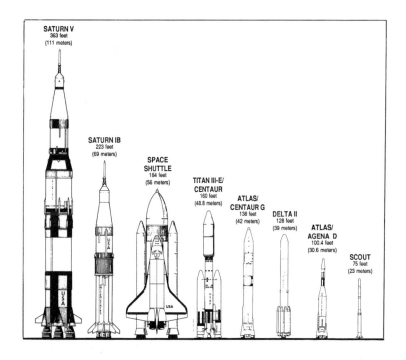

Comparison of missile sizes launched by NASA. Chart courtesy of the National Aeronautics and Space Administration, Washington, D.C.

accomplished by John H. Glenn Jr. in Mercury's Friendship 7 the following February, NASA used a modified air force Atlas missile. The Gemini series of manned spacecraft, which included the first docking in space between Gemini 7 and Gemini 6, was launched by modified air force Titan 2 missiles.

The first NASA-developed rocket capable of launching large loads into orbit was the Saturn V, which was developed at the G.C. Marshall Space Flight Center at Huntsville, Alabama, headed by Wernher von Braun. The engine for the Saturn, designated the H-1, had been developed by the team led by von Braun at the Army Ballistic Missile Agency at the Redstone Arsenal near Huntsville before the agency was transferred to NASA in 1958. The H-1 rocket engine was also used in the Thor and Jupiter missiles.

The Saturn V missile was the main launcher for the Apollo moon program. This program included the moon-orbiting flight by Frank Borman, James Lovell, and William Anders aboard Apollo 8, and the moon landing of Edwin "Buzz" Aldrin, Neil Armstrong, and Michael Collins aboard Apollo 11 during July

1969. The last Saturn to fly launched the Skylab Orbital Workshop in 1973.

Another important engine development started by the military and taken over by NASA was the Centaur. It was used as an upper-stage rocket with Atlas and Titan first stages on a number of NASA satellite and spacecraft launches such as Pioneer, Mariner Surveyor, Viking, and Voyager. The Centaur upper stage continued to be a workhorse of the space program from the 1960s into the 1980s. Its engine, designated the RL-10, burned liquid hydrogen and liquid oxygen. It grew out of research at NASA's Lewis Research Center in the 1940s and 1950s by Dr. Walther Theil, a developer of the German V-2 rocket engine during World War II. In the Centaur, two RL-10s were mounted in parallel. One of its biggest advantages was that it could be stopped and restarted in space.

The Space Shuttle program was conceived in the 1970s as a means of supporting the Skylab Orbital Workshop program. The original concept of developing a true self-contained aerospace vehicle had been dropped early in the program as being too difficult. Consequently the decision was made to launch it into orbit with a rocket but enable the craft to reenter the atmosphere and land as a normal aircraft.

The resulting craft, designated the orbiter, became a delta-winged aerospace craft with a length of 120 feet, a wingspan of 80 feet, and equipped with three rocket engines. At launch, the orbiter is attached to an expendable fuel tank to which are also attached two reusable solid-fuel boosters. The Space Shuttle assembly is capable of lifting a payload of 65,000 pounds into a 230-mile orbit. The entire assembly with payload weighs 4.5 million pounds at launch.

During launch the three orbiter engines and the two boosters fire simultaneously until the shuttle assembly reaches an altitude of 31 miles. At that point the boosters drop off and parachute into the ocean while the orbiter and its external tank continue toward the orbiting altitude. As orbiting altitude is approached, the external fuel tank falls away and the orbiter continues into space.

The first launch of a Space Shuttle was made on April 12, 1981, and a second launch occurred in November of the same year. During the five-year period from 1981 to 1986, the shuttle made 24 successful flights with a variety of missions accomplished, such as in-flight retrieval and repair of a satellite, in-flight launching of a satellite, docking with the Spacelab, and the conduct of a number of experiments in Spacelab. The flight in October 1985 involved a crew of eight, one of whom slept overnight in the Skylab.

The string of successful flights involving increasingly more complex activities came to an abrupt halt with the launching of Challenger in January 1986 when, after 73 seconds of what appeared to be another successful launch, the

The Space Shuttle Columbia *a few seconds after liftoff at 7 a.m. on April 12, 1981. On board were John Young and Bob Crippen. In their 54 hours in orbit they performed a series of tasks designed to test the Space Shuttle's systems. The* Columbia *glided to an airplane-like landing at Edwards Air Force Base, California. Photo courtesy of the National Aeronautics and Space Administration, Washington, D.C.*

shuttle exploded. The loss of the crew of seven and the destruction of the spacecraft with a valuable cargo of two satellites that were to have been launched in orbit, brought about a major review of NASA's shuttle program. Space Shuttle flights were not renewed until 1988, following an extensive refocus and reorganization of the program.

Aviation and Space Museums

❖ *SOUTHERN MUSEUM OF FLIGHT, 4343 North 73rd Street, Birmingham, Alabama 35206. Tel: 205-833-8226. Open Tuesday through Saturday 9:30-5, Sunday 1-5, closed major holidays. Admission $2, student and family discounts.*

The museum was initially conceived in 1965 by the Birmingham Aero Club and is now operated by the city of Birmingham. It contains both military and general aviation planes from eight decades of aviation history. As part of the museum, the state of Alabama authorized the creation of an Alabama Aviation Hall of Fame in 1980. This section of the museum contains displays on important figures in aviation history, including memorabilia from such famous aviators as U.S. Air Force General Claire Lee Chennault of Flying Tigers fame and General Benjamin O. Davis, the first commander of an all-black fighter group.

The collection of aircraft includes planes from the early stages of powered flight, such as a 1912 Curtiss "Pusher." Of special interest are an early Link trainer used during World War II to train pilots in blind flying, a Mini-Mac home-built aircraft, and several ultra-light aircraft. The museum also has a collection of more than 20 aircraft engines, including a French 9-cylinder 1916 Gnome, a cutaway of an 18-cylinder Wright R-3350, and several jet engines. In addition, the museum has a collection of 20 different styles of propellers; exhibits of pilot helmets, goggles, and uniforms, and 400 model planes.

❖ *U.S. ARMY AVIATION MUSEUM, Building 6000, Fort Rucker, Alabama 36362. Tel: 205-255-4507. Open Monday through Friday 9-4, closed major holidays. Admission free.*

Established by the army in 1962, the museum provides displays on the history of the army's role in aviation, with emphasis on the helicopter. The museum's cavernous new building is believed to house the largest collection of vertical-flight aircraft in the world. Exhibits include a history of the army helicopter and features an AH-64 Apache, the newest army attack helicopter.

❖ *PIMA AIR MUSEUM, 6000 E. Valencia Road, Tucson, Arizona 85706. Tel: 602-574-9658. Open daily 9-5, except December 25. Admission $4, student discount.*

The Pima Air Museum was founded by a group of military and civilian aviation enthusiasts with assistance from the Pima County, Arizona, Board of Supervisors. The Tucson Air Museum Foundation of Pima County was formed in 1966 to assume responsibility for operations of the museum. In 1969, the Air Force Museum provided the museum with a nucleus of 35 air force aircraft. By the time the museum officially opened to the public in May 1976, the collection had grown to 75 aircraft. Since then the collection has expanded to more than 200 civilian and military aircraft, and the museum has become the largest privately funded air museum in the world.

The museum's library contains an extensive collection of maintenance and operations manuals as well as historic photographs.

Most aircraft in the collection were built and flown between 1930 and 1960. General aviation and executive aircraft consist of models built by such manufacturers as Beech, Cessna, Piper, Ryan, Stearman, and Waco. Commercial airliners on display include a Lockheed Constellation and an Electra, a French Caravelle, and a British Vickers Viscount. The "Connie" was flown in the United States primarily by TWA from 1946 until replaced by jets around 1960. The two-engine Electra, designed for small

A 1941 Stearman-Boeing. The Stearman was the leading training plane of World War II, with more than 10,000 being built for the army and navy. The plane was very rugged and withstood student abuse. More than 60,000 pilots trained in this type of plane. Photo courtesy of the Owls Head Transportation Museum, Rockland, Maine.

airlines needing a reliable aircraft that could carry up to 10 passengers, was the type of plane used by Amelia Earhart on her fateful attempt to fly around the world in 1937.

The military portion of the display includes an extensive collection of bombers and fighters, as well as cargo and surveillance aircraft and helicopters. In May 1986 the Pima Air

Museum opened the Titan Missile Museum in Green Valley, Arizona. This museum consists of a former Titan II missile installation, which includes a missile in the underground silo, crew facilities, and the command center. This installation is the only Titan facility of the 54 Titan missile sites originally built in Arkansas, Kansas, and Arizona that has been kept intact.

❖ *NEW ENGLAND AIR MUSEUM, Bradley International Airport, Windsor Locks, Connecticut 06096. Tel: 203-623-3305. Open daily 10-5, except major holidays. Admission $5.50, over 60 and pre-teen student discounts.*

Founded by the Connecticut Aeronautical Historical Association in 1960, the museum features exhibits of vintage aircraft and memorabilia with a focus on contributions by Connecticut pioneers. Windsor Locks is situated in the center of a region steeped in aviation history. Nearby are such firms as Pratt & Whitney, United Technology, Sikorsky Helicopter (now part of United Technology), and Kaman Helicopter.

Many of these firms have contributed to the museum's collection. The museum, for example, has a display of almost every engine Pratt & Whitney ever produced. There is also an exhibit paying tribute to the father of the helicopter, Igor Sikorsky (1889-1972), and a number of historically significant helicopters.

The museum has on display 58 of its

total collection of 130 aircraft and is in the process of restoring an additional seven. The oldest plane in the collection is a replica built in 1911 of a French Blériot monoplane. Another early home-built aircraft on display is a biplane built in 1918 by John F. Nixon of Naugatuck, Connecticut, from plans published in a magazine. A later vintage home-assembled kit-craft of interest is a 1976 Rutan Varieze Composite. It was designed by Burt Rutan, the designer of the round-the-world-on-one-tank-of-gas *Voyager*, and is one of the first aircraft constructed of non-metallic carbon-based composite materials.

Also of unusual interest is a 1930 Gee-Bee Model A biplane, the last sports biplane ever built. Jimmy Doolittle flew a Gee Bee when he won the 1931 and 1932 Thompson Trophy races. The stubby monoplane flown in the 1932

Bell 206L-1 Spirit of Texas, *which was flown around the world by H. Ross Perot Jr. and Jay Coburn in 1982. Photo courtesy of the Smithsonian Institution, Washington, D.C.*

race looked like an engine with short wings and a tail. The New England Air Museum also features a number of World War II military aircraft, as well as post-war jets.

❖ *NATIONAL AIR AND SPACE MUSEUM, Sixth Street and Independence Avenue, Washington, D.C. 20560. Tel: 202-357-2700. Open daily 10-5:30, except December 25. Admission free.*

The National Air and Space Museum was opened in 1946 as a bureau within the Smithsonian Institution. The aircraft collection actually dates as far back as 1911 when the Smithsonian acquired a Wright Military Flyer from the War Department. The museum is considered the most outstanding museum in the world on the history of aviation and space exploration. It maintains a collection of more than 350 aircraft, although only a small number of these are on display at the museum at any one time. The majority of the aircraft are kept in storage or are under restoration at the Paul E. Garber Preservation, Restoration, and Storage Facility in nearby Maryland (see separate listing). A portion of the collection is continually on loan to other museums throughout the nation and in foreign countries.

In 1967 the National Air and Space Museum was designated by NASA as the sole custodian of America's relics of space exploration.

The collection includes all manned spacecraft; every major rocket engine (including the Saturn V, the world's largest launch vehicle); space-based astronomical observatories; and backup versions of almost all of the unmanned planetary spacecraft and satellites.

The museum contains more than 20 galleries, each dealing with a specific facet of air and space travel. The wide-ranging number of historically important aircraft and space vehicles in the collection are too numerous to identify here. Even a sampling of the list is impressive:
▪ the Wright brothers' original 1903 experimental Flyer flown at Kitty Hawk, North Carolina;
▪ the Fokker T-2 used by U.S. Army Lieutenants John A. Macready and Oakley G. Kelly in the first non-stop flight from coast to coast made in May 1923;
▪ Charles Lindbergh's Ryan NYP *Spirit of St. Louis,* which he flew across the Atlantic in May 1927;

- the Bell X-1 supersonic test plane, flown by Captain Charles "Chuck" Yeager in October 1947;
- a liquid-fueled rocket of the type used by Dr. Robert H. Goddard in his successful 1926 experiments;

- two Friendship 7 manned spacecraft;
- Gemini 4 and Apollo 11 command modules;
- backup Orbital Workshop, Skylab 4 (the largest object in the museum).

❖ *WEEKS AIR MUSEUM, 14710 Southwest 1328th Street, Tamiami Airport, Miami, Florida 33186. Tel: 305-233-5197. Open daily 10-5, except major holidays. Admission $5, over-65 and pre-teen student discounts.*

Opened in March 1987, the Weeks Air Museum is a non-profit organization devoted to the preservation and restoration of vintage aircraft. It contains more than 35 aircraft, most of which are in operable condition and date from the early days of flight through World War II. The collection was assembled by Kermit Weeks, who is well-known among those interested in aerobatic flying, having participated in aerobatic competitions for many years.

The museum also has on display a variety of engines, propellers, and models of historically significant aircraft.

❖ *NATIONAL MUSEUM OF NAVAL AVIATION, Building 3465, U.S. Naval Air Station, Pensacola, Florida 32508-6800. Tel: 800-327-5002 or 904-452-3604. Open daily 9-5, except major holidays. Admission free.*

The National Museum of Naval Aviation was originally called the Naval Aviation Museum when it was established by authority of the secretary of the navy in 1963. Its purpose is to preserve and present the history of American naval aviation, including contributions by the Marine Corps and the Coast Guard.

Through the efforts of Admiral Arthur W. Radford, USN (Ret.), a Naval Aviation Museum Foundation was established to assist in developing the facility. By 1975 sufficient funds had been accumulated to complete a 64,000-square-foot building on the grounds of the Naval Air Station at Pensacola. The museum has since grown to 110,000 square feet and is the leading naval aviation museum in the country.

The museum collection now consists of more than 100 historic naval aircraft, including:
- a replica of the navy's first aircraft, a Curtiss biplane;
- the first plane to cross the Atlantic (1919), the Curtiss NC-4 flying boat;

- WWII F6F Hellcat and F4U Corsair, plus other historic navy combat aircraft;
- TBM Avenger flown by President George Bush during WWII;
- first F-14 Tomcat on permanent public display; prototype of the navy's newest operational jet, the F/A-18 Hornet;
- Skylab command module in which a navy crew circled the earth for 28 days.

The museum also contains a collection of models depicting almost every class of navy aircraft carrier ever built, and there is an authentic video re-creation of operations in a carrier ready room. Using models and aviation art, the museum features a history of flight from man's first attempts to fly to the exploration of space. Pensacola is the home of the Blue Angels, who periodically provide demonstrations of their precision flying.

❖ *U.S. SPACE CAMP/U.S. ASTRONAUT HALL OF FAME, Titusville, Florida 32780. Tel: 407-269-6100. Open daily 9-5, except December 25. Admission $4.95, under 12 discount.*

Launch of America's first man in space on the Mercury-Redstone-3 from Cape Canaveral launch site on May 5, 1961. Photo courtesy of the National Aeronautics and Space Administration, Washington, D.C.

The Astronaut Hall of Fame was established in 1984 by the Mercury Seven Foundation, which was organized by the six surviving members of the original Mercury Seven astronauts, plus Betty Grissom, widow of the seventh, Gus Grissom. Alan B. Shepard Jr. is currently president of the foundation. Other members include Scott Carpenter, Walter Schirra, Donald Slayton, Gordon Cooper Jr., and John Glenn Jr.

The Astronaut Hall of Fame is a joint project of two non-profit organizations, the Mercury Seven Foundation and the U.S. Space Camp Foundation. The Hall of Fame shares the building with the Space Camp program, which provides classroom and hands-on instruction on space activities to children and adults. The original Space Camp facility and headquarters for the program is located in Huntsville, Alabama.

The Hall of Fame provides exhibits and films recounting the early days of the space program. The Sigma 7 Mercury spacecraft and Gus Grissom's spacesuit are on display. Exhibits describe the personal stories of the seven astronauts, which include personal memorabilia and video presentations of important events in their careers, such as Gus Grissom's escape from his sinking spacecraft. Rare photos of the moon landing and Shepard's walk on the moon are also shown.

❖ *AIRPOWER MUSEUM, Antique Airfield, Blakesburg, Iowa. Tel: 515-938-2773. Open Monday through Friday 9-5, Saturday 10-5, Sunday 1-5, closed major holidays. Admission free, donations appreciated.*

The Airpower Museum was founded in 1965 as an offshoot of the Antique Airplane Association (AAA) for purposes of acquiring and restoring antique aircraft. The AAA, a national organization committed to the restoration and

flying of antique aircraft, is also headquartered at Antique Airfield.

The Air Power Museum and the AAA are devoted to collectors and flyers of small general aviation aircraft. Although the collection of 45 aircraft (typically 25 are on display at any one time) is national in scope, there are a number of unique aircraft on display made by now-defunct midwestern manufacturers that were well-respected in their day, such as Anderson, Porterfield, and Aerosports. The collection focuses on aircraft built during the period between the two world wars, called the Golden Age of Aviation. Aircraft from such well-known manufacturers as Aeronca, Ryan, Stearman, Piper, Fairchild, and Stinson are included.

The museum has an active program of collecting and providing parts for one-of-a-kind aircraft. It also maintains an extensive library of literature and technical manuals of interest to flying enthusiasts and aircraft restorers.

❖ *OWLS HEAD TRANS-PORTATION MUSEUM, State Route 73, Rockland, Maine 04854. Tel: 207-594-4418. Open daily 10-5 from May through October, weekdays 10-5 rest of year. Adult admission $4, over-65 and student discounts.*

The Owls Head Museum was established as a non-profit foundation in 1974 under the leadership of James S. Rockefeller Jr., a member of the famous Rockefeller family, and Stephan Lang. The museum contains collections of antique and classic aircraft, automobiles, horseless carriages, bicycles, and both stationary and aircraft engines.

Replica of a 1911 Bellanca. Photo courtesy of the Owls Head Transportation Museum, Rockland, Maine.

The museum's pioneer collection of approximately 25 aircraft dates from 1909 and extends into the 1960s. All of the aircraft are operational and are frequently flown at shows sponsored by the museum. A separate building contains a number of historic aircraft engines, several of which also date from the 1910 era. The museum also maintains a library containing 5,000 volumes and thousands of periodicals, photographs, and video tapes dealing with transportation subjects.

Among the most interesting early aircraft in the museum is a replica of a 1909 single-wing Blériot Type XI equipped with a 3-cylinder Anzani engine—the model used by Blériot to cross the English Channel. Another early replica is a 1911 Wright Model F dual-propeller biplane, which was America's first production aircraft and built under contract for the Wright brothers by Starling Burgess, a boatbuilder.

Also of interest is a 1912 Curtiss Model D biplane, which was one of the first planes to employ ailerons to control flight instead of the Wright brothers' technique of warping the wings. Of the same vintage is a replica of a 1911 Bellanca. Guiseppi Bellanca built the plane in the back of his brother's grocery store on Long Island, learned to fly in it, and went on to an illustrious career in aviation, which included founding of the Bellanca Aeroplane Company and Flying School.

The collection also encompasses examples of the aircraft flown in World War I, including those made in France, England, Germany, and the United States. Civilian aircraft built during the 1930s and 1940s are represented, most notably by a 1937 Piper J-3 Cub and a 1941 de Havilland Tiger Moth, the latter being the Piper Cub of British aviation.

Examples of planes from the 1950s and 1960s include a 1951 North American AT-6, a single-engine, propeller-driven trainer, and a 1966 Bushmaster Trimotor, a customized version of the Ford Trimotor. The two-seat AT-6 was known as "The Texan" by the air force, "The SNJ" by the navy, and "The Harvard" by the British air force. It is reported to have been the most-produced military plane ever built, with more than 17,000 planes built between 1939 and 1953.

In addition to the antique aircraft, the museum has examples of several historic aircraft engine developments. One is the outstanding engine of the World War I period, the 150-hp, 8-cylinder, water-cooled Hispano-Suiza (c. 1916). Another is a 1917 French 9-cylinder Gnome, an excellent example of a rotary engine. Also in the collection is a 1917 American V-12 water-cooled Liberty engine. Of special interest are a 14-cylinder 1940 Curtiss-Wright Cyclone and a 28-cylinder 1946 Pratt & Whitney Wasp, both of which have been cut away to show the internal workings of the engine.

❖ *PAUL E. GARBER PRESERVATION, RESTORATION, AND STORAGE FACILITY, Old Silver Hill Road and St. Barnabas Road, Suitland, Maryland 20746. Tel: 202-357-1400. Tours available Monday through Friday at 10 a.m., Saturday and Sunday at 10 a.m. and 1 p.m. (reservations required). Open house on last weekend in April. Admission free.*

The Preservation, Restoration and Storage Facility, composed of five buildings, is the support facility for the National Air and Space Museum in Washington, D.C., and holds the primary portion of that museum's aircraft collection. The 160 aircraft and space vehicles stored or under restoration at the facility include the *Enola Gay*, the B-29 Superfortress that delivered the atomic bomb at Hiroshima in 1945.

Tour reservations must be made at least two weeks in advance. Daily tours of the facility last three hours and include visits to the restoration shops as well as to the aircraft collection.

❖ *HENRY FORD MUSEUM, 20900 Oakwood Boulevard, Dearborn, Michigan 48121. Tel: 313-271-1620. Open daily 9-5 except on major holidays. Admission $9.50, school-age and over-62 discounts.*

In 1927 Henry Ford first proposed the idea of an "industrial museum" that would highlight the work ethic of America by displaying the nation's accomplishments in a wide range of industries. The transportation portion of the museum contains one of the nation's outstanding collections of transportation vehicles, including a number of pioneering aircraft.

The aviation exhibit contains an authentic 1909 Blériot—the same model Blériot flew across the English Channel. There is also a 1919 Curtiss flying boat, labelled the Seagull. In 1919, Curtiss flying boats were used in one of the early regularly scheduled passenger services and in the first transatlantic flight, flown by the U.S. Navy. The two trimotors on exhibit, one a 1925 Fokker and the other a 1928 Ford, are the aircraft used by Richard E. Bird to fly over the North and South Poles, the former in 1926 and the latter in 1928. Ford produced almost 200 Ford Trimotors between 1925 and 1932.

Perhaps the most unique aircraft on display is a 1926 Ford "Flivver." This original prototype of Ford's attempt to build an affordable aircraft comparable to the Model T automobile, is the only survivor of the 550-pound, one-seat, low-wing monoplane. Also unique is one of the few surviving Boeing 40-B2 biplanes.

❖ *GLENN CURTISS MUSEUM OF LOCAL HISTORY, Main and Lake Streets, Hammondsport, New York 14840. Tel: 607-569-2160. Open daily 9-5, July through October; Monday through Saturday and holidays 9-5, April 15 through June 30; closed November to mid-April. Admission $3, senior, student, and family discounts.*

The Glenn Curtiss Museum of Local History contains memorabilia and descriptions of early aviation developments achieved by Glenn Curtiss. The museum was first opened in 1963 as a local history museum, with its principal focus on memorabilia concerning Glenn H. Curtiss, a Hammondsport native. Other exhibits include local farm vehicles and equipment, decorative arts, toys, and ladies' costumes. The Curtiss Museum Library and Archives contain the largest collection of photos, books, and periodicals concerning Curtiss in the world. The library and archives are open to researchers by prior appointment.

The aircraft collection includes five Curtiss antique aircraft plus two made by the Mercury Company, another local aircraft manufacturer that was founded by several ex-Curtiss employees. The Curtiss aircraft are replicas of a 1908 June Bug II and a Curtiss Model D Pusher, the original chassis of a JN-T Jenny, a 1919 Oriole, and a 1927 Robin. The two Mercury aircraft are a 1929 Chic and a 1931 S-1 racer. The Curtiss Jenny biplane was one of America's principal contributions to World War I aviation and was used primarily as a trainer.

Among Curtiss's many early contributions to aviation were his engine designs. Before becoming involved in aviation, Curtiss was well-known as a manufacturer and racer of high-speed bicycles and subsequently motorcycles, both of which he produced in Hammondsport. He went on to become a major manufacturer of aviation engines. The museum has on exhibit several of his early motorcycle and aircraft engines.

A 1917 Curtiss JN-4D Jenny. The Jenny trainer was the foremost aircraft of American design to emerge from World War I. Thousands of these planes survived, and in the postwar period sold for as little as $50, bringing aviation to the American public. The Jenny was the Model T Ford of aviation with over 6,000 civilian versions being sold. Photo courtesy of the Owls Head Transportation Museum, Rockland, Maine.

The Wright brothers' first flight. Photo courtesy of the Smithsonian Institution, Washington, D.C.

❖ *WRIGHT BROTHERS NATIONAL MEMORIAL, Kill Devil Hills, North Carolina 27948. Tel: 919-441-7430. Open daily 9-7, June 15 to Labor Day; 9-5 rest of year. Admission $1.*

The Wright Brothers National Memorial is located at the site of the brothers' first experiments in flight. The memorial was founded by the National Park Service in 1928, one of the earliest of the national monuments. The visitor center contains replicas of one of the Wright brothers' 1902 gliders, the 1903 Flyer, and their workshop, wind tunnel, and living quarters. Markers on the ground show where the first flights took place.

❖ *U.S. AIR FORCE MUSEUM, Wright-Patterson Air Force Base, Dayton, Ohio 45433-6518. Tel: 513-255-3284/6518. Open daily 9-5, closed major holidays. Admission free. IMAX® Theater performances $4, student discount. The last bus from the Main Museum to the annex leaves at 2:30 weekdays and 3:30 on Saturdays and Sundays.*

The Air Force Museum is located at Old Wright Field and was established by the Army Air Service, predecessor to the U.S. Air Force, in 1923. The museum has been described as the world's largest and oldest military aviation museum. It is operated by the U.S. Air Force and includes a 300,000-square-foot exhibit building, as well as exhibits located outdoors and at an annex accessible by shuttle bus. Much of the funding for building expansion and acquisitions to the collection have been furnished by private sources through the non-profit Air Force Museum Foundation.

The museum contains exhibits covering the history of aviation starting with the first aircraft acquired by the Army Air Service from the Wright brothers in 1909. It houses a collection of more than 200 aircraft and missiles, plus thousands of related artifacts. Essentially all of the fighters and bombers flown by the air force are on display. Also on display are the only remaining experimental XB-70 bomber, the B-29 that dropped the atomic bomb on Nagasaki, the huge B-36, the X-15 that flew 4,500 mph, and several space capsules. In addition to its own collection, the museum provides air force aircraft and artifacts to more than 100 museums around the world. Currently nearly 1,500 aircraft and 10,000 artifacts are on loan.

Among the museum's historically significant aircraft pre-dating World War II are a Boeing P-12 fighter biplane active in the 1920s, one of two converted Douglas DT-2 torpedo-bombers that made the first aerial circumnavigation of the globe in 1924, and a Martin twin-engine B-10 bomber of the early 1930s. The B-10 carried the U.S. mail during the Post Office's unsuccessful experiment in 1934 to hire the

Army Air Corps to fly its air mail.

The museum annex contains five renovated presidential planes used by Presidents Truman, Eisenhower, Johnson, Nixon, Ford, Carter, and Reagan. Hanging from the ceiling at the annex is the last U-2A "spy plane" ever built. It made 285 surveillance flights before it was retired around 1970.

The memorabilia and artifacts on display at the museum are, to many, as important as the aircraft and spacecraft. Displays on the history of flight go back to Greek mythology and Chinese kites. There are experimental devices used by early pioneers, such as a wind tunnel and an anemometer used by the Wright brothers, and exhibits honoring famous air force heroes, including Billy Mitchell and Eddie Rickenbacker.

❖ *NEIL ARMSTRONG AIR AND SPACE MUSEUM, I-75 and Bellefontaine Road, Wapakoneta, Ohio 45895. Tel: 419-738-8811. Open Monday through Saturday 9:30-5, Sunday noon-5 from March through November, closed major holidays. Admission $3, senior and under 13 discounts.*

The Neil Armstrong Air and Space Museum provides displays on the history of flight, starting with the hot-air balloon and continuing into space exploration, with an emphasis on contributions by Ohioans. Located in Neil Armstrong's hometown of Wapakoneta, Ohio, the museum was organized in 1972 by the Ohio Historical Society with financial help from the state of Ohio. The items on exhibit have been contributed by Neil Armstrong, NASA, the U.S. Air Force Museum, and the Smithsonian Institution.

On view is the Gemini 8 space capsule in which Neil Armstrong and David Scott completed the first space-docking operation in 1966. There are several multi-media presentations that provide the visitor with a sense of traveling in space. Also included are spacesuits and other artifacts associated with space travel, plus several historic aircraft from the post-World War II era. The aircraft include Armstrong's personal 1946 Aeronca 7AC Champion in which he learned to fly and an F5B Skylancer, which he tested for NASA.

❖ *VIRGINIA AIR AND SPACE CENTER/HAMPTON ROADS HISTORY CENTER, 600 Settlers Landing Road, Hampton, Virginia 23669-4033. Tel: 804-727-0800. Open Monday through Wednesday 10-5, Thursday through Saturday 10-7, Sunday noon-7. Admission $6 with feature film, $3 regular, senior and children discounts.*

The Virginia Air and Space Center/ Hampton Roads History Center opened its doors on April 5, 1992. Jointly financed by the commonwealth of Virginia, the city of Hampton, and private contributions, the center offers educational programs and exhibits concerning astronautics, aeronautics, planetary exploration, and space research. Exhibits have been provided by NASA Langley Research Center and the Smithsonian Institution, as well as by local public and private organizations.

Among the most important features at the center are more than 50 exhibits on the history of flight and space exploration. The center also features an IMAX® Theater, which presents spectacular visual images combined with a six-channel, four-way sound system. The initial presentation, titled *The Dream is Alive*, features film footage taken by 14 NASA astronauts on three separate space missions during 1984. New films will be presented three times each year.

The Aeronautics Gallery provides exhibits on the history of aircraft development and on wind tunnel research. Of historical significance is the Langley Aerodrome, designed by Samuel Langley in his unsuccessful attempt to be the first to test a powered aircraft. Among the important space-related exhibits at the center are a moon rock, several spacecraft, and educational exhibits on the solar system and planetary exploration.

❖ *MUSEUM OF FLIGHT, 9404 East Marginal Way South, Seattle, Washington 98108. Tel: 206-764-5720. Open daily 10-5, Thursday until 9, closed December 25. Admission $5, under-19 discount.*

The Museum of Flight was founded in 1964 by a non-profit foundation, the Pacific Northwest Aviation Historical Foundation. The 185,000-square-foot facility is located on seven acres at the southwest corner of Boeing Field and is housed in two buildings, Boeing's original assembly building, called the Red Barn, and a newer, larger building constructed in 1987, called the Great Gallery. In addition to a collection of 40 aircraft, the museum provides exhibits that depict man's efforts to fly since the thirteenth century.

The museum's collection of aircraft includes a Boeing 247 and a Douglas DC-3, two of the world's first commercial aircraft. Also displayed are a number of general aviation, sport, and home-built aircraft. Of particular interest is a 1950 Aerocar, which is one of the few winged automobiles ever certified by the FAA for flight. There are also replicas of a Lilienthal Glider (1896) and a Wright brothers' glider (1902).

Recent additions to the collection are a Goodyear FG-1D Corsair, the outstanding Marine Corps fighter made famous by Major Gregory "Pappy" Boyington, and a Lockheed SR-71A Blackbird, originally built for the Central Intelligence Agency in 1960. The Blackbird is still the highest-flying, fastest air-breathing aircraft in the world, able to fly at Mach 3 at an altitude of 85,000 feet. An outside exhibit area contains a Boeing B-17 Flying Fortress and a B-47 Stratojet.

❖ *EXPERIMENTAL AIRCRAFT ASSOCIATION (EAA) AIR ADVENTURE MUSEUM, 3000 Poberezny Road, Oshkosh, Wisconsin 54903. Tel: 414-426-4800. Open Monday through Saturday and holidays 8:30-5, Sunday 11-5, closed major holidays. Admission $5, senior and student discounts.*

The EAA Air Adventure Museum was founded in 1963 by the Experimental Aircraft Association, which is the largest organization of civilian aircraft enthusiasts in the country. The museum contains 200 professionally displayed military, civilian, and home-built aircraft. A new wing has recently been added to house the museum's extensive collection of World War II aircraft.

The CRIZ was designed and built by Burt Rutan and shown at the July 1972 EAA Fly-in. Rutan is famous for his innovative hand-built canard designs, the most famous of which was Voyager, *which flew around the world on a single fueling in 1986. Photo courtesy of the Smithsonian Institution, Washington, D.C.*

An exhibit of early pioneering developments includes a faithful reproduction of a Wright brothers' 1903 Flyer and an original Glenn Curtiss 1911 Pusher. World War I developments are represented by replicas of a French SPAD VII, a German Fokker DR-1 triplane, a British SE.5, plus an original Curtiss JN-4D Jenny trainer.

The museum displays a number of unusual and innovative planes developed during the Golden Age of Aviation, the 1920s and 1930s. One, developed in the late 1920s, is called the Monocoupe, which was a light, single-engine two-seater with an enclosed cabin. The plane was designed and built by a Davenport, Iowa, advertising man named Donald Luscombe, who went on to build a number of popular lightplanes during the 1930s.

In the early 1930s a number of manufacturers began to offer faster and larger light, cabin aircraft, of which the museum has several on display. Most notable are those of a small manufacturer with the rather pretentious name of the Aeronautical Corporation of America, more commonly known as Aeronca. There is also a Lockheed Vega, made famous by Wiley Post's *Winnie Mae*.

The museum's collection of home-builts and experimental aircraft is the most extensive in the country. In addition to the imposing collection of aircraft, there are displays of various aircraft components such as propellers and engines, many of which are shown with cutaways.

In late July the EAA sponsors the largest annual fly-in in the country. Hundreds of thousands of air enthusiasts flock to Oshkosh to view the hundreds of exhibits and the latest in military, commercial, and individual-built aircraft on display. Each day of the week-long event, the finest in aerobatics and precision-flying teams give demonstrations of their unique capabilities.

National Aeronautics and Space Administration (NASA)

NASA operates nine major research and development facilities around the nation. Each of these facilities maintains a visitor center with exhibits showing the center's activities and pertinent aspects of the history of the country's aviation and space developments.

❖ *GEORGE C. MARSHALL SPACE FLIGHT CENTER, One Tranquility Base, Huntsville, Alabama 35807. Tel: 800-633-7280 or 205-837-3400. Open daily 8-6, June through August; daily 9-5 rest of year; closed December 25. Admission $10.95, over-65 and under-13 discounts.*

The Marshall Space Center is NASA's primary facility for rocket propulsion development. Under the direction of Wernher von Braun, the center's rockets sent the first Americans into space. Its rockets have helped land men on the moon; launch our first space station, Skylab; and lift the Space Shuttle into orbit. Today, this Huntsville facility is heavily involved in the development of the Space Station program.

Tours of the Space Flight Center are conducted by the state-run Alabama Space and Rocket Center, which contains a large number of space-related exhibits and features the world's largest collection of space and rocket hardware. On display is a full-scale Space Shuttle and a Saturn rocket. A regularly scheduled bus takes visitors on a tour of the NASA facility. A Space Station mockup permits visitors to experience the laboratory and living facilities of a permanent space station.

❖ *AMES-DRYDEN FLIGHT RESEARCH FACILITY, Edwards Air Force Base, Lancaster, California 93523. Tel: 805-258-3446. Visitor Center open weekdays 8-3:45, tours conducted at 10:15 a.m. and 1:15 p.m., closed holidays. Admission free. Tours of the facility must be arranged in advance.*

Ames-Dryden is the nation's primary aeronautical flight-test facility and the landing site for many Space Shuttle missions. The facility was the testing site for the X-15. It is currently involved in the testing of the forward-swept-wing X-29 and the Mission Adaptive Wing aircraft, which can vary its wing curvature automatically while in flight. The facility has also been heavily involved in the space program through astronaut training and space shuttle landing tests.

❖ *AMES RESEARCH CENTER, Moffett Field, Mountain View, California 94040. Tel: 415-694-6497. Open Tuesday through Friday 9-5, Saturday 10-5, closed major holidays. Admission free. Tours must be arranged in advance.*

Ames Research Center was founded in 1940 as an aircraft research laboratory by NASA's predecessor, the National Advisory Committee for Aeronautics (NACA). Ames has been a pioneer in aircraft design and operates the largest wind tunnel in the world. The center has expanded into research in space science and the application of the life sciences in space.

❖ *JET PROPULSION LABORATORY, 4800 Oak Grove Drive, Pasadena, California 91109. Tel: 818-354-2337/8594. Visitor Center open weekdays 10-3, except major holidays. Admission free. All visits to the Visitor Center must be arranged in advance.*

The Jet Propulsion Laboratory (JPL) is operated by the California Institute of Technology under contract to NASA. Its mission is the study of the solar system and the exploration of the planets using automated spacecraft. Most of the lunar and planetary missions of the 1960s and 1970s were developed at JPL. These include Ranger and Surveyor, which photographed the moon; Viking, which landed two spacecraft on Mars in 1976; and Voyager, which was launched in the 1970s to explore the outer reaches of the solar system.

The Visitor Center contains various full-size mockups and scale models of spacecraft sent to deep space and displays on the deep space missions. Among the spacecraft on display are Explorer 1, the first orbiting U.S. satellite; Surveyor, which soft-landed on the moon; a Viking spacecraft that landed on Mars; and Mariner, which explored Venus and Mars.

❖ *JOHN F. KENNEDY SPACE CENTER AND CAPE CANAVERAL AIR FORCE STATION, SPACE-PORT, USA, Kennedy Space Center, Florida 32899. Tel: 407-452-2121. Spaceport, USA, is open daily 9 until dusk, except December 25. Bus tours of the Space Center and the Air Force Station operate daily 9:45 to two hours before sunset from the Spaceport. Bus tours $6, under-11 discount.*

The Kennedy Space Center is NASA's primary launch site for manned and unmanned spacecraft. All of America's manned space flights have been flown from here, and it is the home of the family of space shuttles, including the *Atlantis, Columbia, Discovery,* and *Endeavor,* plus the ill-fated *Challenger.* It also contains NASA's "Rock Garden," which consists of many of NASA's launch vehicles.

The Air Force Space Museum contains exhibits dealing with the role of the air force at the AF Station and in the development of the nation's space program. The museum features Mercury and Gemini launch pads, as well as the Explorer I launch pad where America's first satellite was launched on the night of January 31, 1958. Also on display are a number of historically significant rockets and missiles and an authentically restored blockhouse used as the control room for the early manned flights.

❖ *GODDARD SPACE FLIGHT CENTER, Greenbelt, Maryland 20771. Tel: 301-286-8981. Visitor Center open daily 10-4, June to August; Wednesday to Sunday 10-4 rest of year; tours offered by advance arrangement; closed major holidays. Admission free.*

The Goddard Center was established by NASA in 1959 as the first scientific laboratory devoted entirely to research on the exploration of space. Its mission is to design and develop orbiting spacecraft, to manage space projects, and to analyze data from scientific satellites. The center currently manages the Hubble Space Telescope, the National Oceanic and Atmospheric Administration polar-orbiting infrared satellite, and several other satellite projects. Because of its design-to-splash-down mission, Goddard has the largest and most versatile scientific staff of all of the NASA centers.

The Goddard Visitor Center features models of rockets and spacecraft, plus an eight-screen theater for viewing scenes of Earth as well as neighboring planets and distant stars.

❖ *LEWIS RESEARCH CENTER, 21000 Brook Park Road, Cleveland, Ohio 44135. Tel: 216-433-2000. Open Monday through Friday 9-4, Saturday 10-3, Sunday 1-5, and holidays 10-3; closed major holidays plus December 24 and 31. Admission free.*

NASA's Lewis Research Center focuses on research into the improvements of aircraft and spacecraft. The center was built in 1941 by NACA to assist in the World War II effort to improve propeller-driven aircraft engine performance. The center shifted its focus to research on jet engines as the war came to a close, then entered space vehicle propulsion research as the space program accelerated.

The Visitor Center at Lewis, which opened in 1971, is designed to provide a showcase for Lewis's research activities. It contains exhibits on space exploration, space shuttles, and air and space propulsion systems. Lectures and demonstrations on space-related topics are also offered regularly.

❖ *LYNDON B. JOHNSON SPACE CENTER, Building 2, 2101 NASA Road 1, Houston, Texas 77058. Tel: 713-483-4321. Open daily 9-4, except December 25. Admission free.*

The Johnson Space Center has been the focal point for NASA's manned space flight program since Gemini 4 in 1965, including Apollo, Skylab, and Space Shuttle programs. The center is responsible for selecting and training astronauts, designing and testing vehicles and systems for space flight, and the operation of the manned mission.

The Visitor Information Center has a museum with space artifacts and exhibits. Briefings in the Mission Control Center are presented throughout the day. Visitors are allowed to roam about the grounds and visit several of the operational buildings, where the public can observe astronauts being trained and hardware being developed.

❖ *LANGLEY RESEARCH CENTER, Hampton, Virginia 23665. Tel: 804-864-6000. Open Monday through Saturday 8:30-4:30, Sunday noon-4:30; closed major holidays. Admission free.*

Many important developments in aviation and space have occurred at the Langley Research Center. Founded in 1917 by NACA, it focuses primarily on aeronautical research. Langley built one of the world's first full-scale wind tunnels in 1923. The Langley Center managed the X-1 program, which led to the breaking of the sound barrier; the X-15 program, which achieved a speed of Mach 6.7; and the first manned space flight, Project Mercury. Currently the center is involved in developing techniques for building large structures in space and, in a joint program with the Department of Defense, the development of the National Aero-Space Plane.

Effective January 1992, the newly established Virginia Air and Space Center/ Hampton Roads History Center took over the Langley Research Visitor Center function and exhibits (see separate listing).

LIST OF MUSEUMS

MUSEUM SUBJECT CODES: Au—Automobiles, Av—Aviation; CnH—Canals-Historical; CnM—Canals-Modern; Cr—Carriages; M—Maritime; R—Railroads; Sp—Space; TR—Trails and Roads; TR-B—Braddocks Road; TR-F—Forbes Road; TR-M—Bozeman Trail; TR-N—National Road; TR-O—Oregon Trail; TR-SF—Santa Fe Trail; TR-W—Wilderness Road; TR-Z—Natchez Trace; TS—Transit Systems; TV—Taverns and Inns

Alabama
Birmingham, Southern Museum of Flight (Av), 202
Fort Rucker, U.S. Army Aviation Museum (Av), 202
Huntsville, George C. Marshall Space Flight Center (Sp), 213

Alaska
Palmer, Museum of Alaska Transportation and Industry (R), 131

Arizona
Tucson, Pima Air Museum (Av), 202

Arkansas
Morrilton, Museum of Automobiles (Au), 162

California
Danville, The Behring Museum (Au), 162
Lancaster, Ames-Dryden Flight Research Facility (Sp), 213
Monterey, Allen Knight Maritime Museum (M), 96
Mountain View, Ames Res. Center, Moffett Field (Sp), 214
Pasadena, Jet Propulsion Laboratory (Sp), 214
Perris, Orange Empire Railroad Museum (TS), 146
Portola, Portola Railroad Museum (R), 131
Sacramento, California State Railroad Museum (R), 131
Sacramento, Towe Ford Museum of California (Au), 162
San Diego, San Diego Automotive Museum (Au), 164
San Diego, San Diego Maritime Museum (M), 96
San Francisco, San Francisco Cable Car Museum (TS), 147
San Francisco, San Francisco Maritime National Historical Park (M), 97
San Pedro, Los Angeles Maritime Museum (M), 96
Suisun City, Western Railway Museum (R, TS), 147
Sylmar, Merle Norman Classic Beauty Collection (Au), 164
Truckee, Donner Memorial State Park (TR-O), 32

Colorado
Colorado Springs, El Pomar Carriage House Museum (Cr), 48
Denver, Forney Transportation Museum (Au), 164
Golden, Colorado Railroad Museum (R), 133
La Junta, Bents' Old Fort National Historical Site (TR-SF), 27
Trinidad, Pioneer Museum (TR-SF), 28

Connecticut
East Haven, Shore Line Trolley Museum (R-TS), 147
East Windsor, Connecticut Trolley Museum (R-TS), 148
Mystic, Mystic Seaport Museum (M), 98

New London, U.S. Coast Guard Museum (M), 98
Ridgefield, Keeler Tavern Preservation Society (Tv), 33
Windsor Locks, New England Air Museum (Av), 203

District of Columbia
National Museum of American History (R), 133
National Air and Space Museum (Av, Sp), 204

Florida
Miami, Gold Coast Railroad Museum (R), 134
Miami, Weeks Air Museum (Av), 205
Naples, Collier Automotive Museum (Au), 165
Kennedy Space Center (Sp), 214
Pensacola, National Museum of Naval Aviation (Av), 205
Ocala, Don Garlits Museum of Drag Racing (Au), 166
Sarasota, Bellm Cars and Music of Yesterday (Au), 167
Titusville, U.S. Astronaut Hall of Fame (Sp), 206

Georgia
Savannah, The Ships of Sea Maritime Museum (M), 98

Hawaii
Honolulu, Hawaii Maritime Center (M), 99

Idaho
Sand Point, Vintage Wheel Museum (Au), 167

Illinois
Lockport, Illinois and Michigan Canal Museum (CnH), 70
Rock Island, Mississippi River Locks /Dam #15 (CnM), 76
Union (McHenry County), Illinois Railroad Museum (R), 134
Utica, Illinois Waterway Visitor Center (CnM), 76

Indiana
Auburn, Auburn-Cord-Duesenberg Museum (Au), 167
Cambridge City, Huddleston Farmhouse Inn Museum (Tv), 33
Indianapolis, Indianapolis Motor Speedway Hall of Fame (Au), 168
South Bend, Studebaker National Museum (Cr, Au), 48, 169

Iowa
Blakesburg, Airpower Museum (Av), 206
Dubuque, Fred W. Woodward Riverboat Museum (M), 99
Keokuk, Keokuk River Museum (M), 99
Keokuk, Mississippi River Keokuk Lock /Dam #19 (CnM), 76
Mason City, Van Horn's Antique Truck Collection (Au), 169

Bibiliography

Allen, G.F. *North American Railroads Today.* London: Brian Trodd, 1990.

Andrews, Wayne. *Concise Dictionary of American History.* New York: Charles Scribner's Sons, 1961.

Athearn, Robert G. *Union Pacific Country.* Chicago: Rand McNally, 1971.

Baer, Christopher T. *Canals and Railroads of the Mid-Atlantic States — 1800-1860.* Wilmington, Delaware: Eleutherian Mills-Hagley Foundation, 1981.

Beebe, Lucius. *The Age of Steam.* New York: Rinehart, 1957.

Berry, Robert L. *1830-1870 Western Immigrant Trails* (map). Independence, Missouri: Oregon-California Trails Association, 1991.

Birkebile, Donald H. *Horse-Drawn Commercial Vehicles.* New York: Dover Publications, 1989.

Botkin, B.A. and Alvin F. Harlow. *A Treasury of Railroad Folklore.* New York: Bonanza Books, 1989.

Boyne, Walter J. *The Leading Edge.* New York: Stewart, Tabori & Chang, 1986. Reprinted New York: Artabras, 1991.

_____. *Power Behind the Wheel.* New York: Stewart, Tabori & Chang, 1988.

Brown, William E. *The Santa Fe Trail: National Park Service 1963 Historic Sites Survey.* St. Louis: The Patrice Press, 1988.

Burgess-Wise, David; Denis Miller; and Erwin Tragatsch. *The Illustrated History of Road Transport.* London: Quarto Publishing, 1986.

Cahill, Marie and Lynne Piade. *The History of The Union Pacific.* Greenwich, Connecticut: Brompton Books, 1989.

Chappelle, Howard I. *The History of American Sailing Ships.* New York: W. W. Norton, 1935. Reprinted by Bonanza Books, 1982.

Cox, Fletcher. *The Complete Steam Locomotive Companion.* Alexandria, Virginia: Fletcher Cox, 1987.

Cudahy, Brian J. *Cash, Tokens, and Transfers—A History of Urban Mass Transit in North America.* New York: Fordham Univ. Press, 1990.

Drury, George H. *The Historical Guide to North American Railroads.* Waukesha, Wisconsin: Kalmbach Publishing, 1991.

_____. *Guide to Tourist Railroads and Railroad Museums.* Waukesha, Wisconsin: Kalmbach Publishing, 1991.

Elliott, Stephen P. and Alan Isaacs, eds. *New Webster's Universal Encyclopedia.* New York: Bonanza Books, 1987.

Eves, Edward and Dan Berger. *Great Car Collections of the World.* New York: Multimedia Publications (UK), 1986.

Fox, Charles Philip. *Horses in Harness.* Greendale, Wisconsin: Reiman Associates, 1987.

Greenwood, John T., ed. *Milestones of Aviation: Smithsonian Institution, National Air and Space Museum.* New York: Hugh Lauter Levin Associates, 1989.

Hafer, Erminie Shaeffer. *A Century of Vehicle Craftsman ship.* Boyerttown, Pennsylvania: The Hafer Foundation, 1972.

Hahn, Thomas F. *The C. & O. Canal Boatmen—1892-1924.* York, Pennsylvania: American Canal and Transportation Center, 1980.

Harlow, Alvin F. *When Horses Pulled Boats, A Story of Early Canals.* York, Pennsylvania: American Canal and Transportation Center, 1983.

Hawkes, Nigel. *Vehicles.* New York: MacMillan, 1991.

Hayes, Bill. *Steam Trains.* London, England: Albany Books, 1981; New York: Galahad Books, 1981.

Kemp, Peter. *The History of Ships.* Stamford, Connecticut: Longmeadow Press, 1988.

Kennedy, Gregory P., compiler. *Rockets, Missiles and Spacecraft of the National Air and Space Museum.* Washington, D.C.: Smithsonian Institution Press, 1976. Revised edition, 1983.

Jacobs, Timothy, ed. *The History of the Pennsylvania Railroad.* Greenwich, Connecticut: Brompton Books, 1988.

_____. *The History of the Baltimore & Ohio.* Greenwich, Connecticut: Brompton Books, 1989.

Jensen, Oliver. *The American Heritage History of Railroads in America.* New York: American Heritage Publishing, 1975. New edition New York: Bonanza Books, 1981.

Klein, Aaron E., *The History of the New York Central System.* Greenwich, Connecticut: Brompton Books, 1985.

_____. *Encyclopedia of North American Railroads.* New York: Bison Books, 1985.

Manchester, Albert D. *Trails Begin Where Rails End; Early-day Motoring Adventures in the West and Southwest.* Glendale, California: Trans-Anglo Books, 1987.

Millar, John Fitzhugh. *Early American Ships.* Williamsburg, Virginia: Thirteen Colonies Press, 1986.

Mulhearn, Daniel J. and John R. Taibi. *General Motors' F-Units, The Locomotives that Revolutionized Railroading.* Westfield, New Jersey: Bells & Whistles, 1982.

Neill, Peter. *Maritime America.* New York: Balsam Press in affiliation with Harry M. Abrams, 1988.

Oakes, Claudia M and Kathleen L. Brooks-Pazmany, compilers; F. Robert van der Linden, ed. *Aircraft of the National Air and Space Museum.* Washington, D.C.: Smithsonian Institution, 1976. Fourth edition, 1991.

Phillips, Lance. *Yonder Comes the Train.* New York: Galahad Books, 1986.

Rand McNally & Company. *Handy Railroad Maps of the United States—1948.* Chicago: Rand McNally, 1948. Reproduced Waukesha, Wisconsin: Kalmbach Publishing.

Riegel, Robert Edgar. *The Story of the Western Railroads.* New York: MacMillan, 1926. Reprinted Univ. of Nebraska Press, 1964.

Ruiz, Marco. *The History of the Automobile.* New York: Gallery Books, W. H. Smith Publishers, 1988.

Schnieider, Norris F. *The National Road: Main Street of America.* Columbus, Ohio: Ohio Historical Society, 1975.

Shank, William H. *The Amazing Pennsylvania Canals.* York, Pennsylvania: American Canal and Transportation Center, 1986.

_____. *Pennsylvania Transportation History.* York, Pennsylvania: American Canal and Transportation Center, 1990.

_____, ed. *The Best from American Canals.* Vol. 1-5. York, Pennsylvania: American Canal and Transportation Center, 1982-1991.

_____. *Towpaths to Tugboats, A History of American Canal Engineering.* York, Pennsylvania: American Canal and Transportation Center, 1982.

_____. *Vanderbilt's Folly, A History of the Pennsylvania Turnpike.* York, Pennsylvania: American Canal and Transportation Center, 1989.

Shaw, Ronald E. *Erie Water West, A History of the Erie Canal 1792-1854.* Lexington, Kentucky: Univ. of Kentucky Press, 1966.

_____. *Canals for a Nation, The Canal Era in the United States 1790-1860.* Lexington, Kentucky: Univ. of Kentucky Press, 1990

Singer, Alan, ed. *Railroads of North America.* Secaucus, New Jersey, Chartwell Books, 1978.

Smith, Mark. *25th Annual Steam Passenger Service Directory.* Richmond, Vermont: Empire State Railway Museum, 1990.

Stanford, Joseph M. *Sea History's Guide to American and Canadian Maritime Museums.* Peekskill, New York: National Maritime Historical Society, 1990.

Taylor, John. *North American Railroads.* London: Studio Editions, 1991. New York: Random House, 1991.

Villiers, Capt. Allan. *Men Ships and the Sea.* Washington, D.C.: National Geographic Society, 1962.

Walker, Henry Pickering. *The Wagonmasters; High Plains Freighting from the Earliest Days of the Santa Fe Trail to 1880.* Norman, Oklahoma: University of Oklahoma Press, 1986.

Wamsley, James S. *American Ingenuity; Henry Ford Museum and Greenfield Village.* New York: Harry N. Abrams, 1985.

Warp, Harold. *A History of Man's Progress, from 1830 to Present.* Minden, Nebraska: Harold Warp Pioneer Village, 1987.

Westwood, John. *Trains.* London: Octopus Books, 1979.

Yenne, Bill. *The History of the U.S. Air Force.* Greenwich, Connecticut: Brompton Books, 1984.

_____. *The History of The Southern Pacific.* Greenwich, Connecticut, Brompton Books, 1985.

_____, ed. *Pictorial History of NASA.* New York: Gallery Books, 1989.

Index